PRINCIPLES OF
EUROPEAN ANTITRUST ENFORCEMENT

After 1 May 2004, European antitrust law entered a new era. At the same time as 10 new Member States joined the European Union, Regulation No 17, which had governed the enforcement of Articles 81 and 82 EC since 1962, was replaced by Regulation No 1/2003, which has ushered in far-reaching changes. This book brings together six essays which analyse the background and main characteristics of the new enforcement system, as well as a number of outstanding questions and potential areas of further reform, including the question whether private antitrust enforcement should be encouraged, and the question whether the decisional power in antitrust matters should be transferred to the courts. Special attention is given to the issues of the compatibility of the new enforcement system and of the practice of European antitrust enforcement with the requirements of the European Convention on Human Rights and the Charter of Fundamental Rights of the European Union, including the principle of *ne bis in idem*, the privilege against self-incrimination, and the right to an independent and impartial tribunal. On many of these issues, the discussion contained in this book is not only legal, but also includes an economic analysis from the perspective of efficient law enforcement.

Principles of European Antitrust Enforcement

DR WOUTER P J WILS

HART
PUBLISHING

OXFORD AND PORTLAND, OREGON
2005

Hart Publishing
Oxford and Portland, Oregon

Published in North America (US and Canada) by
Hart Publishing c/o
International Specialized Book Services
5804 NE Hassalo Street
Portland, Oregon
97213-3644
USA

Hart Publishing is a specialist legal publisher based in Oxford, England.
To order further copies of this book or to request a list of other
publications please write to:

Hart Publishing, Salter's Boatyard, Folly Bridge,
Abingdon Road, Oxford OX1 4LB
Telephone: +44 (0)1865 245533 or Fax: +44 (0)1865 794882
e-mail: mail@hartpub.co.uk
WEBSITE: http//www.hartpub.co.uk

British Library Cataloguing in Publication Data
Data Available
ISBN 1–84113–526–7 (hardback)

Typeset by Hope Services (Abingdon) Ltd
Printed and bound in Great Britain on acid-free paper by
MPG Books, Bodmin, Cornwall

Introduction and Acknowledgements

Since 1 May 2004, the enforcement of Articles 81 and 82 EC has entered a new era. At the same time as 10 new Member States joined the European Union, Regulation No 17,[1] which had governed the enforcement of Articles 81 and 82 EC since 1962, was replaced by Regulation No 1/2003,[2] which has ushered in far-reaching changes.

This book brings together six essays which analyse the main characteristics of the new enforcement system, as well as a number of outstanding questions and potential areas of further reform. The essays are all based on reports or articles that have been published previously, but have been updated to varying degrees so as to include recent developments as well as the evolution of my thinking. Tables and a subject index have been added at the end of the book.

Chapter 1 gives an overview of the main content of Regulation No 1/2003 in its historical context, and discusses a number of issues about which concerns have been raised during the period leading up to or following the adoption of the Regulation. This chapter is based on my Community Report for the XXI FIDE Congress in Dublin in June 2004, published in D Cahill and JD Cooke (eds), *The Modernisation of Competition Law Enforcement in the EU* (Cambridge University Press, 2004) 661–736.

Chapter 2 focuses on one of the main novelties under Regulation No 1/2003, namely the European Competition Network, bringing together the European Commission and the competition authorities of the Member States. More specifically, it addresses the question whether the structure and functioning of this network is compatible with the requirements of the European Convention on Human Rights and of the Charter of Fundamental Rights of the EU. This chapter contains a significantly updated version of a paper first presented at the Seventh Annual EC Competition Law and Policy workshop at the European University Institute in Florence in April 2002, published in CD Ehlermann and I Atanasiu (eds), *European Competition Law Annual 2002: Constructing the EU Network of Competition Authorities* (Hart, 2004) 433–64.

Chapter 3 deals with the principle of *ne bis in idem* (double jeopardy), including in particular its application within the European Competition Network. This chapter is based on WPJ Wils, 'The Principle of *Ne Bis in Idem* in EC Antitrust Enforcement: A Legal and Economic Analysis', published in (2003) 26 *World Competition* 131–48, by permission of the editor of *World Competition*, José Rivas, and the publisher, Kluwer Law International.

---

[1] Council Regulation No 17 [1962] OJ 13/204 (Special English Edition 1959–62, p 87).
[2] Council Regulation (EC) No 1/2003 of 16 December 2002 on the implementation of the rules on competition laid down in Articles 81 and 82 of the Treaty [2003] OJ L1/1.

Chapter 4 deals with private enforcement of Articles 81 and 82 EC. It is widely considered that the promotion of private enforcement was one of the aims of the reform brought about by Regulation No 1/2003, but that the actual impact of the Regulation is likely to be limited.[3] In this chapter I take a step back and address the policy question whether private enforcement should be encouraged beyond its existing level. This chapter is based on WPJ Wils, 'Should Private Antitrust Enforcement Be Encouraged in Europe?' published in (2003) 26 *World Competition* 473–88, by permission of the editor of *World Competition*, José Rivas, and the publisher, Kluwer Law International.

Chapter 5 deals with the collection of intelligence and evidence from antitrust violators, including a discussion of the authorities' powers of investigation, the privilege against self-incrimination and the instrument of leniency. This chapter is based on WPJ Wils, 'Self-incrimination in EC Antitrust Enforcement: A Legal and Economic Analysis' (2003) 26 *World Competition* 567–88, by permission of the editor of *World Competition*, José Rivas, and the publisher, Kluwer Law International.

Finally, chapter 6 analyses the advantages and disadvantages of the current EC antitrust enforcement system,[4] in which the European Commission combines the investigative and prosecutorial function with the adjudicative or decision-making function, in comparison with a system in which the adjudicative function is separated from the investigative and prosecutorial function. This chapter is based on WPJ Wils, 'The Combination of the Investigative and Prosecutorial Function and the Adjudicative Function in EC Antitrust Enforcement: A Legal and Economic Analysis', published in (2004) 27 *World Competition* 201–24, by permission of the editor of *World Competition*, José Rivas, and the publisher, Kluwer Law International.

I am grateful to Daniel Beard, Margaret Bloom, Terry Calvani, Fernando Castillo de la Torre, Thomas Deisenhofer, Barry Doherty, Claus Dieter Ehlermann, Leo Flynn, Céline Gauer, Eric Gippini Fournier, Barry Hawk, Alberto Heimler, Per Hellström, Erling Hjelmeng, Nicholas Khan, Kirsi Leivo, François Lelièvre, Xavier Lewis, Thalia Lingos, Richard Lyal, Eugenio de March, Giuliano Marenco, Kirti Mehta, Walter Mölls, Sven Norberg, Peter Oliver, Laura Pignataro, José Rivas, Jacques Steenbergen, Hanns Ullrich, Denis Waelbroeck and Anthony Whelan for their stimulating comments on earlier versions of parts or the whole of this book, and to Huguette Boumans for her kind and efficient help. All views expressed in this book are strictly personal, and should not be construed as reflecting the opinion of the European Commission, its Legal Service, or any of the persons mentioned above. Comments are welcome at Wouter.Wils@cec.eu.int.

Dr Wouter PJ Wils
Brussels, 20 June 2004

[3] See among others, J Venit, 'Brave New World: The Modernization and Decentralization of Enforcement under Articles 81 and 82 of the EC Treaty' (2003) 40 *Common Market Law Review* 545, 570–72; PJ Slot, 'A View from the Mountain: 40 Years of Developments in EC Competition Law' (2004) 41 *Common Market Law Review* 443, 466–67.
[4] Not only under Regulation No 1/2003 but also under Council Regulation (EC) No 139/2004 of 20 January 2004 on the control of concentrations between undertakings (the EC Merger Regulation), [2004] OJ L24/1.

Contents

1

The Reform of Competition Law Enforcement Brought About by Regulation No 1/2003

1. This chapter consists of two parts. The first part gives an overview of the main content of Regulation No 1/2003 in its historic context. The second part deals with a number of areas of potential concern, ie issues about which questions have been raised either during the period leading up to the adoption of the Regulation or following its adoption. For each of these areas of potential concern, I have tried to explain how the concerns have been taken into account in the Regulation and its implementing measures, or why there is no real ground for concern.

1.1 THE REFORM OF COMPETITION LAW ENFORCEMENT BROUGHT ABOUT BY REGULATION NO 1/2003

1.1.1 Regulation No 1/2003 and its Implementing Measures

2. The EC Treaty itself does not set out how the prohibitions laid down in Articles 81 and 82 EC are to be enforced.[1] Article 83 EC instead delegates to the Council, acting by a qualified majority on a proposal from the Commission and after consulting the European Parliament, the task of laying down 'the appropriate regulations or directives to give effect to the principles set out in Articles 81 and 82'. The second paragraph of Article 83 EC further indicates that these implementing regulations shall be designed 'to ensure compliance with the prohibitions laid down in Article 81(1) and in Article 82 by making provision for fines and periodic penalty payments' and 'to lay down detailed rules for the application of Article 81(3), taking into account the need to ensure effective supervision on the one hand, and to simplify administration to the greatest possible extent on the other'.

---

[1] Apart from the word 'prohibited' in both provisions, and Article 81(2) EC, which provides that 'any agreements (...) prohibited pursuant to this Article shall be automatically void'. Regard should also be had to Article 85(1) EC, which, in the words of the Court of First Instance, Judgment of 20 April 1999 in Joined Cases T–305/94 etc *Limburgse Vinyl Maatschappij and Others v Commission* ('*PVC II*') [1999] ECR II–987 para 148: 'constitutes the specific expression in [the] area [of competition law] of the general supervisory role conferred on the Commission by Article [211] of the Treaty'. See also Judgment of the Court of Justice of 14 December 2000 in Case C–344/98 *Masterfoods* [2000] ECR I–11427 para 46.

3. On the basis of Article 83 EC (then Article 87 of the EEC Treaty) the Council adopted in 1962 Regulation No 17,[2] which has governed the enforcement of Articles 81 and 82 EC for four decades.

4. As from 1 May 2004, Regulation No 17 is replaced by Regulation No 1/2003,[3] again based on Article 83 EC. The Council adopted the Regulation following the Commission's proposal of 27 September 2000,[4] which had been preceded by a White Paper published by the Commission in 1999.[5]

5. Pursuant to Article 33(1) of the Regulation, some implementing provisions are contained in Commission Regulation No 773/2004 relating to the conduct of proceedings by the Commission pursuant to Articles 81 and 82 of the EC Treaty.[6]

6. The Regulation and the Commission Implementing Regulation are further accompanied by six Commission notices:

— a Commission Notice on cooperation within the Network of Competition Authorities;[7] this Notice is based to a significant extent on the Joint Statement of the Council and the Commission on the functioning of the network of competition authorities, entered in the Council Minutes at the time of the adoption of the Regulation;[8]
— a Commission Notice on the cooperation between the Commission and the courts of the EU Member States in the application of Articles 81 and 82 EC;[9]
— a Commission Notice on the handling of complaints by the Commission under Articles 81 and 82 of the EC Treaty;[10]

---

[2] Council Regulation No 17 [1962] OJ 13/204 (Special English Edition 1959–62, p 87).

[3] Council Regulation (EC) No 1/2003 of 16 December 2002 on the implementation of the rules on competition laid down in Articles 81 and 82 of the Treaty [2003] OJ L1/1. Article 45, second sentence, of the Regulation provides that 'it shall apply from 1 May 2004'. Article 43(1) provides that 'Regulation No 17 is repealed with the exception of Article 8(3) which continues to apply to decisions adopted pursuant to Article 81(3) of the Treaty prior to the date of application of this Regulation until the date of expiry of those decisions'. The Regulation also replaces the procedural provisions governing the application of Articles 81 and 82 EC in the transport sector previously contained in Regulations No 1017/68, No 4056/86 and No 3975/87. See Recital 36 and Articles 36, 38, 39 and 43(2) of the Regulation. The Regulation has already been amended (deletion of point (c) in Article 32) by Council Regulation (EC) No 411/2004 of 26 February 2004 repealing Regulation (EEC) No 3975/87 and amending Regulations (EEC) No 3976/87 and (EC) No 1/2003, in connection with air transport between the Community and third countries [2004] OJ L68/1.

[4] [2000] OJ C365E/284; for the explanatory memorandum, see Commission document COM (2000) 582 of 27 September 2000.

[5] [1999] OJ C132/1.

[6] Commission Regulation (EC) No 773/2004 of 7 April 2004 relating to the conduct of proceedings by the Commission pursuant to Articles 81 and 82 of the EC Treaty, [2004] OJ L123/18.

[7] [2004] OJ C101/43.

[8] Council Document 15435/02 ADD 1 of 10 December 2002, available at http://register.consilium.eu.int. According to its paras 3 and 4, 'this Joint Statement is political in nature and does therefore not create any legal rights or obligations. It is limited to setting out common political understanding shared by all Member States and the Commission on the principles of the functioning of the Network. Details will be set out in a Commission notice which will be drafted and updated as necessary in close cooperation with Member States'.

[9] [2004] OJ C101/54.

[10] [2004] OJ C101/65.

— a Commission Notice on informal guidance relating to novel questions concerning Articles 81 and 82 of the EC Treaty that arise in individual cases (guidance letters);[11]

— a Commission Notice—Guidelines on the effect on trade concept contained in Articles 81 and 82 of the Treaty;[12]

— a Commission Notice—Guidelines on the application of Article 81(3) of the Treaty.[13]

7. Most provisions of the Regulation do not require any implementing measures by the Member States to become effectively applicable, even if Member States may want to adopt some further measures in connection with these provisions.[14]

8. However, some provisions of the Regulation require national implementing measures. Pursuant to Article 35 of the Regulation, 'the Member States shall designate the competition authority or authorities responsible for the application of Articles 81 and 82 of the Treaty in such a way that the provisions of this regulation are effectively complied with. The measures necessary to empower those authorities to apply those Articles shall be taken before 1 May 2004'.[15]

9. Finally, it should be kept in mind that all existing block exemption regulations remain in force, and that a number of Commission notices and guidelines retain their full usefulness alongside Regulation No 1/2003 and the above listed implementing and accompanying measures. A list of those block exemption regulations, notices and guidelines can be found in the Annex to the Commission Notice on cooperation between the Commission and the national courts.[16]

1.1.2 The Core of the Reform: The Replacement of the Centralised Notification and Authorisation System for Article 81(3) EC by a Directly Applicable Exception System

10. As is apparent from recitals 2 to 4, and from the Commission's proposal and the White Paper which preceded the adoption of Regulation No 1/2003,[17] the core of the reform brought about by the Regulation is the replacement of the

---

[11] [2004] OJ C101/78.

[12] [2004] OJ C101/81.

[13] [2004] OJ C101/97.

[14] For instance, in connection with Article 3 of the Regulation, Member States might want to adopt transitional provisions, so as to preserve the validity of procedural steps taken on the basis of national competition law only, and Member States might want to reconsider existing notification systems under national competition law.

[15] The provisions compliance must thus be ensured with are in particular those contained in Articles 5, 11 and 14 of the Regulation. See also paras 134–37 below.

[16] See n 9 above. This list is also available and updated on the Commission's website at http://europa.eu.int/comm/competition/antitrust/legislation/. On block exemption regulations, see paras 69–72 below.

[17] See n 4 and n 5 above.

centralised notification and authorisation system for Article 81(3) EC by a directly applicable exception system.

11. Already under Regulation No 17, Articles 81(1) and 82 EC were directly applicable.[18] These provisions could thus be applied, not only by the Commission, but also by national courts in private litigation and (as long as the Commission had not initiated a procedure regarding the same agreement or practice)[19] by those national competition authorities which had been empowered by national law to apply these provisions.

12. As to the application of Article 81(3) EC, however, Regulation No 17 provided for a centralised notification and authorisation system. Indeed, Article 4(1) of Regulation No 17 provided that agreements falling under Article 81(1) EC in respect of which the parties sought application of Article 81(3) EC had to be notified to the Commission. Article 6(1) of Regulation No 17 added that exemption decisions pursuant to Article 81(3) EC could not take effect at a date earlier than the date of notification. This condition of prior notification did not apply to agreements falling within Article 4(2) of Regulation No 17. The latter provision initially covered only a few relatively unimportant types of agreements, but from 18 June 1999 it included all vertical agreements.[20] These agreements were also covered, however, by Article 9(1) of Regulation No 17, which provided that the Commission had sole power to declare Article 81(1) EC inapplicable pursuant to Article 81(3) EC.

13. Regulation No 1/2003 does away with this centralised notification and authorisation system, and makes Article 81(3) EC directly applicable.[21] Indeed, Article 1(2) of the Regulation provides that 'agreements, decisions and concerted practices caught by Article 81(1) of the Treaty which satisfy the conditions of Article 81(3) of the Treaty shall not be prohibited, no prior decision to that effect being required'. The Regulation does not provide any more for any possibility to notify agreements to the Commission, nor for exemption decisions.[22] Article 6 of

---

[18] See Article 1 of Regulation No 17 and Judgment of the Court of Justice of 30 January 1974 in Case 127/73 *BRT v SABAM* [1974] ECR 62 para 16.

[19] See Article 9(3) of Regulation No 17.

[20] Council Regulation (EC) No 1216/1999 amending Regulation No 17 [1999] OJ L148/5.

[21] It can however be deduced from Article 43(1) of Regulation No 1/2003, which repeals Regulation No 17 'with the exception of Article 8(3) which continues to apply to decisions adopted pursuant to Article 81(3) of the Treaty prior to the date of application of this Regulation until the date of expiry of those decisions', that, as a transitional measure, exemption decisions adopted before 1 May 2004 remain in principle valid until the date of expiry mentioned in those decisions. This concerns in practice only a few decisions for a few years after 1 May 2004.

[22] Applications for negative clearance (see Article 2 of Regulation No 17) are no longer provided for either. Article 10 of Regulation No 1/2003 (see full text in para 38 below) gives the Commission the power to take decisions finding that Article 81 EC is not applicable to an agreement or practice, either because the conditions of Article 81(1) EC are not fulfilled, or because the conditions of Article 81(3) EC are satisfied, but the Commission can only take such non-infringement decisions 'acting on its own initiative' and 'where the Community public interest relating to the application of Articles 81 and 82 of the Treaty so requires'. In the light of Article 1(2) of the Regulation, non-infringement decisions under Article 10 of the Regulation that are based on a finding that the conditions of Article 81(3) EC are satisfied can only be of a declaratory nature, whereas exemption decisions under Regulation No 17 were of a constitutive nature.

the Regulation further confirms that 'national courts shall have the power to apply Articles 81 and 82 of the Treaty', thus also Article 81(3) EC, and the first sentence of Article 5 of the Regulation similarly provides that 'the competition authorities of the Member States shall have the power to apply Articles 81 and 82 of the Treaty in individual cases'.[23]

1.1.3 The Historic Justification for a Centralised Notification and Authorisation System, and Why This Justification is No Longer Valid Today

14. The abolition of the centralised notification and authorisation system for Article 81(3) EC raises the question why Regulation No 17 introduced this system, and why the reasons justifying its introduction are no longer valid today.[24]

15. The answer, I believe, lies in the fact that, at the time Regulation No 17 was adopted, the prohibition on restrictive agreements was entirely revolutionary in Europe. The prohibition on abuse of a dominant position, first in the ECSC Treaty of 1951 and subsequently in Article 86 of the EEC Treaty of 1957 (now Article 82 EC), was not without precedent: in Germany, for instance, an 'Ordinance against the Abuse of Economic Power' had been enacted in 1923.[25] However, the prohibition on restrictive agreements first laid down in Article 65 of the ECSC Treaty and then also in Article 85 of the EEC Treaty (now Article 81 EC), was 'a fundamental innovation in Europe'.[26] Before the second world war, cartels were a wide-spread and highly esteemed institution throughout Europe.[27] The insertion of the prohibition on restrictive agreements in European law, as well as around the same time in German national law, was due to American influence, if not pressure.[28] As an entirely new and revolutionary import, the meaning of the

---

[23] The powers of the national competition authorities are however limited by the following sentences of Article 5, which restrict the type of decisions these authorities can take, by Article 11(6) of the Regulation, which provides that the initiation of proceedings by the Commission shall relieve the national competition authorities of their competence to apply Articles 81 and 82 EC in the same case, and by Article 16(2) of the Regulation. See paras 45–50 below.

[24] The choice between a centralised authorisation system and a directly applicable exception system had indeed been the object of intense discussion, not only at the time of the adoption of Regulation No 17 but already before, at the stage of the drafting of the then Articles 85 and 87 of the EEC Treaty (now Articles 81 and 83 EC). See G Marenco, 'Does a Legal Exception System Require an Amendment of the Treaty?' in CD Ehlermann and I Atanasiu (eds), *European Competition Law Annual 2000: The Modernisation of EC Antitrust Policy* (Hart Publishing, Oxford, 2001) 145–84.

[25] K Nörr, 'Law and Market Organization: The Historical Experience in Germany From 1900 to the Law Against Restraints of Competition (1957)' (1995) 151 *Journal of Institutional and Theoretical Economics / Zeitschrift für die gesamte Staatswissenschaft* 5, 10.

[26] J Monnet, *Mémoires* (Fayard, 1976) 413.

[27] HG Schröter, 'Cartelization and Decartelization in Europe, 1870–1995: Rise and Decline of an Economic Institution' (1996) 25 *Journal of European Economic History* 129, 137, who also writes at p 140 that Yugoslavia was the only European country where cartels were prohibited at that time.

[28] See J Monnet, n 26 above, p 356–57 and 411–13; D Spierenburg and R Poidevin, *The History of the High Authority of the European Coal and Steel Community* (Weidenfeld and Nicholson, 1994) 26–28, and, with a detailed description of the strong resistance to be overcome in Germany,

prohibition on restrictive agreements must have been rather unclear to most European business people and lawyers.

16. The revolutionary character of Article 85 EEC (now Article 81 EC) pleaded for a centralised notification and authorisation system.[29] Indeed, given the radical novelty of the rule, companies and their legal advisors could not be relied upon to assess themselves the compatibility of their agreements with the provisions of Article 81 EC. Similarly, leaving the application of Article 81(3) EC to the courts and authorities of the Member States, steeped in the European tradition favourable to cartel agreements, would have entailed a major risk of the prohibition laid down in Article 81 EC not being applied in practice, or at least not in a sufficiently uniform manner. The centralised notification and authorisation system guaranteed that the new provision would be interpreted and applied by the Commission, which was specifically dedicated to the new religion.[30] The notification system also had an educational function, as companies and their lawyers were educated by the Commission through the authorisation process.[31]

17. This historic justification is no longer valid today. Article 81 EC is no longer revolutionary: after several decades of application, European business people and lawyers have acculturated; virtually all Member States have now also adopted similar provisions in their national laws.[32] The novel character of Article 81 EC can thus no longer justify a centralised notification and authorisation system.

18. The choice of a centralised notification system in Regulation No 17 may also have been influenced by some confusion as to the nature of Article 81(3) EC. At the time Regulation No 17 was adopted, it may have been considered that the application of Article 81(3) EC depended or should depend on discretionary political decisions. Indeed, without the benefit of subsequent case law and practice, this Treaty provision could have been read in two different ways. Under the first reading, Article 81(3) EC is nothing but a codified form of the American rule of reason. Indeed, Article 81 EC is the European equivalent of Section 1 of the Sherman Act. Whereas the latter reads as a single rule prohibiting all agreements in restraint of trade (similar to Article 81(1) EC), it has been interpreted by the

V Berghahn, *The Americanization of West German Industry* 1945–1973 (Berg, 1986). In the national laws of other European countries, a similar prohibition on restrictive agreements was introduced much later: for instance in the Netherlands only in 1997 and in Luxembourg only in 2004. See also para 199 below.

[29] For a more systematic and more detailed discussion, see my book *The Optimal Enforcement of EC Antitrust Law* (Kluwer, 2002) ch 5 and s 6.2.

[30] See BE Hawk, 'EU "modernisation": a latter-day Reformation' (August/September 1999) *Global Competition Law Review* 12, and, more generally, RH Nelson, *Economics as Religion* (Penn State UP, 2001).

[31] See Recital 1 of Regulation No 1/2003.

[32] The new Member States from Central and Eastern Europe have also already adopted similar national laws. Indeed, the Europe Agreements between the EC and the accession candidates obliged these countries to apply the principles of Articles 81 and 82 EC and to harmonize their national competition law with EC competition law. See for instance Articles 63 and 69 of the Europe Agreement between the European Communities and their Member States, of the one part, and the Republic of Poland, of the other part [1993] OJ L348/1.

courts as condemning only unreasonable restraints.[33] Article 81(3) EC simply codifies this case law. Under this first reading, there is of course no scope for discretionary political decisions in the application of Article 81(3) EC, the American rule of reason being a true rule of law. Unter the second reading, which could draw on the word 'may' in the text of Article 81(3) EC ('The provisions of paragraph 1 may, however, be declared inapplicable in the case of ...'), the application of Article 81(3) EC would not be a right whenever the four conditions listed therein are met, but rather depend on a discretionary political decision. In the perspective of this second reading, a centralised notification and authorisation system would have appeared logical.

19. There can be no doubt any more today that the first reading is the right one. In 40 years of application of Regulation No 17, the Commission has never refused an exemption when the four conditions of Article 81(3) EC were met, nor has it granted an exemption for other reasons than the fulfilment of those conditions.[34] As to the Community Courts, the underlying conception of the case law is that fulfilment of the conditions entitles an undertaking to the benefit of Article 81(3) EC.[35] Notwithstanding the Courts' declarations regarding the 'margin of discretion' which the Commission enjoys in the 'complex economic appraisals' it makes under Article 81(3) EC,[36] the case law shows how punctiliously the Courts control the assessment made by the Commission in accepting or refusing the fulfilment of a condition.[37] In French, the internal working language of the Courts, the Courts have never used the term '*marge de discrétion*' but instead '*marge d'appréciation*', suggesting no more than a margin of economic assessment. Such a margin also exists in the application of Article 81(1) EC,[38] or Article 82 EC,[39] as they equally require complex economic assessments. This is not a political discretion, and it does not therefore require a centralised notification and authorisation system.

---

[33] *Standard Oil v United States* 221 US 1 (1911).

[34] See G Marenco, n 24 above, p 164–67.

[35] In its Judgment of 14 July 1994 in Case T–17/93 *Matra v Commission* [1994] ECR II–595 para 85, the Court of First Instance considered that 'in principle, no anticompetitive practice can exist which, whatever the extent of its effects on a given market, cannot be exempted, provided that all the conditions laid down in Article 81(3) of the Treaty are satisfied and that the practice in question has been properly notified to the Commission'.

[36] Judgment of the Court of Justice of 25 October 1977 in Case 26/76 *Metro v Commission* [1977] ECR 1875 paras 45 and 50; Judgment of the Court of First Instance of 23 February 1994 in Joined Cases T–39/92 and T–40/92 *CB and Europay v Commission* [1994] ECR II–49 para 109.

[37] G Marenco, n 24 above; S Kon, 'Article 85, Para 3: A Case for Application by National Courts' (1982) 19 *Common Market Law Review* 541; contra R Wesseling, 'The Commission White Paper on Modernisation of EC Antitrust Law: Unspoken Consequences and Incomplete Treatment of Alternative Options' [1999] *European Competition Law Review* 420.

[38] Judgments of the Court of Justice of 11 July 1985 in Case 42/84 *Remia v Commission* [1985] ECR 2566 para 34; of 17 November 1987 in Joined Cases 142 and 156/84 *BAT and Reynolds v Commission* [1987] ECR 4487 para 62; and of 21 January 1999 in Joined Cases C–215/96 and C–216/96 *Bagnasco* [1999] ECR I–179 para 50.

[39] See n 147 below.

1.1.4 The Benefits Resulting from the Introduction of a Directly Applicable Exception System

20. Compared with the centralised notification and authorisation system under Regulation No 17, the directly applicable exception system for Article 81(3) EC as introduced by Regulation No 1/2003 has a number of major advantages.

1.1.4.1 Impact on Private Litigation in which Article 81 EC is Used as a Shield

21. The reform brought about by Regulation No 1/2003 will have important effects on private litigation in which Article 81 EC is used as a 'shield'.[40] The antitrust prohibitions are used as a shield when they are invoked in defence against a contractual claim for performance or for damages because of non-performance or against some other claim, for instance in an intellectual property infringement action.[41] Here the reform has had a double impact.[42]

1.1.4.1.1 Agreements which Fulfil the Conditions of Article 81(3) EC are No Longer Void

22. Under Regulation No 17, agreements which fell under Article 81(1) EC, which were not covered by a block exemption regulation and which had not previously been notified to the Commission, were void under Article 81(2) EC, even if they fulfilled the four conditions of Article 81(3) EC.[43] Many agreements appeared to be in this situation.[44]

23. Under Regulation No 1/2003, agreements falling under Article 81(1) EC and not covered by a block exemption regulation are only void if the conditions of Article 81(3) EC are not fulfilled.[45]

24. This change is obviously to be welcomed, as the enforcement of the substantive rule laid down in Article 81 EC, namely the prohibition on restrictive

---

[40] On the distinction between the use of Articles 81 and 82 EC as a 'shield' and as a 'sword', see FG Jacobs and T Deisenhofer, 'Procedural Aspects of the Effective Private Enforcement of EC Competition Rules: A Community Perspective' in CD Ehlermann and I Atanasiu (eds), *European Competition Law Annual 2001: Effective Private Enforcement of EC Antitrust Law* (Hart Publishing, 2003) 187, 189–190.

[41] The use of Article 81 EC as a shield in contractual disputes has its basis directly in the EC Treaty. Indeed, Article 81(2) EC provides that 'any agreements [...] prohibited pursuant to this article shall be automatically void'. In *BRT v SABAM* (n 18 above, para 16), on a preliminary reference from a national court before which Article 82 EC was invoked in an intellectual property infringement case, the Court of Justice held more generally that 'as the prohibitions of Articles 81(1) and 82 tend by their very nature to produce direct effects in relations between individuals, these articles create direct rights in respect of the individuals concerned which the national courts must safeguard'.

[42] See para 85 below as to the question whether this impact will lead to an increase or a decrease in the number of cases in which Article 81 is invoked as a shield in private litigation before national courts.

[43] This did not apply to agreements covered by Article 4(2) of Regulation No 17, including since 18 June 1999 all vertical agreements. See para 12 above.

[44] See CD Ehlermann, 'The Modernization of EC Antitrust Policy: A Legal and Cultural Revolution' (2000) 37 *Common Market Law Review* 537, 546.

[45] See Article 1(2) of the Regulation, and para 13 above.

agreements without redeeming virtue, cannot possibly be served by rendering agreements which do not violate this prohibition unenforceable.

1.1.4.1.2 *National Courts are Now Able to Apply the Four Conditions of Article 81(3) EC Themselves*

25. Under Regulation No 17, national courts could not themselves apply the four conditions of Article 81(3) EC. Even in the case of vertical agreements and other types of agreements covered by Article 4(2) of Regulation No 17,[46] national courts which were called upon to apply Article 81(1) EC, by virtue of its direct effect, could not themselves apply Article 81(3) EC. They instead had to suspend their proceedings and wait for a decision of the Commission on whether or not the four conditions of Article 81(3) EC were met. Only if the conditions for the application of Article 81(3) EC were clearly not satisfied and there was, consequently, scarcely any risk of the Commission taking a different decision, could the national court continue the proceedings and rule on the agreement in question.[47]

26. Regulation No 1/2003 does away with this impossibility for the national courts to apply Article 81(3) EC themselves.[48]

27. This change should to be welcomed for several reasons. First, it is manifestly more economical to have one single decision-maker decide whether the same agreement falls under Article 81(1) EC and fulfils the conditions of Article 81(3) EC. Both assessments require knowledge of largely the same facts, and in substance both provisions are closely linked.[49] Splitting the assessment between the national court and the Commission slows down contractual litigation, increases its overall cost, and increases the risk of inconsistencies.

28. Secondly, all the resources which the Commission has to spend on making Article 81(3) EC assessments for the purposes of resolving contractual disputes are necessarily diverted from its other work. The Commission should rather spend these resources on the detection and punishment of the most serious infringements, such as secret price-fixing or market-sharing arrangements. For this task, the Commission is really needed, whereas the application of Article 81(3) EC in a contractual dispute can be perfectly left to the national courts.[50]

29. Thirdly, entrusting national courts with the task of applying Article 81(3) EC has the benefit of consolidating the interpretation of Article 81(3) EC as a true rule of law. As already mentioned above,[51] this Treaty provision, read in isolation, could originally have been read either as a true rule of law or as a discretionary political tool. The case law and decisional practice of the last 40 years make it clear

---

[46] See para 12 above.
[47] Judgment of the Court of Justice of 28 February 1991 in Case C–234/89 *Delimitis* [1991] ECR I–935 para 50.
[48] See Article 6 of the Regulation, and para 13 above.
[49] In its Judgment of 6 April 1962 in Case 13/61 *Bosch v Van Rijn* [1962] ECR 52, the Court of Justice speaks of them 'forming an indivisible whole'.
[50] See paras 30–32 and 85–88 below.
[51] Paras 18 and 19.

today that the first reading is the correct one. Regulation No 1/2003 has the merit of consolidating this interpretation.[52]

1.1.4.2 Impact on the Commission's Enforcement Priorities

1.1.4.2.1 What Should the Commission's Enforcement Priorities Be?

30. The resources which the Commission can devote to the enforcement of Articles 81 and 82 EC are inevitably limited. The Commission should thus set its priorities so as to use its scarce resources to the best possible effect.

31. The main priority for the Commission should be to prosecute and punish the most serious violations of Articles 81 and 82 EC, such as secret price-fixing or market-sharing cartels, more specifically those of a Community dimension.[53]

32. Secondly, the Commission may also have a role to play in clarifying the law and ensuring its consistent application throughout the Community.[54] All the more so now that the Commission no longer has exclusive competence to apply Article 81(3) EC, there can be no doubt that giving authoritative interpretations of the law is the task of the Court of Justice, together with the Court of First Instance and in cooperation with the national courts. The Commission can however make a valuable contribution by collecting, ordering and disseminating available information about the law, thus reducing the cost and enhancing the accuracy of the self-assessment by undertakings and of ex post enforcement proceedings.[55]

1.1.4.2.2 The Notification System Distorted the Commission's Enforcement Priorities

33. The notification system under Regulation No 17 had a serious distorting effect on the Commission's enforcement priorities. The most serious infringements of Article 81 EC, such as price-fixing or market-sharing cartels, were never notified

---

[52] See also J Burrichter, 'The Application of Article 81(3) by National Courts: Some Remarks from the Point of View of a Practitioner' in CD Ehlermann and I Atanasiu (eds), *European Competition Law Annual 2000: The Modernisation of EC Antitrust Policy* (Hart Publishing, 2001) 539.

[53] See Recital 2 of the Regulation.

[54] The wording 'clarifying the law' is used in Recital 14 of the Regulation. In point 11 of the Notice on the handling of complaints, n 10 above, the language 'define Community competition policy' is used. I would personally take the view that the use of the term 'policy' is inappropriate in this context. Articles 81 and 82 EC being directly applicable rules of law, the clarification of the material content of these provisions (ie, what exactly is prohibited) is not a matter of 'policy'. See also paras 18 and 19 above. Only in the adoption of block exemption regulations is there some scope for policy as to the material content of the prohibitions. There is also scope for the Commission to have a policy concerning the use of its prosecutorial discretion. The Commission's Guidelines on the method of setting fines, [1998] OJ C9/3, and its Notice on immunity from fines and reduction of fines in cartel cases, [2002] OJ C45/3, are expressions of such enforcement policy. The term 'competition policy' is also appropriate outside the area of Articles 81 and 82 EC, for instance for state aid policy, deregulation and trade liberalization. See *The Optimal Enforcement of EC Antitrust Law*, n 29 above, section 6.2.3.3, and B Hoekman and PC Mavroidis, 'Economic Development, Competition Policy and the World Trade Organization' (2003) 37 *Journal of World Trade* 1, 4–5.

[55] See *The Optimal Enforcement of EC Antitrust Law*, n 29 above, sections 6.2.3.3 and 6.2.3.4.

to the Commission.[56] The notifications which the Commission received tended to reveal either no infringement at all or only relatively minor problems. In 40 years of application of Regulation No 17 there have been only 9 decisions in which a notified agreement was prohibited without a complaint having been lodged against it.[57] However, given that the Commission was under an obligation to act upon all notifications within a reasonable period,[58] notification-related work consumed about half of the resources of the parts of the Commission's Directorate-General for Competition not dealing with mergers or state aid.[59]

34. Moreover, in recent years most notifications were of little or no value for the purpose of clarifying the law, as they did not raise novel questions. In any event, the instrument of comfort letters, which was used to deal with the overwhelming majority of notifications, was particularly unsuited for the purpose of clarifying the law, since comfort letters were not published and in general barely (if at all) reasoned.[60]

35. The notification system may also have had further negative effects on the culture of the Commission's Directorate-General for Competition and on the interpretation of Article 81 EC. Indeed, dealing with notifications is a very different type of work from investigating infringements such as secret price cartels. Notification work is unlikely to be a good training for conducting dawn raids, and a service where a large proportion of the work consists of reading notifications is unlikely to attract and retain people naturally suited for (quasi-) criminal investigatory work.[61] As to the interpretation of Article 81 EC, the Commission's very wide interpretation of Article 81(1) EC, which was much criticised until it was reversed in the last few years,[62] may have been caused in part by the understandable tendency of highly qualified officials in the Directorate-General for Competition to bring some intellectual sparkle to dull notification work by discovering some new, esoteric restriction of competition.

---

[56] Nor did undertakings ever request a negative clearance for the worst abuses of a dominant position.

[57] White Paper, n 5 above, para 77.

[58] Judgment of the Court of First instance of 22 October 1997 in Joined Cases T–213/95 and T–18/96 *SCK and FNK v Commission* [1997] ECR II–1764 para 55.

[59] The problem could not have been solved by giving more resources to the Directorate-General for Competition. Indeed, if more resources had been available, notifications would have been dealt with more swiftly, and this would have made notification more attractive to industry. Many agreements which fell under Article 81(1) EC and which benefited neither from a block exemption regulation nor from Article 4(2) of Regulation No 17, and which were not unlikely to meet the substantive conditions of Article 81(3) EC, were not notified, notwithstanding the resulting unenforceability. See para 22 above. If the Commission had provided a better service, more of these agreements would have been notified. See also para 60 below regarding the impact of enlargement.

[60] See also para 159 below.

[61] On the 'criminal' or not 'criminal' nature of the enforcement of Articles 81 or 82 EC by the Commission, see n 88 below.

[62] For the criticism, see B Hawk, 'System Failure: Vertical Restraints and EC Competition Law' (1995) 32 *Common Market Law Review* 973; for the reversal, see para 41 below.

1.1.4.2.3 *Regulation No 1/2003 Allows the Commission to Set its Enforcement Priorities Correctly*

36. By abolishing the notification system, Regulation No 1/2003 has removed the distortions of the Commission's enforcement priorities. The Commission is no longer obliged to deal with cases that involve no infringement at all or only minor competition problems, and which have not much value either for clarifying the law. The Commission is now free to concentrate its resources on the most serious infringements of Articles 81 and 82 EC.

37. Apart from its primary task of prosecuting the most serious antitrust infringements, the Commission can also, to the extent necessary, fulfil its role in clarifying the law and ensuring its consistent application throughout the Community. Regulation No 1/2003 has provided the appropriate (reasoned and published) instruments for this task. Apart from guidelines, which already existed under Regulation No 17,[63] these instruments are non-infringement decisions under Article 10 of the Regulation and guidance letters as provided for in the Commission Notice on informal guidance relating to novel questions.[64]

38. Article 10 of the Regulation reads as follows:

> Where the Community public interest relating to the application of Articles 81 and 82 of the Treaty so requires, the Commission, acting on its own initiative, may by decision find that Article 81 of the Treaty is not applicable to an agreement, a decision by an association of undertakings or a concerted practice, either because the conditions of Article 81(1) of the Treaty are not fulfilled, or because the conditions of Article 81(3) are satisfied.
>
>   The Commission may likewise make such a finding with reference to Article 82 of the Treaty.

39. It is clear from this provision that undertakings do not have a right to force the Commission to adopt such decisions, which will only be taken in those (probably rather exceptional) cases where there is a need to clarify the law and to ensure its consistent application throughout the Community.[65] Decisions taken pursuant to Article 10 of the Regulation will be reasoned and published.[66]

40. In the Notice on informal guidance relating to novel questions, the Commission announces that it may issue a guidance letter at the request of undertakings if:

> the substantive assessment of an agreement or practice with regard to Articles 81 and/or 82 of the Treaty poses a question of application of the law for which there is no

---

[63] See in particular the Guidelines on vertical restraints, [2000] OJ C291/1, and the Guidelines on the applicability of Article 81 EC to horizontal co-operation agreements, [2001] OJ C3/2. In fact neither Regulation No 17 nor Regulation No 1/2003 mention the instrument of guidelines.

[64] Above, n 11. See also Recital 38 of the Regulation, and the statement by the Commission entered in the Council Minutes, Council Document 15435/02 ADD 1, of 10 December 2002, available at http://register.consilium.eu.int.

[65] See also E Paulis and C Gauer, 'La Réforme des Règles d'Application des Articles 81 et 82 du Traité' (2003) 11 *Journal des Tribunaux Droit Européen* 65, paras 35–37.

[66] Article 253 EC and Article 30 of the Regulation.

clarification in the existing EC legal framework including the case law of the Community Courts, nor publicly available general guidance or precedent in decision-making practice or previous guidance letters.[67]

The Commission retains however full discretion to refuse to deal with a request for guidance, in particular to ensure that the provision of informal guidance would not interfere with its enforcement priorities.[68] Guidance letters will be reasoned, and posted on the Commission's web-site.[69]

41. Finally, the abolition of the notification system also removes the further negative effects on the culture of the Commission's Directorate-General for Competition and on the interpretation of Article 81 EC.[70] The detection, prosecution and punishment of serious antitrust violations is now the core task of all parts of the Directorate-General for Competition not dealing with mergers or state aid.[71] As to the interpretation of Article 81 EC, the Guidelines on vertical restraints and the Guidelines on the applicability of Article 81 EC to horizontal co-operation agreements[72] have already before the entry into force of Regulation No 1/2003 restored balance in the interpretation of Article 81(1) EC.

1.1.4.3 The Application of Articles 81 and 82 EC by National Competition Authorities

1.1.4.3.1 Regulation No 17 Discouraged the Application of Articles 81 and 82 EC by National Competition Authorities

42. Under Regulation No 17, the competition authorities of the Member States have only rarely prosecuted infringements of Articles 81 or 82 EC. This inactivity can be explained by two factors. The first is that national law empowered national competition authorities to apply Articles 81(1) and 82 EC in only about half of the Member States. As to those countries which had a national authority empowered to apply Community competition law, the other factor explaining the lack of prosecution of infringements of Article 81(1) EC is that the Commission's power to grant exemptions under Article 81(3) EC, combined with Article 9(3) of Regulation No 17, discouraged national authorities from taking up Article 81(1) EC cases.[73] Indeed, if a national competition authority had started prosecuting an

---

[67] Para 8, point a, of the Notice on informal guidance relating to novel questions, n 11 above.

[68] Idem, paras 6 and 7.

[69] Idem, paras 19 and 21.

[70] Para 35 above.

[71] See the announcement of 25 July 2003 on the web-site of the Commission's Directorate-General for Competition concerning the abolition of the specific cartel units as part of the internal reorganisation linked to Regulation No 1/2003: http://europa.eu.int/comm/competition/older_headlines_en.html.

[72] Above, n 63.

[73] See also AW Kist and ML Tierno Centella, 'Coherence and Efficiency in a Decentralised Enforcement of EC Competition Rules: Reflections on the White Paper on Modernisation' in CD Ehlermann and I Atanasiu (eds), European Competition Law Annual 2000: The Modernisation of EC Antitrust Policy (Hart Publishing, 2001) 369.

infringement of Article 81(1) EC, the undertakings concerned could have decided to notify their agreement or practice to the Commission, which, because of the legal obligation to act upon the notification, might have been forced to initiate a procedure, thus taking away the national authority's competence. In its 1997 notice on cooperation between national competition authorities and itself, the Commission tried to reduce this problem by announcing that 'it consider[ed] itself justified in not examining as a matter of priority' such 'dilatory notifications'.[74] This attempted solution was however not easy to implement, and its legality was never confirmed by the Community Courts.

1.1.4.3.2   *Regulation No 1/2003 Encourages the Application of Articles 81 and 82 EC by National Competition Authorities*

43. Regulation No 1/2003 has removed both obstacles to the prosecution of infringements of Articles 81 and 82 EC by national competition authorities. As to the first problem, Article 35 of the Regulation obliges the Member States to designate the competition authority or authorities responsible for the application of Articles 81 and 82 EC, and to take before 1 May 2004 the measures necessary to empower those authorities to apply those Articles. As to the second problem, it has disappeared together with the notification system. It is true that Article 11(6) of Regulation No 1/2003 still provides that the initiation by the Commission of proceedings for the adoption of a decision relieves the national competition authorities of their competence to apply Articles 81 and 82 EC,[75] but this should not discourage action by the national authorities. Indeed, as explained below,[76] Article 11(3) of the Regulation provides that a national competition authority shall, when acting under Articles 81 or 82 EC, inform the Commission before or without delay after commencing the first formal investigative measure. If the Commission then considers that it is better placed to deal with the case,[77] it will take over the case swiftly, normally within a period of two months after the information is received.[78] After this initial allocation phase, the Commission will in principle only apply Article 11(6) of the Regulation in a limited number of special situations listed in the Notice on cooperation within the network.[79]

44. The application of Articles 81 and 82 EC by national competition authorities is further encouraged through Article 3(1) of Regulation No 1/2003, which provides that where national competition authorities apply national competition law to agreements, decisions of undertakings or concerted practices within the meaning of Article 81(1) EC which may affect trade between Member States or to

---

[74] [1997] OJ C313/03 paras 55–57.
[75] See para 181 below for the full text of Article 11(6) of the Regulation.
[76] Para 106.
[77] See paras 100–3 below for the criteria to decide which authority is best placed to deal with a case.
[78] Para 18 of the Notice on cooperation within the network, n 7 above.
[79] Idem, para 54.

any abuse prohibited by Article 82 EC, they shall also apply Article 81 or 82 EC.[80]

1.1.4.3.3 *The Powers of National Competition Authorities as Compared to Those of the Commission*

45. The powers of the national competition authorities are circumscribed by Regulation No 1/2003 as to the types of decisions that can be taken.[81] Article 5 of the Regulation reads as follows:

> The competition authorities of the Member States shall have the power to apply Articles 81 and 82 of the Treaty in individual cases. For this purpose, acting on their own initiative or on a complaint, they may take the following decisions:
>
> — requiring that an infringement be brought to an end,
> — ordering interim measures,
> — accepting commitments,
> — imposing fines, periodic penalty payments or any other penalty provided for in their national law.
>
> Where on the basis of the information in their possession the conditions for prohibition are not met they may likewise decide that there are no grounds for action on their part.

46. National competition authorities thus do not have the power to adopt non-infringement decisions similar to the decisions which the Commission may adopt under Article 10 of the Regulation.[82]

47. The power of the Commission to adopt non-infringement decisions under Article 10 of the Regulation, the rule laid down in Article 11(6) of the Regulation, according to which the initiation by the Commission of proceedings relieves the national competition authorities of their competence to deal with the same case,[83] and the rule laid down in Article 16(2) of the Regulation, according to which national competition authorities cannot take decisions which would run counter to an earlier decision by the Commission concerning the same agreement or practice,[84] differentiate the position of the Commission from that of the national competition authorities.

48. These three differences all relate to the Commission's specific role in clarifying the law and ensuring its consistent application throughout the Community,[85] as provided in Article 85(1) EC.[86]

---

[80] The rationale and interpretation of Article 3 of the Regulation are further discussed in paras 145–57 below. The provisions of Article 3 of the Regulation apply not only to national competition authorities but also to national courts.

[81] Apart from the powers listed in Article 5 of the Regulation, national competition authorities are also empowered by Article 29(2) of the Regulation to withdraw the benefit of a block exemption regulation under certain conditions. See also n 122 below.

[82] See para 38 above.

[83] See para 43 above and para 181 below.

[84] See para 165 below.

[85] See para 32 above, and para 9 of the Joint Statement on the functioning of the network, n 8 above.

[86] See the judgments of *Masterfoods* and *PVC II*, n 1 above.

49. Otherwise, the idea of the Regulation is that the Commission and the national competition authorities have parallel competences and that they should form together a network of authorities applying Articles 81 and 82 EC in close cooperation.[87]

50. In fact national competition authorities could have stronger powers than the Commission under Regulation No 1/2003. Indeed, whereas the Regulation only empowers the Commission to impose fines on undertakings for infringements of Articles 81 or 82 EC,[88] Article 5 of the Regulation allows national competition authorities to impose also 'any other penalty provided for in their national law', including imprisonment or criminal sanctions on natural persons.[89]

1.1.4.3.4 Why Should National Competition Authorities Prosecute Violations of Articles 81 and 82 EC?

51. The question could be asked why prosecution by national competition authorities of violations of Articles 81 and 82 EC should be encouraged. Why not leave this task exclusively to the Commission? Three reasons can be given.[90]

52. The first reason is one of resources. By adding those of the competition authorities of the Member States, substantially more resources can be devoted to the detection and punishment of violations of Articles 81 and 82 EC.[91] Given the

---

[87] See Recital 15 of the Regulation, the Joint Statement on the functioning of the network, n 8 above, and the Notice on cooperation within the network, n 7 above.

[88] Article 23(2) of the Regulation. According to Article 23(5) of the Regulation, decisions imposing such fines 'shall not be of a criminal nature'. The latter provision may have some importance as to the status of such fines under national law (for instance whether they are tax deductable). The Council may also have considered that it had some relevance as to the necessary legal basis under the EC Treaty (see Articles 29 and 47 EU; Case C–176/03 *Commission v Council*, currently pending before the Court of Justice; and *The Optimal Enforcement of EC Antitrust Law*, n 29 above, sections 8.7.4.1 and 8.7.4.2). The provision does however not prevent such fines from being qualified as 'criminal' within the meaning of the European Convention of Human Rights and the Charter of Fundamental Rights of the EU (see Opinion of Judge Vesterdorf acting as Advocate General in Case T–1/89 *Rhône-Poulenc v Commission* [1991] ECR II–867, 885; Opinion of Advocate General Léger in Case C–185/95 P *Baustahlgewebe v Commission* [1998] ECR I–8422 para 31; Judgment of the Court of Justice of 8 July 1999 in Case C–199/92 P *Hüls v Commission* [1999] ECR I–4383 paras 149–50; K Lenaerts and J Vanhamme, 'Procedural Rights of Private Parties in the Community Administrative Process' (1997) 34 *Common Market Law Review* 531, 557; WPJ Wils 'La Compatibilité des Procédures Communautaires en Matière de Concurrence Avec la Convention Européenne des Droits de l'Homme' (1996) 32 *Cahiers de Droit Européen* 329; and section 2.5.2.3 and 6.1.4.1 below). However, even if Article 23(5) of the Regulation does not prevent the fines provided for in Article 23(2) of the Regulation from being qualified as 'criminal' within the meaning of the European Convention of Human Rights and the Charter of Fundamental Rights of the EU, the provision may still be relevant under the Convention and the Charter, as the requirements of the Convention may be stricter for proceedings which are not only 'criminal' within the wider sense of the Convention but also criminal under domestic law or relating to traditional areas of criminal law. See n 14 of section 6.1.4.1 below. On the different meanings of 'criminal', see also *The Optimal Enforcement of EC Antitrust Law*, n 29 above, section 8.7.2.

[89] See also paras 153–57 and 185–89 below.

[90] Contra A Riley, 'EC Antitrust Modernisation: The Commission Does Very Nicely—Thank You! Part Two: Between the Idea and the Reality: Decentralisation under Regulation No 1' [2003] *European Competition Law Review* 657, 671.

[91] According to figures cited in para 44 of the White Paper, n 5 above, in 1998 there were around 1222 officials responsible for investigating antitrust cases in the Member States as opposed to 153 in the Commission.

limited resources of the Commission, and the current inadequate level of effective deterrence,[92] this is certainly to be welcomed. This first reason is however not a very profound one, as the same result could be obtained by increasing the resources of the Commission's Directorate General for Competition.

53. The second reason is that for cases where the relevant markets are local, national or regional, the competition authority or authorities concerned are likely to have better access to the relevant information than the Commission.[93]

54. The third reason is that multiple enforcement is likely to lead to more innovation in the interpretation and application of the law. Enforcement by several authorities is likely to be more creative, innovative and adaptive to change than enforcement by a monopolist authority.[94]

1.1.4.4 The Direct and Hidden Costs of the Notification System Have Disappeared

55. A system of prior notification and authorisation is inherently a very costly system to enforce a prohibition such as the one laid down in Article 81 EC, in particular because of the enormous number of contracts and business decisions which should be assessed to avoid violations of Article 81 EC.[95] A notification system is both costly for the undertakings making the notifications and for the competition authority dealing with them.

56. The authors of Regulation No 17 must have been aware of the risk of a huge number of notifications, and the resulting impossibility for the Commission to deal with them swiftly. Indeed, no time limit was provided for the Commission's decision:[96] the undertakings were free to implement the notified agreement and when the Commission later adopted an exemption decision, this decision could have retroactive effect back to the date of notification. In the meantime the undertakings benefited from immunity from fines.[97] These modalities made the notification system much more manageable, but the price to be paid was that violations could go on undisturbed for quite some time.[98]

---

[92] See The Optimal Enforcement of EC Antitrust Law, n 29 above, chs 8 and 9.

[93] Part of the advantage of national authorities relates to language. See para 223 below.

[94] See also E Fox, 'Modernization: Efficiency, Dynamic Efficiency, and the Diffusion of Competition Law' in CD Ehlermann and I Atanasiu (eds), European Competition Law Annual 2000: The Modernisation of EC Antitrust Policy (Hart Publishing, 2001) 123; JS Venit, 'Brave New World: The Modernization of Enforcement under Articles 81 and 82 of the EC Treaty' (2003) 40 Common Market Law Review 545, 562–63.

[95] For a more systematic and more detailed discussion, including a comparison with merger control, see The Optimal Enforcement of EC Antitrust Law, n 29 above, ch 5 and section 6.2.

[96] However, according to later case law, the decision had to be taken within a reasonable period. See n 58 above.

[97] So-called 'old agreements', ie agreements which were already in existence on 22 February 1962, the date of entry into force of Regulation No 17, provided that they were notified to the Commission before 1 November 1962, even benefited from provisional validity. See also para 60 below as to the similar arrangements later added at the occasion of the accession of new Member States.

[98] For the most extreme cases of blatant violations being notified and consequently immune from fines until the day the Commission dealt with the notification, a possibility of withdrawal of immunity

57. These modalities which made the notification system manageable for the Commission, and thus reduced some of the administrative cost, did not however affect the number of notifications made and the corresponding cost borne by the notifying parties. In the first years of the application of Regulation No 17, almost 40,000 agreements were notified to the Commission. From 1967 on the Commission adopted a number of block exemption regulations, which exempted entire categories of agreements.[99] The cost of notifying and examining these agreements was thus avoided. On the other hand, a price had to be paid: as block exemption regulations clear entire categories of agreements defined in the abstract, errors may be made in that certain agreements which upon individual analysis would appear to violate the substantive rule are exempted. For instance, from 1 May 1967 until 31 May 2000,[100] all exclusive purchase agreements were block exempted, irrespective of the market power of the undertakings concerned.[101]

58. It should be recalled that, even outside the scope of the block exemption regulations and of its Article 4(2), Regulation No 17 did not impose an obligation to notify agreements falling under Article 81(1) EC. Undertakings could thus avoid the cost of notification by choosing not to notify. In practice many undertakings made this choice.[102] However, they then paid a different price in that their agreement, if it was indeed found to fall under Article 81(1) EC, was not legally enforceable, even if it met the substantive conditions of Article 81(3).[103]

59. Finally, even if in the last years of application of Regulation No 17 only a relatively small number of agreements were thus notified to the Commission (on average 233 per year for the 1995–1999 period), notification-related work still

was provided for in Article 15(6) of Regulation No 17. An (admittedly not representative) example of an agreement which was notified to the Commission in 1962 and which was implemented until 1998 without its legality having been settled is the industry-wide agreement governing retail prices for books in the Netherlands. See Judgment of the Court of Justice of 24 April 1997 in Case C–39/96 *KVBBB v Free Record Shop* [1997] ECR I–2303. For another example, see para 38 of the Judgment of the Court of First Instance of 13 January 2004 in Case T–67/01 *JCB Service*, not yet published in ECR.

[99] Over the years, block exemption regulations were adopted for exclusive distribution agreements, exclusive purchase agreements, motor vehicle distribution and servicing agreements, franchising agreements, technology transfer agreements, specialization agreements, research and development agreements, as well as for certain types of agreements in the insurance and transport sectors; for the list of current block exemption regulations, see para 9 above; as to the role of block exemptions under Regulation No 1/2003, see paras 69–72 below.

[100] The former date is that of entry into force of Commission Regulation No 67/67, [1967] OJ L847/67. The latter is the date until which Commission Regulation No 1984/83, which succeeded Regulation No 67/67, was prolonged by Article 12(1) of Commission Regulation No 2790/1999, [1999] OJ L336/21. By virtue of Article 12(2) of the latter Regulation, agreements already in force on 31 May 2000 continued to benefit from the exemption until 31 December 2001.

[101] Block exemption regulations usually provide for a possibility to withdraw the benefit of the exemption for an agreement which does not meet the substantive conditions of Article 81(3) EC, but doing so is administratively costly, with the result that the Commission used this power only once in more than 30 years: see Commission Decision of 23 December 1992, *Langnese-Iglo*, [1993] OJ L183/19. Moreover the withdrawal only has effect for the future. As to withdrawal of the benefit of block exemptions under Regulation No 1/2003, see n 122 below.

[102] See para 22 above.
[103] Idem.

consumed approximately half of the resources of the parts of the Commission's Directorate-General for Competition not dealing with mergers or state aid.[104]

60. The costs of the notification system would have increased significantly with the accession of ten new Member States on 1 May 2004, assuming that, like on the occasion of previous accessions, notification within six months from the date of accession of existing agreements to which Article 81 EC became applicable by virtue of the accession had been provided for.[105]

61. Under Regulation No 1/2003 all these costs have disappeared. There are no longer violations of Article 81 EC which have immunity from fines or even provisional validity because they have been notified to the Commission and the Commission has not yet been able to deal with them. The urge to get rid of unmanageably high numbers of notifications no longer leads to excessively generous block exemptions. Indeed, recent block exemptions all contain a market share threshold.[106] Agreements which are caught by Article 81(1) EC that do not benefit from a block exemption regulation but which fulfil the conditions of Article 81(3) EC are no longer void merely because they have not been notified to the Commission.[107] Finally, no resources are spent anymore by industry and by the Commission on making notifications or dealing with them.[108]

1.1.4.5 Impact on Private Litigation in which Article 81 EC is Used as a Sword

62. The antitrust rules are used as a 'sword' when they are used proactively by private parties as a basis for claiming damages or injunctive relief.[109]

63. The EC Treaty is silent as to the use of Articles 81 or 82 EC as a sword.[110] Regulation No 17 did not in any way hint at this possibility either. When it was consulted in 1961 on the Commission's proposal for what became Regulation No 17, the European Parliament expressed its view that rules should be laid down not only for administrative sanctions for violation of articles 81 and 82 EC but also for the recovery of damages.[111] The Commission did however not propose such rules, and the Council did not include any in Regulation No 17. Since 1973, when it first expressed this view in response to a parliamentary question,[112] the Commission has with some regularity expressed the view that private actions for damages could provide useful support for its own enforcement actions.[113]

---

[104] See para 33 above.

[105] See Article 25 of Regulation No 17, as added by the 1972, 1979, 1985 and 1995 Accession Acts, and Recital 1 of Regulation No 1/2003.

[106] See for instance the 30% market share threshold in the block exemption for vertical agreements, Commission Regulation No 2790/1999 [1999] OJ L336/21.

[107] See para 23 above.

[108] See para 33 above.

[109] See n 40 above.

[110] Compare with n 41 above.

[111] OJ 1410/61 of 15 November 1961, para 11.

[112] Answer of 10 April 1973 to Written Question No 519/72 by Mr Vredeling [1973] OJ C67/55.

[113] See list of statements from the Commission referred to in n 112 of the Opinion of Advocate General Van Gerven of 27 October 1993 in Case C–128/92 Banks [1994] ECR I–1251.

64. Relatively recently, in *Courage v Crehan*, the Court of Justice has held that 'the full effectiveness of Article 81 of the Treaty and, in particular, the practical effect of the prohibition laid down in Article 81(1) would be put at risk if it were not open to any individual to claim damages for loss caused to him by a contract or by conduct liable to restrict or distort competition',[114] thereby confirming the possibility of actions for damages for violation of Article 81 EC before the national courts.

65. Article 6 of Regulation No 1/2003 provides that 'national courts shall have the power to apply Articles 81 and 82 of the Treaty'. That this is meant to cover not only the use of the antitrust provisions as a shield but also their use as a sword, is apparent from recital 7 of the Regulation according to which 'national courts have an essential part to play in applying the Community competition rules. When deciding disputes between private individuals, they protect the subjective rights under Community law, for example by awarding damages to the victims of infringements'.

66. In practice it appears that the use of Articles 81 and 82 EC as a sword in private litigation has been rare.[115] I do not expect Regulation No 1/2003 to bring about a major change in this respect. By abolishing the notification system and the exclusive competence of the Commission to apply Article 81(3) EC, the Regulation removes an obstacle for private enforcement of Article 81 EC, as it will no longer be possible in practice to bring court proceedings to a halt by lodging a notification with the Commission. As the experience with Article 82 EC shows, however, the relative absence of private enforcement is mainly due to other factors.[116]

67. If private actions for damages or injunctive relief are rare, it should however be noted that private complainants play an important role in the public enforcement of Articles 81 and 82 EC.[117] Indeed, under Article 7 of Regulation No 1/2003 (and before under Article 3 of Regulation No 17), any natural or legal person who can show a legitimate interest can lodge a complaint requesting the Commission to take action against a violation of Articles 81 or 82 EC. Many Commission actions start this way. If the Commission does not intend to act upon the complaint, it has to take a reasoned decision rejecting the complaint, and this decision can be subjected to judicial review by the Court of First Instance.[118]

---

[114] Judgment of 20 September 2001 in Case C–453/99 *Courage v Crehan* [2001] ECR I–6314 para 26. In para 104 of his Opinion of 22 May 2003 in Joined Cases C–246/01, C–306/01, C–354/01 and C–355/01, *AOK Bundesverband*, not yet published in ECR, Advocate General Jacobs has expressed the view that the same analysis would apply equally to injunctive relief.

[115] See R Whish, *Competition Law*, 5th edn (Lexis-Nexis Butterworths, 2003) 302, for references to some of the few examples known of. It is difficult to estimate the exact amount of private litigation because cases may be settled without much publicity.

[116] See FG Jacobs and T Deisenhofer, n 40 above; and *The Optimal Enforcement of EC Antitrust Law*, n 29 above, section 6.4.2.1.

[117] See Notice on the handling of complaints by the Commission, n 10 above.

[118] See Judgment of the Court of First instance of 18 September 1992 in Case T–24/90 *Automec II* [1992] ECR II–2250.

68. For the reasons set out in chapter 4 below, I personally find it far from obvious that private actions for damages should be encouraged. Indeed, from the perspective of ensuring that the antitrust prohibitions are not violated, public antitrust enforcement is inherently superior to private enforcement, because of more effective investigative and sanctioning powers, because private antitrust enforcement is driven by private profit motives which often diverge from the general interest in this area, and because of the high cost of private antitrust enforcement. I have argued that there does not even appear to be a case for a supplementary role for private enforcement, as the adequate level of sanctions and the adequate number and variety of prosecutions can be ensured more effectively and at a lower cost through public enforcement. In particular the argument that private damages actions following prosecutions by the Commission or by national authorities could provide useful additional deterrence does not convince me. If additional financial sanctions were indeed required for deterrence, these could be provided for in a much cheaper and more reliable way by increasing the fines imposed in the public enforcement proceeding.[119] It also seems difficult in my view to justify an increased role for private antitrust enforcement by the pursuit of corrective justice, as there does not appear to be a clear social need for such action, and because truly achieving corrective justice in the antitrust context is in practice a very difficult task. Any attempts to do so are likely to be very costly or to lead to results which do not really serve corrective justice.[120]

---

[119] It can moreover be doubted whether it would be desirable to have additional financial sanctions on companies on top of the already high fines imposed by the Commission today, as the result risks becoming anti-competitive in that companies are weakened as competitors (or are even bankrupted) or are led to raise their prices to pay for the fines and damages. See J-F Bellis, 'La Détermination des Amendes Pour Infraction au Droit Communautaire de la Concurrence—Bilan de Cinq Années d'Application des Lignes Directrices de 1998' (2003) Cahiers de Droit Européen 373, 396–97. It would appear much more desirable to increase deterrence by adding other types of penalties, such as director disqualification and imprisonment. See The Optimal Enforcement of EC Antitrust Enforcement, n 29 above, chs 8 and 9; and CD Ehlermann and I Atanasiu (eds), European Competition Law Annual 2001: Effective Private Enforcement of EC Antitrust Law (Hart Publishing, 2003) panel four.

[120] The victims most deserving of compensation would be those consumers who have been priced out of the market as a result of the antitrust violation. But determining who would have purchased the good or service if its price had been lower, is exceedingly difficult. If the good or service is an input rather than a final product, it will also be necessary to trace the indirect effects produced by this substitution. In the US system of private enforcement, no attempt is even made to identify these victims. As to those purchasers who paid an overcharge, unless they are final consumers, they are most likely to have passed on at least part of the overcharge to other, indirect purchasers. In the US, direct purchasers can recover the whole overcharge, even if they have entirely passed it on to their customers, and indirect customers cannot sue, at least not under federal law. If corrective justice is the objective, this simplifying rule appears undefendable, as it grants direct purchasers unjustified windfalls. Factually determining how much of an overcharge has been passed on, is however a very difficult task. On the side of the antitrust offender, equally complex problems arise. Indeed, the companies which committed the antitrust violations are unlikely to have retained their gains. It is more likely that the profits have been paid out in taxes, dividends, salaries and wages. In the US, empirical studies have estimated that unions are able to capture most of the monopoly profits earned by manufacturing firms. See GJ Werden and MJ Simon, 'Why price fixers should go to prison' [1987] Antitrust Bulletin 917 n 35. The shareholders who received the dividends or the benefit of the increased share prices may very well have sold on their shares by the time damages are imposed.

1.2 AREAS OF POTENTIAL CONCERN

1.2.1 Block Exemption Regulations

69. Whereas Regulation No 1/2003 does away with individual exemption decisions,[121] it does not abolish block exemption regulations.[122] The continued use of the instrument of block exemption regulations does not appear to pose any particular problems.

70. Since Article 83 EC has left the Council the choice how to implement Article 83(3) EC, it is perfectly compatible with the Treaty for the Council to abolish individual exemption decisions but to keep the instrument of block exemption regulations.

71. The legal nature and the effects of block exemption regulations are not different under Regulation No 1/2003 than under Regulation No 17. Block exemption regulations are general legislative acts which circumscribe a portion of the field where Article 81 EC is not applicable.[123] Like all regulations, they are binding in their entirety and directly applicable.[124]

72. It is true that the function of block exemptions has in part changed. As explained above,[125] block exemption regulations were initially adopted as an instrument to reduce the huge number of notifications which the Commission could not handle administratively. This historical justification is of course no longer relevant. However, block exemptions remain useful as a mechanism to save on enforcement costs. Indeed, for any category of agreements (i) which are very frequently concluded in business practice, (ii) for which a full individual assessment would in the overwhelming majority of cases lead to the conclusion that the conditions of Article 81(3) EC are fulfilled, and (iii) which can be sufficiently clearly defined, the cost saving, including the reduction of risk, at the level of self-assessment by the undertakings when concluding these agreements as well as at the level of ex post litigation is likely to outweigh the cost of adopting the block exemption regulation.[126]

---

[121] See n 22 above as to Article 10 of the Regulation.

[122] Even if the text of Article 9(1) of Regulation No 17 appeared to grant the Commission sole power not only to adopt individual exemption decisions but also block exemption regulations, the Commission has never claimed this. Instead the Commission has always accepted that its power to adopt block exemption regulations was based on later Council Regulations such as Regulation No 19/65 and Regulation No 2821/71. These Council Regulations remain in force. See Recital 10 and Article 40 of Regulation No 1/2003. Article 29 of Regulation No 1/2003 only generalises the possibility, already provided for in Article 7 of Regulation No 19/65, as amended by Regulation No 1215/1999 [1999] OJ L148/1, not only for the Commission but also, within certain conditions, for national competition authorities to withdraw the benefit of a block exemption in individual cases. See also n 81 above.

[123] See G Marenco, n 24 above, p 173.

[124] Second sentence of Article 249 EC.

[125] Para 57.

[126] See The Optimal Enforcement of EC Antitrust Law, n 29 above, section 6.2.3.2.

1.2.2 Burden of Proof

73. The move to a directly applicable exception system for Article 81(3) EC, as first announced in the White Paper,[127] had led to concerns among some commentators that the protection of competition would be weakened in that it would become more difficult for the competition authorities as well as for claimants using Article 81 EC as a sword in private litigation to establish violations of Article 81 EC.[128]

74. It is of course true that under Regulation No 1/2003 agreements falling under Article 81(1) EC and not covered by a block exemption regulation are no longer void for the sole reason that they have not been notified to the Commission, even if they fulfil the substantive conditions of Article 81(3) EC.[129] As explained above,[130] this change is however entirely desirable. The objectives underlying Article 81 EC are not served by voiding agreements which do not violate the substantive standard laid down in that Article.

75. The concern was however also that the competition authorities or the claimants using Article 81 EC as a sword in private litigation would have to shoulder the burden of proof as to the conditions of Article 81(3) EC not being fulfilled, whereas under Regulation No 17 it was incumbent on the undertaking requesting an exemption from the Commission 'to submit all evidence necessary to substantiate the economic justification for an exemption and to prove that it satisfies each of the four conditions laid down in Article 81(3) EC'.[131]

76. This concern about a possible change in the distribution of the burden of proof has led to the inclusion in the Regulation of Article 2, which reads as follows:

> In any national or Community proceedings for the application of Articles 81 and 82 of the Treaty, the burden of proving an infringement of Article 81(1) or of Article 82 of the Treaty shall rest on the party or the authority alleging the infringement. The undertaking or association of undertakings claiming the benefit of Article 81(3) of the Treaty shall bear the burden of proving that the conditions of that paragraph are fulfilled.

77. The last sentence of recital 5 of the Regulation explains that this provision 'affects neither national rules on the standard of proof nor obligations of competition authorities and courts of the Member States to ascertain the relevant facts of a case, provided that such rules and obligations are compatible with general principles of Community law'. Recital 37 further recalls that the provisions of the Regulation should be interpreted and applied with respect to the fundamental

---

[127] See n 5 above.
[128] See E Paulis and C Gauer, n 65 above, para 11.
[129] See paras 22 and 23 above.
[130] Para 24.
[131] Judgment of the Court of First Instance of 13 January 2004 in Case T–67/01 *JCB Service v Commission*, not yet published in ECR, para 162, referring to well-established case law.

rights and principles recognised in particular by the Charter of Fundamental Rights of the EU.[132]

78. In its recent judgment in the *Cement cartel* case, the Court of Justice has referred as follows to recital 5 and thus indirectly to Article 2 of the Regulation:

> As the Council very recently stated in the fifth recital of [Regulation No 1/2003], it should be for the party or the authority alleging an infringement of the competition rules to prove the existence thereof and it should be for the undertaking or the association of undertakings invoking the benefit of a defence against a finding of an infringement to demonstrate that the conditions for applying such defence are satisfied, so that the authority will then have to resort to other evidence.
>
> Although according to those principles the legal burden of proof is borne either by the Commission or by the undertaking or association concerned, the factual evidence on which a party relies may be of such a kind as to require the other party to provide an explanation or justification, failing which it is permissible to conclude that the burden of proof has been discharged.[133]

1.2.3 Self-Assessment

79. With the abolition of the notification system, companies envisaging an agreement or practice which could possibly violate Articles 81 or 82 EC no longer have the option to notify the agreement or practice to the Commission, thus obliging the Commission to take a position on its compatibility with Articles 81 and 82 EC.[134]

---

[132] At the time of adoption of the Regulation, the German delegation made the following statement, entered into the Council Minutes:

With a view to supplementing in particular Recital 5 of this Regulation, the Government of the Federal Republic of Germany confirms its view that Article 83 of the Treaty is not a sufficient legal basis for introducing or amending criminal law or criminal procedural law provisions. This applies in particular to fundamental procedural safeguards in criminal proceedings such as the presumption of innocence on the part of the defendant. The Government of the Federal Republic of Germany would point out that these procedural safeguards also apply to criminal-law-related proceedings such as monetary fine proceedings and enjoy constitutional status. It accordingly assumes that the present Regulation, and in particular Article 2 thereof, cannot amend or adversely affect such criminal law or criminal procedural law provisions applicable to criminal proceedings or criminal-law-related proceedings and legal principles of the Member States.

As to the question whether Article 83 EC is a sufficient legal basis for affecting criminal-law provisions, the answer to which I personally believe is positive, see Articles 29 and 47 EU; Case C–176/03 *Commission v Council*, currently pending before the Court of Justice; and *The Optimal Enforcement of EC Antitrust Law*, n 29 above, sections 8.7.4.1 and 8.7.4.2. See also para 200 below.

[133] Judgment of 7 January 2004 in Joined Cases C–204/00 P *Aalborg Portland A/S and Others v Commission*, not yet published in ECR, paras 78 and 79.

[134] The notification and authorisation system under Regulation No 17 only concerned Article 81(3) EC, but Article 2 of Regulation No 17 provided for the additional possibility of requesting a negative clearance concerning Articles 81(1) and 82 EC, which has also been abolished by Regulation No 1/2003. According to para 55 of the judgment of the Court of First Instance of 22 October 1997 in Joined Cases T–213/95 and T–18/96 *SCK and FNK v Commission* [1997] *ECR* II–1764, the Commission was under an obligation to act within a reasonable period upon receipt of either a notification or a request for negative clearance.

80. Given that in the last years of operation of the notification system, most companies already chose not to notify their agreements to the Commission, even if this meant that they were not legally enforceable,[135] the abolition of the notification system should not make much of a difference in this respect.[136]

81. Indeed, the content of the prohibitions of Articles 81 and 82 EC has been clarified to a very large extent through the existing block exemption regulations, the case law of the Community Courts, the decisions of the Commission, and the guidelines issued by the Commission, such as the Guidelines on vertical restraints and the Guidelines on the applicability of Article 81 EC to horizontal co-operation agreements.[137]

82. Moreover, the Commission may, where appropriate, issue guidance letters under the terms of the Notice on informal guidance relating to novel questions.[138]

83. It should also be recalled that it is the practice of the Commission to impose more than symbolic fines only in cases where it is established, either in horizontal instruments or in the case law and practice, that a certain behaviour constitutes an infringement.[139]

84. Finally, as I have argued in detail elsewhere,[140] provided that all existing information about the law is made publicly available, that the underlying conceptions of the law are broadly understood by the business and legal communities, and that the content of the law is not dependent on discretionary political decisions—three conditions which are fulfilled in the case of Articles 81 and 82 EC today[141]—companies, with the help of their legal and economic advisors, are better able than any competition authority to assess in advance whether envisaged agreements or practices comply with the antitrust prohibitions, as they have better access to all relevant information. Moreover, under the same conditions, the socially optimal level of investment is induced when companies internalize any remaining antitrust risk.[142]

1.2.4 Capability of National Courts to Apply Article 81(3) EC

1.2.4.1 The Issue Put in Perspective

85. As explained above, the reform brought about by Regulation No 1/2003 is unlikely to lead to a substantial increase in the number of cases before national

---

[135] See para 22 above.

[136] As explained in paras 20–61 above, the abolition of the notification system does make a major difference in several other respects.

[137] See n 63 above.

[138] See para 40 above.

[139] See para 4 of the Notice on informal guidance, n 11 above. See also Judgment of the Court of First Instance of 30 September 2003 in Joined Cases T–191/98 *Atlantic Container Line and Others v Commission*, not yet published in ECR, paras 1611–33.

[140] The Optimal Enforcement of EC Antitrust Law, n 29 above, section 6.2.2.3.

[141] See paras 37–40, 17, and 19 and 29 above.

[142] For a more detailed argumentation, see *The Optimal Enforcement of EC Antitrust Law*, n 29 above, section 6.2.2.3.

courts in which Articles 81 or 82 EC are used as a sword.[143] The reform will however have important effects on private litigation in which Article 81 EC is used as a shield. First, a number of agreements (all agreements falling under Article 81(1) EC and fulfilling the conditions of Article 81(3) EC but not benefiting from a block exemption regulation and never notified to the Commission) which were void under Regulation No 17 have become legally enforceable under Regulation No 1/2003. Second, in all cases in which Article 81 EC is invoked as a shield, national courts will now themselves apply Article 81(3) EC.[144] It is unclear whether the combined effect of these two changes will be an increase or a decrease in the number of cases in which Article 81 EC is invoked as a shield in contractual litigation before national courts.[145]

86. As also explained above, the fact that national courts themselves will now apply in such cases not only Article 81 (1) EC but also Article 81(3) EC is to be welcomed, because it better allows an integrated assessment of the two provisions, which require knowledge of largely the same facts and which are closely linked in substance, and because it consolidates the interpretation of Article 81(3) EC as a true rule of law.[146]

87. The fact that the application of Article 81(3) EC may require complex economic assessments should not pose any particular problem. Indeed, Article 81(3) EC is not different in this respect from Article 81(1) EC, Article 82 EC or Article 86(2) EC, the application of which equally requires complex economic assessments to be carried out by national courts.[147] National courts also deal with many other problems and areas of law which are not less complex or technical than the application of competition law,[148] where necessary with the help of experts.

88. National courts can find guidance which may assist them in the application of Article 81(3) EC in the existing block exemption regulations, the case law of the Community Courts, the decisions of the Commission, and the guidelines issued by the Commission, such as the Guidelines on vertical restraints and the Guidelines on the applicability of Article 81 EC to horizontal co-operation

---

[143] Para 66 above. See also E Paulis and C Gauer, n 65 above, para 77; A Riley, n 90 above, p 670.

[144] Paras 21–29 above.

[145] On the one hand, the number of contractual actions for performance or for damages because of non-performance is likely to increase. On the other hand, the percentage of cases in which Article 81 EC is invoked as a defence is likely to decrease.

[146] Paras 27–29.

[147] As to Article 81(1) EC, see Judgments of the Court of Justice of 11 July 1985 in Case 42/84 *Remia v Commission* [1985] ECR 2566 para 34; of 17 November 1987 in Joined Cases 142 and 156/84 *BAT and Reynolds v Commission* [1987] *ECR* 4487 para 62; and of 21 January 1999 in Joined Cases C–215/96 and C–216/96 *Bagnasco* [1999] *ECR* I–179 para 50. As to Article 82 EC, see for instance Judgment of the Court of Justice of 26 November 1998 in Case C–7/97 *Bronner v Mediaprint* [1998] *ECR* I7819. As to Article 86(2) EC, see for instance Judgment of the Court of Justice of 19 May 1993 in Case C–320/91 *Corbeau* [1993] *ECR* I–2563. As has been pointed out by G Marenco, n 24 above, p 165 and n 31, the analyses under Articles 81 and 82 EC are in fact closely intertwined in some cases, such as the Irish ice cream case. See Judgment of the Court of First Instance of 23 October 2003 in Case T–65/98 *Van den Bergh Foods v Commission*, not yet published in ECR.

[148] See also CD Ehlermann, n 44 above, p 585.

agreements,[149] and the new general Guidelines on the application of Article 81(3) of the Treaty.[150]

1.2.4.2 Article 15 of the Regulation

89. Article 15(1) of Regulation No 1/2003 provides that 'in proceedings for the application of Article 81 or Article 82 of the Treaty, courts of the Member States may ask the Commission to transmit to them information in its possession or its opinion on questions concerning the application of the Community competition rules'. This provision confirms the possibility, already existing before Regulation No 1/2003 on the basis of Article 10 EC, for national courts to call upon the Commission as a legal or economic expert.[151]

90. In the Notice on the cooperation between the Commission and the courts of the EU Member States in the application of Articles 81 and 82 EC, the Commission has stated that it will endeavour to provide the national court with any requested information within one month, and with any requested opinion within four months from the date it receives the request.[152]

91. As also explained in the Notice, 'the Commission is committed to remaining neutral and objective in its assistance. Indeed, the Commission's assistance to national courts is part of its duty to defend the public interest. It has therefore no intention to serve the private interest of the parties involved in the case before the national court'.[153]

> When giving its opinion, the Commission will limit itself to providing the national court with the factual information or the economic or legal clarification asked for, without considering the merits of the case pending before the national court. Moreover, unlike the authoritative interpretation of Community law by the Community Courts, the opinion of the Commission does not legally bind the national court.[154]

92. In the same logic, the Commission will not hear any of the parties in the case before the national court.[155] Respect for the right to adversarial proceedings

---

[149] See n 63 above.

[150] See n 13 above. As has been pointed out by G Marenco, n 24 above, p 165, more guidance is thus available for the interpretation of Article 81 EC than for the interpretation of Article 82 EC, which the national courts were already competent to apply before Regulation No 1/2003.

[151] See the Commission's 1993 Notice on cooperation between national courts and the Commission, [1993] OJ C39/5 (replaced by the new Notice on the cooperation between the Commission and the courts of the EU Member States in the application of Articles 81 and 82 EC, n 9 above); and Judgment of 11 January 2000 in Joined Cases C–174/98 P and C–189/98 P *Netherlands and Van der Wal v Commission* [2000] ECR I–47 paras 20–25.

[152] See n 9 above, paras 22 and 28.

[153] Idem, para 19.

[154] Idem, para 29.

[155] Idem, paras 19 and 30. If the Commission has been contacted by one of the parties on issues which are raised before the national court, it will inform the national court thereof, irrespective of whether these contacts took place before or after the national court's request for cooperation.

can be fully ensured by the national court after it has received the information or opinion from the Commission.[156]

93. The possibility for national courts to seek an opinion from the Commission under Article 15(1) of the Regulation is of course without prejudice to the possibility or the obligation for national courts to ask the Court of Justice for a preliminary ruling regarding the interpretation or the validity of Community law in accordance with Article 234 EC.[157] Where national law provides for this possibility, national courts may also seek advice from national competition authorities. Especially where the relevant markets are national or local, the latter may actually be better placed than the Commission to give assistance.

94. Article 15(1) of the Regulation only concerns the courts of the Member States,[158] not arbitration tribunals. This reflects the fact that this provision merely restates the Commission's obligations under Article 10 EC. Nothing would however prevent the Commission from also providing assistance to arbitration tribunals, if it were to receive requests for such assistance and if this would not unduly interfere with its enforcement priorities.

95. Whereas Article 15(1) of the Regulation provides for the right for national courts to ask assistance from the Commission (the possibility for national courts to request assistance from national competition authorities being a matter of national law), Article 15(3) of the Regulation gives both national competition authorities and the Commission the right to submit written observations to the national courts of their Member States on issues relating to the application of Articles 81 and 82 EC.[159]

96. The right of the Commission to submit written observations to national courts under Article 15(3) of the Regulation is more limited than that of national competition authorities, in that the Commission can only do so 'where the coherent application of Article 81 or Article 82 of the Treaty so requires'.[160] Both national competition authorities and the Commission can only submit observations 'acting on their own initiative', which means that the parties in the case pending before the national court do not have any right to ask for such intervention. Finally, the last sentence of Article 15(3) of the Regulation provides that, 'for the purposes of the preparation of their observations only, the competition

---

[156] Idem, para 30; as to the case law of the European Court of Human Rights on the right to adversarial proceedings, see section 2.7.2.2 below.

[157] Idem, para 27.

[158] Including those national competition authorities that are courts. See Recital 21 and Article 35(1) of the Regulation, para 2 of the Notice on the cooperation between the Commission and the courts, n 9 above. See also para 184 below.

[159] Article 15(3) of the Regulation adds that oral observations may also be made 'with the permission of the court in question'. Article 15(4) of the Regulation provides that Article 15 of the Regulation is 'without prejudice to wider powers to make observations before national courts conferred on competition authorities of the Member States under the law of their Member State'.

[160] Article 15 (3) of Regulation No 1/2003. See also Article 15(4) of the Regulation, n 159 above. Moreover, Article 15(2) of the Regulation, which imposes an obligation on Member States to forward to the Commission copies of judgments of their national courts deciding on the application of Articles 81 or 82 EC, suggests that the Commission is likely only to submit observations to appeal courts.

authorities of the Member States and the Commission may request the relevant court of the Member State to transmit or ensure the transmission to them of any documents necessary for the assessment of the case'.

1.2.4.3 Training and Specialisation

97. Some Member States have taken initiatives to provide training for their national judges in the application of Articles 81 and 82 EC, or to create a certain level of specialisation within their judiciary, so as to ensure that cases involving more complex questions of application of Articles 81 and 82 EC could be dealt with by judges with specific expertise.

98. On 21 April 2004 the European Parliament and the Council adopted a Decision establishing a Community action programme to promote bodies active at European level and support specific activities in the field of education and training.[161] This decision, based on Articles 149(4) and 150(4) EC, allows Community financial support for training of national judges in the application of Articles 81 and 82 EC.[162]

1.2.5 Allocation of Cases Within the Network of Competition Authorities

99. Regulation No 1/2003 creates a system of parallel competences in which the Commission and the national competition authorities can apply Articles 81 and 82 EC in individual cases.[163] This raises the question as to how cases are to be allocated within the network of competition authorities.

1.2.5.1 Principles of Allocation

100. The Regulation does not itself contain any rules on case allocation, only a set of instruments which allow a flexible allocation of cases to be organised.[164] However, recital 18 of the Regulation indicates that 'the objective [is] that each case should be handled by a single authority'.

101. Further principles of allocation are contained in the Commission Notice on cooperation within the network.[165] Paragraph 8 of this Notice reads as follows:

---

[161] Decision No 791/2004/EC, [2004] OJ L138/31.

[162] Idem, Recital 8 and action 3C listed in the annexe.

[163] See para 11 of the Joint Statement of the Council and the Commission on the functioning of the network, n 8 above, and para 1 of the Notice on cooperation within the network, n 7 above.

[164] These instruments are the possibility to suspend or terminate duplicative proceedings (Article 13), the possibility for members of the network to assist each other in fact-finding (Article 22), the possibility to exchange information and transfer entire cases (Article 12), the information and consultation mechanisms within the network and the Commission's power to withdraw a case from a national authority (Article 11).

[165] See n 7 above.

An authority can be considered to be well placed to deal with a case if the following three cumulative conditions are met:

(1) the agreement or practice has substantial direct actual or foreseeable effects on competition within its territory, is implemented within or originates from its territory;
(2) the authority is able to effectively bring to an end the entire infringement ie it can adopt a cease and desist order the effect of which will be sufficient to bring an end to the infringement and it can, where appropriate, sanction the infringement adequately;
(3) it can gather, possibly with the assistance of other authorities, the evidence required to prove the infringement.

102. Paragraph 9 of the same Notice adds that 'the above criteria indicate that a material link between the infringement and the territory of a Member State must exist in order for that Member State's competition authority to be considered well placed'.

103. As to the Commission, it considers itself—

particularly well placed if one or several agreement(s) or practice(s), including networks of similar agreements or practices, have effects on competition in more than three Member States (cross-border markets covering more than three Member States or several national markets). Moreover, the Commission is particularly well placed to deal with a case if it is closely linked to other Community provisions which may be exclusively or more effectively applied by the Commission, if the Community interest requires the adoption of a Commission decision to develop Community competition policy when a new competition issue arises or to ensure effective enforcement.[166]

1.2.5.2 Re-Allocation

104. As the above principles of allocation have been set out by the Commission in close cooperation with the Member States,[167] and are also brought to the attention of potential complainants,[168] it is expected that 'in most instances the authority that receives a complaint or starts an ex-officio-proceeding will remain in charge of the case'.[169]

105. Re-allocation could possibly arise at the outset of proceedings either because an authority receiving a complaint considers itself not well placed to deal with it, or because other authorities, informed about the fact that an authority has started to act on a certain case, express an interest in dealing with that case.[170]

106. Such mutual provision of information regarding new cases is provided for under Articles 11(3) of the Regulation, which reads as follows:

The competition authorities of the Member States shall, when acting under Article 81 or Article 82 of the Treaty, inform the Commission in writing before or without delay after

---

[166] Notice on cooperation within the network, n 7 above, paras 14 and 15.
[167] See Recital 15 of the Regulation and the Joint Statement of the Council and the Commission, n 8 above.
[168] See paras 19–25 of the Notice on the handling of complaints by the Commission, n 10 above.
[169] Notice on cooperation within the network, n 7 above, para 6.
[170] Idem.

commencing the first formal investigative measure. This information may also be made available to the competition authorities of the other Member States.

107. That the information will as a rule be made available to all members of the network can be deduced from paragraph 10 of the Joint Statement of the Council and the Commission on the functioning of the network.[171]

108. Article 11(2) of the Regulation similarly provides, but without an indication as to the timing, that 'the Commission shall transmit to the competition authorities of the Member States copies of the most important documents it has collected' when dealing with a case.

109. The Notice on cooperation within the network states:

Network members will inform each other of pending cases by means of a standard form containing limited details of the case such as the authority dealing with the case, the product, territories and parties concerned, the alleged infringement, the suspected duration of the infringement, and the origin of the case. [...]

Where case re-allocation issues arise, they will be resolved swiftly, normally within a period of two months starting from the date of the first information sent to the network pursuant to [Article 11(2) or (3) of the Regulation]. During this period, competition authorities will endeavour to reach an agreement on a possible re-allocation and, where relevant, on the modalities for parallel action.

In general, the competition authority or authorities that is/are dealing with a case at the end of the re-allocation period should continue to deal with the case until the completion of the proceedings. Re-allocation of a case after the initial allocation period of two months should only occur where the facts known about the case change materially during the course of the proceedings.[172]

110. The mechanism of case allocation set up by the Regulation and by the Notice on cooperation within the network is thus flexible and consensual. However, if the members of the network were not to reach an agreement as to which of them should deal with a case, or if a national authority were to fail to respect the principles of allocation set out in the Notice, in particular the requirement of a material link between the infringement and the national territory,[173] the Commission could always under Article 11(6) of the Regulation initiate proceedings itself, thus relieving all national authorities of their competence to deal with the case.[174]

1.2.5.3 Rights of the Private Parties Concerned

111. Paragraph 34 of the Notice on cooperation within the network states that, 'if a case is reallocated within the network, the undertakings concerned and the complainant(s) are informed as soon as possible by the competition authorities involved'.

---

[171] See n 8 above. See however para 219 below for the special case of leniency applications.
[172] See n 8 above, paras 17–19.
[173] Para 102 above.
[174] See paras 43 above and 182 below.

112. As to complainants, Article 13(1) of the Regulation provides that the fact that another member of the network is dealing with the case shall be sufficient grounds for the Commission or a national competition authority to reject the complaint. If the complainant does not want the authority to which the case has been reallocated to deal with its complaint, it can always withdraw the complaint.[175]

113. If an undertaking or a person being investigated is dissatisfied with the re-allocation, could it bring an application for judicial review against any decision?

114. If the case is reallocated from one national competition authority to another, up to four decisions could possibly be identified: (1) a decision by the first authority to terminate its proceedings, (2) a decision by the second authority to open proceedings, and possibly also (3) a decision by the first authority to transfer to the second authority the information in its file, and (4) a decision by the second authority to take into its file this information received from the first authority. Whether the first and the third decisions are challengeable acts depends on the national law of the Member State of the first authority, and whether the second and fourth decisions constitute challengeable acts depends on the national law of the second Member State. In any event, it would seem unlikely that such appeals, if admissible under national law, could be successful. Indeed, the first decision does not harm the undertaking or person concerned.[176] The second decision does not appear in any relevant sense different from any other opening of proceedings by a competent competition authority. The third and fourth decisions are covered by Article 12(1) of the Regulation, which provides that, 'for the purpose of applying Articles 81 and 82 of the Treaty the Commission and the competition authorities of the Member States shall have the power to provide one another with and use in evidence any matter of fact and law, including confidential information', as long as the fourth decision respects the limitations set out in Articles 12(2) and (3) of the Regulation.[177]

115. If a case is reallocated to the Commission, there will be a decision by the Commission to open proceedings (which, pursuant to Article 11(6) of the Regulation, automatically relieves the national competition authority previously dealing with the case from its competence). While the Member States could no doubt bring an action for annulment of this decision before the Court of Justice, an action brought by a company or other person being investigated before the Court of First Instance would appear inadmissible, because the decision is simply a preliminary step in the Commission's procedure.[178] Apart from the decision to open proceedings, the Commission may also request the national competition

---

[175] The authority could of course continue or reopen the case on its own motion.

[176] The harm consisting of the sanctions possibly later imposed by the second authority does not flow from the decision by the first authority to terminate its proceedings. This harm would only arise later, if and when the second authority imposes these sanctions. Of course the possible later decision in which the second authority imposes the sanctions will be challengeable.

[177] See n 264 and para 195 below.

[178] Compare with the Judgment of the Court of Justice of 11 November 1981 in Case 60/81 *IBM v Commission* [1981] ECR 2639.

authority, pursuant to Article 18(6) of the Regulation, to transmit the information in its file. Again an application for annulment by a company being investigated before the Court of First Instance would appear inadmissible, as it would simply relate to a preliminary step in the Commission's proceedings. Alternatively, the national competition authority could decide on its own motion to transfer the information in its file to the Commission. Whether this would constitute a challengeable act depends on the national law of the Member States concerned, but it is hard to see how an appeal could ever be successful, as such transfer is covered by Article 12(1) of the Regulation. Finally, a decision by the Commission to include the information thus received in its file would again appear non-challengeable, as it is simply a preliminary step in its proceedings.

1.2.5.4 Parallel Action and the Principle of Ne Bis In Idem

116. According to recital 18 of the Regulation, 'the objective [is] that each case should be handled by a single authority'. However, the Joint Statement of the Council and the Commission on the functioning of the network[179] and the Notice on cooperation within the network[180] do not exclude the possibility of parallel action by several national competition authorities.[181]

117. This raises the question to what extent such parallel action is compatible with the principle of *ne bis in idem* as recognised in Article 50 of the Charter of Fundamental Rights of the European Union.[182] According to recital 37 of the Regulation, 'this Regulation respects the fundamental rights and observes the principles recognised in particular by the Charter of Fundamental Rights of the European Union. Accordingly, this Regulation should be interpreted and applied with respect to those rights and principles'.

118. Article 50 of the Charter restates the principle of *ne bis in idem* as follows:

> No one shall be liable to be tried or punished again in criminal proceedings for an offence for which he or she has already been finally acquitted or convicted within the Union in accordance with the law.

119. According to the explanatory memorandum provided by the Secretariat of the body which drafted the Charter,[183] this provision—

---

[179] See n 8 above, in particular paras 16 and 18.

[180] See n 7 above, in particular paras 12–13.

[181] Parallel action by the Commission and one or more national competition authorities is excluded by Article 11(6) of the Regulation.

[182] [2000] OJ C364/1. On the legal status of the Charter in general, see 'European Union Law and National Constitutions', FIDE XX Congress (London, 30 October–2 November 2002) and its reports: J Dutheil de la Rochère and I Pernice, 'General Report: European Union Law and National Constitutions, FIDE XX Congress (London, 2002); P Oliver, Community Report: European Union Law and National Constitutions, FIDE XX Congress (London, 2002), both available at http://www.fide2002.org. See also section 2.4.3 below.

[183] Council of the EU, Charter of Fundamental Rights of the European Union—Explanations relating to the complete text of the Charter (December 2000), available at http://ue.eu.int/df/docs/en/EN_2001_1023.pdf.

corresponds to Article 4 of Protocol No 7 to the ECHR, but its scope is extended to European Union level between the Courts of the Member States.[184]

In accordance with Article 50, the *non bis in idem* principle applies not only within the jurisdiction of one State but also between the jurisdictions of several Member States. That corresponds to the acquis in Union law; see Articles 54 to 58 of the Schengen Convention, Article 7 of the Convention on the Protection of the European Communities' Financial Interests and Article 10 of the Convention on the Fight Against Corruption.[185]

120. As to the scope of the right guaranteed, Article 52 of the Charter provides generally:

1. Any limitation on the exercise of the rights and freedoms recognised by this Charter must be provided for by law and respect the essence of those rights and freedoms. Subject to the principle of proportionality, limitations may be made only if they are necessary and genuinely meet objectives of general interest recognised by the Union or the need to protect the rights and freedoms of others.
2. [...]
3. In so far as this Charter contains rights which correspond to rights guaranteed by the Convention for the Protection of Human Rights and Fundamental Freedoms, the meaning and scope of those rights shall be the same as those laid down by the said Convention. This provision shall not prevent Union law providing more extensive protection.

121. As argued in chapter 3 below, the principle of *ne bis in idem* prohibits multiple prosecution or punishments of the same defendants for the same offence, not merely for the same effects of an offence.[186] In my view, if for example two national competition authorities were to impose fines on the same companies for the same cartel agreement covering a market comprising the territories of the two Member States concerned, a violation of the principle of *ne bis in idem* could not be avoided with the argument that each national competition authority was only taking into account the effects of the violation of Article 81 EC on its own national territory.[187]

---

[184] Idem, at 76.

[185] Idem, at 69. Convention of 19 June 1990 implementing the Schengen Agreement [2000] OJ L239/19; Convention of 26 July 1995 on the protection of the European Communities' financial interests [1995] OJ C316/49; Convention of 26 May 1997 on the fight against corruption involving officials of the European Communities or officials of Member States of the European Union [1997] OJ C195/2.

[186] See also Opinion of 11 February 2003 of Advocate General Ruiz-Jarabo Colomer in Case C–213/00 P *Italcementi v Commission*, not yet published in ECR, paras 88–98, and the speech by Judge Bo Vesterdorf, President of the Court of First Instance of the EC, 'Double Jeopardy by Parallel International Prosecution of Cartels—Ne Bis in Idem Principle in Competition Matters' (5th International Cartel Workshop, European Commission, Brussels, 3 October 2003).

[187] See also n 88 above as to the 'criminal' nature of EC competition fines, and paras 125–31 below as to the territorial scope of fining decisions by national competition authorities. The situation is of course different with regard to countries outside the European Union, to which Article 50 of the Charter does not apply. See Judgment of the Court of First Instance of 9 July 2003 in Case T–224/00 *Archer Daniels Midland v Commission*, not yet published in ECR, paras 85–112; and Judgment of the Court of First Instance of 29 April 2004 in Joined Cases T–236/01 etc *Tokai Carbon and Others v Commission*, not yet published in ECR, para 137.

122. The prohibition of double prosecution and punishment does not exclude the possibility of parallel proceedings being conducted by several members of the network of competition authorities at the same time against the same defendants, as long as none of these proceedings has already reached the stage of final acquittal or conviction. This means that at a preliminary stage, when it may not yet be clear which member of the network is the best placed to deal with the case, several competition authorities may investigate the same agreement or practice. However, at the latest at the moment when the first proceeding is closed by a final acquittal or conviction, the other authorities have to discontinue their proceedings with regard to the same defendants.[188]

1.2.6 Extraterritorial Powers of National Competition Authorities

123. As discussed above, Article 5 of the Regulation provides that 'the competition authorities of the Member States shall have the power to apply Articles 81 and 82 of the Treaty in individual cases' and that, for this purpose, they may take decisions requiring that an infringement be brought to an end, ordering interim measures, accepting commitments and/or imposing fines, periodic penalty payments or any other penalty provided for in their national law.[189] The Joint Statement of the Council and the Commission on the functioning of the network explains that the national competition authorities 'will be fully competent to apply Articles 81 and 82 of the Treaty' and that 'without prejudice to Article 11(6) of the Regulation, all Network members have full parallel competence to apply Articles 81 and 82 of the Treaty'.[190]

124. As far as fact-finding powers are concerned, the Regulation expressly provides for the means to enable national competition authorities to exercise this full competence. Indeed, Article 22(1) of the Regulation provides:

> the competition authority of a Member State may in its own territory carry out any inspection or other fact-finding measure under its national law on behalf and for the account of the competition authority of another Member State in order to establish whether there has been an infringement of Article 81 or Article 82 of the Treaty.[191]

---

[188] As to what constitutes a final acquittal or conviction, see Judgment of the Court of Justice of 11 February 2003 in Joined Cases C–187/01 and C–385/01 *Hüseyin Gözütok and Klaus Brügge* [2003] ECR I–1378 and section 2.5.2.4.2 below.

[189] Para 45 above.

[190] See n 8 above, paras 6 and 11.

[191] It is true that this provision does not contain an obligation for the requested national competition authority to provide fact-finding assistance. However, if a national competition authority were to refuse unreasonably a request from another national competition authority under Article 22(1) of the Regulation to carry out an inspection, the Commission could arguably oblige it carry out the inspection under Article 22(2) of the Regulation and subsequently transfer the information obtained to the requesting national competition authority under Article 12 of the Regulation.

Article 12 of the Regulation allows the transfer and subsequent use of the information thus obtained.[192]

125. As far as sanctioning powers are concerned, the Regulation does not expressly provide for the power for national competition authorities, when imposing fines or other penalties, to take into account the effects of violations of Articles 81 or 82 EC in the territory of other Member States. The Regulation does not provide either for mechanisms allowing the decisions of national competition authorities imposing fines, requiring termination of an infringement or ordering interim measures to be enforced in other Member States.

126. Emil Paulis and Céline Gauer have argued that, because:

the limitations inherent in public international law, which prohibits a sovereign State to exercise its police powers outside its territory have not been abolished by the Regulation, each national authority can thus in principle order the termination and sanction the effects of infringements only on its territory. A Community act or a bilateral or even multilateral agreement could change this state of affairs, but under the existing law this limited power of the Member States must be considered as given.[193]

127. Dr Alan Riley has expressed the view that the absence of provisions in the Regulation giving extraterritorial sanctioning powers to national competition authorities reflects 'a refusal of the Commission to accept a real partnership with the [national competition authorities], which would involve real sharing of the caseload and the development of the law'.[194]

128. On the other hand, Laura Pignataro has pointed out that, according to well established case law of the Court of Justice, where Community legislation refers to national law for the purpose of penalties for an infringement, Article 10 EC requires the Member States to make the penalties effective, proportionate and dissuasive.[195] Applied to Article 5 of Regulation No 1/2003, she draws the conclusion that the combined reading of recital 18 of the Regulation, which states that the objective is that each case should be dealt with by a single authority,[196] and

---

[192] See n 264 and para 195 below as to the restrictions contained in Article 12(2) and (3) of the Regulation, and paras 218 and 219 below as to information provided by leniency applicants.

[193] E Paulis and C Gauer, n 65 above, para 58. This is my translation:

Les limitations inhérentes au droit international public qui interdit à un Etat souverain d'exercer ses pouvoirs de police à l'extérieur de son territoire n'ont cependant pas été abolies par le règlement. Chaque autorité nationale ne peut donc en principe ordonner la cessation et sanctionner les effets des infractions que sur son territoire. Un acte communautaire ou un accord bilatéral ou même multilatéral pourrait changer cette situation mais à droit constant, ce pouvoir limité des Etats membres doit être considéré comme une donnée.

See also the last sentence of the explanations on Article 5 in the Commission's Explanatory Memorandum to the proposal for Regulation No 1/2003, n 4 above, which states (without further explanation) that 'decisions adopted by national competition authorities do not have legal effects outside the territory of their Member State'.

[194] A Riley, n 90 above, p 665.

[195] Judgments of the Court of Justice of 21 September 1989 in Case 68/88 *Commission v Greece* [1989] ECR 2984 paras 23 and 24, and of 18 October 2001 in Case C–354/99 *Commission v Ireland* [2001] *ECR* I–7684 para 46.

[196] See para 116 above.

Article 10 EC requires that national competition authorities, when sanctioning an infringement of Articles 81 or 82 EC, take into account the effects of the infringement in the territory of other Member States.[197]

129. I would personally tend to agree with the latter view.[198] The scope of the powers to apply Articles 81 and 82 EC granted by Article 5 of the Regulation to national competition authorities should be determined on the basis of Community law alone. Reading Article 5 of the Regulation, in the light of the Joint Statement of the Council and the Commission describing the system set up by the Regulation as one of 'full parallel competence' of the Commission and all national competition authorities,[199] and in the light of the need for effective enforcement of Articles 81 and 82 EC in full respect for the principle of *ne bis in idem*,[200] I would personally take the view that the Regulation has given the national competition authorities the power (and, where necessary for the effective enforcement of Articles 81 and 82 EC, also the obligation, in the light of Articles 10 and 12 EC), when imposing fines or other penalties, to take into account the effects of violations of Articles 81 or 82 EC in the territory of other Member States.[201] I would equally consider that national competition authorities have been granted the power by the Regulation to order termination of infringements or interim measures throughout the Community.

130. These conclusions should not be affected by the absence of mechanisms allowing a national competition authority to call upon the authorities and courts of other Member States to enforce its decisions on its behalf,[202] and the practical difficulties which might result in some situations where undertakings or persons based in other Member States did not obey the decisions of a national competition authority.[203]

131. Finally, as explained above,[204] there is no risk that for instance the Irish competition authorities would deal with a case where the relevant market is Scandinavia, because the principles of allocation set out in the Notice on

---

[197] L Pignataro, 'La Riforma del Diritto Comunitario Della Concorrenza: Il Regolamento N 1/2003 Sull'Applicazione Degli Articoli 81 e 82 del Trattato CE' (2003) 8 *Contratto e Impresa / Europa* 1–233, 264.

[198] See also n 54 of ch 3 below.

[199] See para 123 above.

[200] See paras 117–22 above.

[201] I would personally also take the view, at a more philosophical level, that the idea of a national authority 'sanctioning the effects of infringements only on its territory' reflects an undesirable conception of fines as instruments not to deter infringements but merely to price their effects. See RD Cooter, 'Prices and Sanctions' (1984) 84 *Columbia Law Review* 1523–60; C Harding, 'Business Cartels as a Criminal Activity: Reconciling North American and European Models of Regulation' (2002) 9 *Maastricht Journal of European and Comparative Law* 393–419.

[202] To the extent that such mechanisms are not provided for in other provisions of Community law, provisions under Title VI of the EU Treaty, the national laws of the other Member States, or international agreements between the Member States concerned.

[203] I would personally not expect such practical difficulties to arise in many cases. The Commission is potentially faced with similar practical problems when for instance it imposes fines on companies based in third countries. However, it appears that companies based in third countries usually pay the fines imposed on them by the Commission.

[204] Paras 102 and 110.

cooperation within the network indicate that a material link between the infringement and the territory of a Member State must exist in order for that Member State's competition authority to be considered well placed, and the Commission can ensure respect for these principles of allocation through the possible use of Article 11(6) of the Regulation.

1.2.7 Capability of National Competition Authorities

132. There are significant differences in the levels of resources and experience of the competition authorities of the different Member States.[205]

133. However, it should be recalled that the system set up by Regulation No 1/2003 is one of parallel competences between the Commission and all national competition authorities.[206] If for instance the Belgian or the Luxembourg competition authorities were not to have sufficient resources to deal with a case for which the relevant geographic market is the Benelux, the case could be dealt with by the Dutch competition authority or by the Commission.[207]

134. Article 35(1) of the Regulation provides that 'the Member States shall designate the competition authorities responsible for the application of Articles 81 and 82 of the Treaty in such a way that the provisions of this regulation are effectively complied with'.

135. This provision, read together with the provisions of Articles 14, 20 and 22 of the Regulation, imposes on Member States the obligation to ensure that their national competition authorities have the necessary resources to be represented in the Advisory Committee, to provide assistance in inspections conducted by the Commission on their territory and to undertake inspections requested by the Commission.

136. Article 5 of Regulation No 1/2003 provides that 'the competition authorities of the Member States shall have the power to apply Articles 81 and 82 of the Treaty in individual cases'.[208] Focusing on the word 'effectively' in Article 35(1) of the Regulation, it can be argued that Articles 35(1) and 5 of the Regulation, read together, impose on Member States the obligation to ensure that their national competition authorities have not only the legal power to apply Articles 81 and 82 EC in individual cases, but also a minimum of resources to enable them to make effective use of these powers.

137. The adoption and entry into application of Regulation No 1/2003 has in fact led a number of Member States to increase the resources available to their competition authorities.[209]

---

[205] See also A Riley, n 90 above, p 658–59.

[206] See paras 49 and 123 above.

[207] See n 209 below as to the resources of the Belgian and Luxembourg competition authorities.

[208] See para 45 above.

[209] For example, the Regulation has led to a radical reform in Luxembourg, involving the creation of a new competition authority. In Belgium, the government has recently started allocating more resources to the national competition authorities.

1.2.8 NATIONAL BIAS AND RENATIONALISATION

1.2.8.1 Article 11 of the Regulation Insures Against National Bias

138. Dr Alan Riley has observed that,

the Commission has, over 40 years, established a remarkable degree of perceived independence in dealing with the Member States on core antitrust matters. Even if an individual [national competition authority] does have a degree of real independence of action from its government, it is likely to find it more difficult to establish the perception that it is acting independently amongst the other actors in the field compared with the supranational Commission.[210]

139. I have no reason to suspect that the competition authorities of the 25 Member States would not be sufficiently independent or professional to avoid bias in favour of national interests. The issue should, however, be considered, if only because, even in the absence of any real national bias, there may indeed be a problem of perceptions. In particular, undertakings or persons unhappy with a decision of a competition authority of another Member State may be led to believe that they were the victims of national bias.

140. One could distinguish two situations of national bias. The first would be where the competition authority of a Member State is excessively severe in that it wrongly prohibits or punishes, at the request of a national complainant, the behaviour of a foreign undertaking, for instance aggressive competition on the merits by a foreign dominant undertaking, harming less efficient national competitors. The second situation would be where a national competition authority is excessively lax in that it refuses to act upon complaints by foreigners against violations committed by domestic undertakings, for instance complaints by foreign entrants about foreclosure of distribution channels by the domestic incumbent.

141. The second situation is less of a problem, because the foreign complainants always have the alternative to bring their complaint before the Commission, national courts, or possibly the competition authority of another Member State. The first situation is much more problematic. Article 11(4) and (6) of the Regulation address this risk.[211]

142. Article 11(4) of the Regulation reads as follows:

No later than 30 days before adoption of a decision requiring an infringement to be brought to an end, accepting commitments or withdrawing the benefit of a block exemption Regulation, the competition authorities of the Member States shall inform the Commission. To that effect, they shall provide the Commission with a summary of the case, the envisaged decision or, in the absence thereof, any other document indicating

---

[210] A Riley, n 90 above, p 660.

[211] As explained in paras 162 and 163 below, Article 11(4) and (6) of the Regulation also serve more generally to ensure consistent application of Articles 81 and 82 EC, and, as explained in para 110 above, Article 11(6) of the Regulation also plays a role in the system of case allocation.

the proposed course of action. This information may also be made available to the competition authorities of the other Member States. At the request of the Commission, the acting competition authority shall make available to the Commission other documents it holds which are necessary for the assessment of the case. The information supplied to the Commission may be made available to competition authorities of the other Member States. National competition authorities may also exchange between themselves information necessary for the assessment of a case that they are dealing with under Article 81 or Article 82 of the Treaty.

143. Article 11(4) of the Regulation thus obliges national competition authorities to consult the Commission before adopting a negative decision.[212] It can be deduced from paragraph 10 of the Joint statement of the Council and the Commission on the functioning of the network[213] that the information received by the Commission will as a rule also be made available to the competition authorities of the other Member States, who might thus raise concerns over national bias. If the Commission were to share such concerns, it could take away the case from the acting national authority by application of Article 11(6) of the Regulation.[214] Even if it is unlikely that the Commission will often, or ever, have to use this mechanism to prevent a biased decision being adopted, its presence will have a preventive effect, to the extent necessary, as well as reassure against perceptions of national bias.

144. Finally, at a deeper level, the Regulation, which leads to much closer and more intensive exchange and cooperation within the network of national competition authorities and the Commission, tends to reduce the risk of national bias. Indeed, if there exists a problem of bias in favour of national interests, it must be because the competition authorities of the Member States would each be accountable or feel accountable to domestic interests.[215] By making all national competition authorities and the Commission act in close cooperation, as its Article 11(1) provides for, the Regulation will tend over time to make national authorities feel accountable towards the other authorities in the network, and susceptible to their peer pressure, which will reduce any risk of national bias.[216]

[212] When comparing the list of types of decisions in the first sentence of Article 11(4) with the list of decisions in Article 5 of the Regulation, it would appear that there is no obligation for national competition authorities to consult the Commission on decisions imposing fines or other penalties, unless these decisions also include an order requiring the infringement to be brought to an end (which may not be the case in decisions regarding past infringements). As can be deduced *a contrario* from para 24 of the Joint Statement of the Council and the Commission on the functioning of the network, n 8 above, and para 48 of the Notice on cooperation within the network, n 7 above, the understanding within the network is that consultation will take place on all decisions imposing fines or other penalties. The legality of this understanding cannot be doubted in the light of Article 11(5) of the Regulation, which provides that 'the competition authorities of the Member States may consult the Commission on any case involving the application of Community law'.

[213] See n 8 above.

[214] See paras 43 above and 181 below.

[215] See also P Mavroidis and D Neven, 'The White Paper: A Whiter Shade of Pale: Of Interest and Interests' in CD Ehlermann and I Atanasiu (eds), *European Competition Law Annual 2000: The Modernisation of EC Antitrust Policy* (Hart Publishing, 2001) 207.

[216] See also G Majone, 'The Credibility Crisis of Community Regulation' (2000) 38 *Journal of Common Market Studies* 273, 296–98.

1.2.8.2 Article 3 of the Regulation Prevents Renationalisation

145. If national competition authorities had been left free to choose whether to apply Articles 81 and 82 EC or national competition law in any individual case, there would have been a risk that they might in some cases choose to apply national law rather than Articles 81 and 82 EC so as to avoid being submitted to the cooperation mechanisms set out in Article 11 of the Regulation.

146. For this reason, and also more generally to encourage the application of Articles 81 and 82 EC,[217] Article 3(1) of the Regulation provides as follows:

> Where the competition authorities of the Member States or national courts apply national competition law to agreements, decisions by associations of undertakings or concerted practices within the meaning of Article 81(1) of the Treaty which may affect trade between Member States within the meaning of that provision, they shall also apply Article 81 of the Treaty to such agreements, decisions or concerted practices. Where the competition authorities of the Member States or national courts apply national competition law to any abuse prohibited by Article 82 of the Treaty, they shall also apply Article 82 of the Treaty.

147. When dealing with an agreement, decision or practice within the meaning of Article 81(1) EC which may affect trade between Member States or an abuse prohibited by Article 82 EC, national competition authorities will thus have the choice either to apply only Articles 81 or 82 EC, or to apply both national competition law and Articles 81 or 82 EC. In both cases, they will have to inform the Commission at the beginning of their proceedings pursuant to Article 11(3) of the Regulation and inform the Commission of their envisaged decision at the latest 30 days before its adoption in accordance with Article 11(4) of the Regulation. In both cases the Commission can remove the case from them by opening proceedings under Article 11(6) of the Regulation. Indeed, it follows from Articles 11(6) and 3(1) of the Regulation, read together, that an initiation of proceedings by the Commission relieves national competition authorities not only of their competence to apply Articles 81 or 82 EC, but also of their competence to apply national competition law in the same case.

148. With regard to Article 81 EC only, Article 3(2) of the Regulation goes even further in encouraging the application of Community law by excluding the possibility of prohibiting under national competition law agreements or practices which fall within the scope of application of Article 81 EC but which are not prohibited by it.[218]

---

[217] See the first sentence of Recital 8 of the Regulation. Article 3(1) of the Regulation also applies to national courts, thus ensuring the applicability of the cooperation mechanisms provided for in Article 15 of the Regulation. See paras 89–96 above. As to the origin of Article 3 of the Regulation, see also E Paulis and C Gauer, n 65 above, paras 16–24.

[218] That national competition authorities or national courts cannot authorise under national law agreements or practices prohibited by Article 81 or 82 EC is so obvious an application of the general principle of primacy of Community law that the Council did not need to state so in the Regulation.

149. Indeed, Article 3(2) of the Regulation reads as follows:

The application of national competition law may not lead to the prohibition of agreements, decisions by associations of undertakings or concerted practices which may affect
trade between Member States but which do not restrict competition within the meaning
of Article 81(1) of the Treaty, or which fulfil the conditions of Article 81(3) of the Treaty
or which are covered by a Regulation for the application of Article 81(3) of the Treaty.
Member States shall not under this Regulation be precluded from adopting and applying on their territory stricter national laws which prohibit or sanction unilateral conduct
engaged in by undertakings.

150. As is apparent from the text of Article 3(1) of the Regulation, the obligation to apply also Articles 81 or 82 EC, with all the consequences as to the applicability of the provisions of Article 11 and 15 of the Regulation, only exists when
national competition authorities or national courts 'apply national competition
law to agreements [...] or concerted practices [...] which may affect trade between
Member States within the meaning of [Article 81 EC]' or 'apply national competition law to any abuse prohibited by Article 82 [EC]'. As appears from the text of
Article 82 EC, an abuse is only prohibited by that provision 'in so far as it may
affect trade between Member States'.

151. The concept of 'may affect trade between Member States' within the
meaning of Articles 81 and 82 EC has been interpreted in a substantial number of
judgments of the Community Courts. The Commission has made available its
understanding of this concept, as interpreted by the Community Courts, in its
Guidelines on the effect on trade concept contained in Articles 81 and 82 of the
Treaty.[219]

152. As to the question what constitutes 'national competition law', Article
3(3) of the Regulation expressly provides that Article 3(1) and (2) do not apply
'when the competition authorities and the courts of the Member States apply
national merger control laws nor do they preclude the application of provisions of
national law that predominantly pursue an objective different from that pursued
by Articles 81 and 82 of the Treaty'.[220]

153. The last sentence of recital 8 of the Regulation adds the following:

This Regulation does not apply to national laws which impose criminal sanctions on natural persons except to the extent that such sanctions are the means whereby competition
rules applying to undertakings are enforced.

154. I personally find this sentence difficult to understand.[221]

---

[219] See n 12 above.

[220] Recital 9 of the Regulation adds that 'Articles 81 and 82 of the Treaty have as their objective the
protection of competition on the market', and confirms in particular that 'Member States may under
this Regulation implement on their territory national legislation that prohibits or imposes sanctions on
acts of unfair trading practice, be they unilateral or contractual'.

[221] The difficulty of interpreting it is only increased when one examines the other language versions.
For instance, whereas the Italian, Spanish and Dutch versions use the equivalent of the words 'the
means' in the English version (*gli strumenti, el medio, het middel*), the French and German versions
rather use the equivalent of 'a means' (*un moyen, Mittel*). The sentence did not figure in the

155. In the absence of other indications, I would personally take the view that it should be interpreted in the light of the following four elements: (i) its place, not in the operative part of the Regulation but in a recital, more precisely at the end of the first of the two recitals accompanying Article 3 of the Regulation, (ii) the fact that 'competition rules applying to undertakings' is the expression used in the EC Treaty itself in the chapter and section headings covering Articles 81 and 82 EC, (iii) the fact that, even if the Regulation allows the Commission only to impose fines and periodic penalty payments of a non-criminal nature[222] on undertakings, which are usually not natural persons,[223] it is clear from Article 5 of the Regulation,[224] read also in the light of Article 12(3) of the Regulation,[225] that the Regulation does apply in principle to all types of penalties which national law may provide for violations of Articles 81 and 82 EC, including criminal sanctions on natural persons, and (iv) the clear objective of Article 3 of the Regulation of avoiding that national authorities or national courts would circumvent the application of the Regulation, in particular of the provisions of its Articles 11 and 15, by applying only national competition law.

156. In the light of these elements, I would personally interpret the last sentence of recital 8 of the Regulation as merely specifying, with regard to national laws which impose criminal sanctions on natural persons, what already follows from Article 3(3) of the Regulation, namely that Article 3(1) and (2) of the Regulation do not preclude the application of provisions of national law that predominantly pursue an objective different from that pursued by Articles 81 and 82 EC.[226] Article 3(1) and (2) of the Regulation do however apply to all national laws that do not predominantly pursue an objective different from that pursued by Articles 81 and 82 EC, irrespective of the question whether those laws impose criminal sanctions on natural persons.

157. Whenever national competition authorities (which may include courts)[227] take decisions of the kind listed in the second sentence of Article 5 of the Regulation (requiring that an infringement be brought to an end, ordering interim measures, accepting commitments, imposing fines or any other penalty, including criminal sanctions on natural persons) under national laws that do not predominantly pursue an objective different from that pursued by Articles 81 and 82 EC, Article 3(1) and (2) and consequently Article 11(4) and (6) of the Regulation

---

Commission's proposal, n 4 above, so no explanations can be found in the explanatory memorandum of that proposal. For other attempts at interpreting this sentence, see L Idot, 'Le Nouveau Système Communautaire de Mise en Oeuvre des Articles 81 et 82 CE (Règlement 1/2003 et Projets de Textes d'Application' (2003) 39 *Cahiers de Droit Européen* 283 para 40; A Riley, 'EC Antitrust Modernisation: The Commission Does Very Nicely—Thank You! Part One: Regulation No 1 and the Notification Burden' [2003] *European Competition Law Review* 604, 606–7 and note 11.

[222] See n 88 above.
[223] In some cases undertakings are natural persons. See *The Optimal Enforcement of EC Antitrust Law*, n 29 above, ch 7.
[224] Para 45 above.
[225] Para 195 below.
[226] Para 152 above.
[227] See the second sentence of Article 35(1) of the Regulation, and paras 173–184 below.

would apply,[228] except where there is no potential effect on trade between Member States, or if the national law prohibits or sanctions unilateral conduct not prohibited by Article 82 EC,[229] or in the case of national merger control laws.[230]

1.2.9 Consistent Application of Articles 81 and 82 EC

1.2.9.1 The Issue Put in Perspective

158. The fear has often been expressed that the loss of the Commission's monopoly to apply Article 81(3) EC would lead to unacceptably greater inconsistency in the application of that provision. More generally the question arises whether, as a result of increased application of Articles 81 and 82 EC by national competition authorities and possibly also national courts,[231] there would be an unacceptable increase in conflicting or inconsistent decisions.

159. As to the situation under Regulation No 17, it should be kept in mind that a monopoly does not necessarily guarantee its consistent use. The Commission's few formal exemption decisions may on the whole have been consistent, but it is impossible to know whether the same could be said about the much more numerous comfort letters, which were not published and were, in general, barely (if at all) reasoned, and which, because they were not acts of the Commission but only of its services, were not subjected to the same quality and consistency controls before being issued.[232]

160. On the other hand, national courts have already been applying Articles 81(1) and 82 EC, without particular problems of inconsistency. Indeed, in virtually all areas other than competition, EC law is applied fully by the many national courts.[233] The Court of Justice ensures the uniform application of EC law, mainly via the mechanism of requests by national courts for preliminary rulings.[234] There is nothing about Articles 81 and 82 EC, or Article 81(3) EC in particular, which would suggest a greater threat of inconsistency than in other areas of EC law.[235]

---

[228] An example would be a conviction in the United Kingdom under Section 188 (Cartel offence) of the Enterprise Act 2002 (http://www.hmso.gov.uk/acts/acts2002/20020040.htm), provided that the price-fixing, supply-limiting, market-dividing or bid-rigging arrangements within the meaning of section 188, subsection (2) of the Enterprise Act 2002 may affect trade between Member States within the meaning of Article 81 EC.

[229] See last sentence of Article 3(2) of the Regulation, para 149 above.

[230] See Article 3(3) of the Regulation, para 152 above.

[231] As to whether there will be an increased application of Articles 81 and 82 by national courts, see para 85 above.

[232] There was for instance no obligatory consultation of the Commission's Legal Service, nor consultation of the Advisory Committee.

[233] See also C Ehlermann, n 44 above, p 575–77.

[234] On the question whether national competition authorities can make references under Article 234 EC, see AP Komninos, 'Article 234 EC and National Competition Authorities in the Era of Decentralisation' (2004) 29 European Law Review 106.

[235] As explained in paras 15 and 16 above, the situation was different for Article 81 EC (then Article 85 EEC) at the time Regulation No 17 was adopted, because of the novelty of the prohibition on restrictive agreements in Europe at that time.

161. In any event, as explained immediately below, several provisions in Regulation No 1/2003 guarantee a high level of consistency in the application of Articles 81 and 82 EC.

1.2.9.2 Articles 11, 15 and 16 of the Regulation Ensure Consistency

162. As already explained above,[236] Article 11(4) of the Regulation obliges national competition authorities to consult the Commission before adopting negative decisions, and the Commission has the power under Article 11(6) of the Regulation to withdraw the case from the national authorities by initiating proceedings.

163. The Joint Statement of the Council and the Commission on the functioning of the network[237] and the Notice on cooperation within the network,[238] acknowledge in particular the possibility for the Commission to use its power under Article 11(6) of the Regulation when 'network members envisage conflicting decisions' or when,

> network members envisage a decision which is obviously in conflict with consolidated case law; the standards defined in the judgments of the Community courts and in previous decisions and regulations of the Commission should serve as a yardstick; concerning the assessment of the facts (eg market definition), only a significant divergence will trigger an intervention of the Commission.

164. As already explained above, Article 15 of the Regulation provides for cooperation between the Commission and/or national competition authorities and the national courts, which should also help ensure consistent application of Articles 81 and 82 EC.[239]

165. Finally, conflicting decisions in the same case are prevented by the provisions of Article 16 of the Regulation, which reads as follows:

> 1. When national courts rule on agreements, decisions or practices under Article 81 or Article 82 of the Treaty which are already the subject of a Commission decision, they cannot take decisions running counter to the decision adopted by the Commission. They must also avoid giving decisions which would conflict with a decision contemplated by the Commission in proceedings it has initiated. To that effect, the national court may assess whether it is necessary to stay its proceedings. This obligation is without prejudice to the rights and obligations under Article 234 of the Treaty.
>
> 2. When competition authorities of the Member States rule on agreements, decisions or practices under Article 81 or Article 82 of the Treaty which are already the subject of a Commission decision, they cannot take decisions which would run counter to the decision adopted by the Commission.

---

[236] See paras 142 and 143 above.
[237] See n 8 above, para 21.
[238] See n 7 above, para 54.
[239] Paras 89–96. As indicated in Recital 21 of the Regulation, Article 15 also applies to national competition authorities which are courts. See also the last sentence of Article 35(1) of the Regulation and, as to the concept of 'court', para 1 of the Notice on the cooperation between the Commission and the courts, n 9 above.

166. The first paragraph of this Article codifies the *Masterfoods* case law of the Court of Justice,[240] whereas the second paragraph should be read together with Article 11(6) of the Regulation.[241]

1.2.10 Separation of Investigative, Prosecutorial and Adjudicative Functions

1.2.10.1 The Various Systems for the Public Enforcement of Articles 81 and 82 EC

167. At the level of the Community and of the different Member States, there exists a wide variety of institutional systems for the public enforcement of Articles 81 and 82 EC.

168. The Commission, when dealing itself with an individual case using its powers under Chapters III, V and VI of Regulation No 1/2003, combines investigative, prosecutorial and adjudicative functions.[242]

169. This combination of investigative and prosecutorial with adjudicative functions has led to a legal debate relating to Article 6(1) of the European Convention of Human Rights. In scholarly articles as well as in (so far always unsuccessful) applications before the Community Courts,[243] it has been argued that the current system in which the Commission investigates and prosecutes as well as decides is incompatible with the requirements of Article 6(1) ECHR.

170. Although the Commission combines the investigative and prosecutorial with adjudicative functions, and thus cannot be qualified as an independent and impartial tribunal within the meaning of Article 6(1) ECHR, this does not as such make the current system incompatible with Article 6(1) ECHR. Indeed, the European Court of Human Rights has ruled that, for reasons of efficiency, the determination of civil rights and obligations or the prosecution and punishment of offences which are 'criminal' within the wider meaning of Article 6 ECHR[244] can be entrusted to administrative authorities, provided that the persons concerned are able to challenge any decision thus made before a judicial body that has full jurisdiction and that provides the full guarantees of Article 6(1) ECHR.[245] The

---

[240] See n 1 above.

[241] See paras 43 above and 181 below.

[242] See ch 6 below. As paraed out in n 1 of ch 6, it could be argued that in the system of Chapters III, V and VI of the Regulation there is not really a prosecutorial function, only investigative and adjudicative functions. The prosecutorial function only emerges in a system in which the adjudicative function is separated from the investigative function.

[243] See D Waelbroeck and D Fosselard, 'Should the Decision-Making Power in EC Antitrust Procedures be left to an Independent Judge?—The Impact of the European Convention on Human Rights on EC Antitrust Procedures' (1994) 14 *Yearbook of European Law* 111–42; and Judgment of the Court of First Instance of 15 March 2000 in Joined Cases T–25/95 etc *Cimenteries CBR and Others v Commission* [2000] ECR II–700 paras 712–24.

[244] As to the concept of 'criminal', see n 88 above.

[245] Judgments of 23 June 1981, *Le Compte, Van Leuven and De Meyere v Belgium*, A/43 para 51; of 1 February 1983, *Albert and Le Compte v Belgium*, A/58 para 29; of 21 February 1984, *Öztürk v Germany*, A/73 para 56; and of 24 February 1994, *Bendenoun v France*, A/284 para 46. This alternative

latter condition is currently satisfied because the addressees of Commission decisions imposing fines can bring an action for annulment before the Court of First Instance, which manifestly provides the full guarantees of Article 6(1) ECHR and which undertakes a comprehensive review of the Commission's decisions.[246]

171. Some national authorities, such as the German *Bundeskartellamt* or the Italian *Autorità garante della Concorrenza e del Mercato* are comparable to the Commission in that they also combine the investigative and prosecutorial function with the adjudicative function, with a possibility for their decisions to be challenged before a court that fulfils the requirements of Article 6(1) ECHR.

172. A number of other Member States have opted for a public enforcement system in which the investigative, prosecutorial and adjudicative functions are separated in varying ways. As far as concerns the separation between, on the one hand, the investigative and prosecutorial function or functions and, on the other hand, the adjudicative function, Member States may have opted for such separation on (possibly a combination of) three possible grounds. First, their national courts may interpret the requirements of Article 6 ECHR more strictly than the European Court of Human Rights. This appears to be the case for instance in France.[247] Second, national constitutional law may require a separation. Third, national legislators may, as a matter of policy, prefer a system of separation of functions.[248]

1.2.10.2 The Regulation Recognises the Wide Variation in the Public Enforcement Systems of the Member States

173. According to the third sentence of recital 35 of the Regulation, 'this Regulation recognises the wide variation which exists in the public enforcement systems of Member States'.

174. Article 35(1) and (2) of the Regulation read as follows:

1. The Member States shall designate the competition authority or authorities responsible for the application of Articles 81 and 82 of the Treaty in such a way that the provisions of this regulation are effectively complied with. [...] The authorities designated may include courts.

---

means of satisfying the requirements of Article 6(1) ECHR does not appear to be available in more traditional areas of criminal law or in areas considered criminal under domestic law. See Judgments of 26 October 1984, *De Cubber v Belgium*, A/86 paras 31–32; and of 25 February 1997, *Findlay v United Kingdom*, Reports 1997–I para 79.

[246] See Judgment in *Cimenteries CBR and Others v Commission*, n 243 above, para 719: 'When the Court of First Instance reviews the legality of a decision finding an infringement of [Article 81(1) and/or Article 82 EC], the applicants may call upon it to undertake an exhaustive review of both the Commission's substantive findings of fact and its legal appraisal of those facts.'

[247] See I Luc, 'L'application du Principe d'Impartialité aux Autorités de Concurrence Françaises' *Petites Affiches* No 34 (15 February 2002) 4–12; and No 35 (18 February 2002) 4–8; and D Waelbroeck and M Griffiths, 'Comment on French *Cour de Cassation: TGV Nord et Pont de Normandie*, Judgment of 5 October 1999' (2000) 37 *Common Market Law Review* 1465–76.

[248] As to the question whether a combination of functions or a separation of functions is preferable from an economic perspective of efficient antitrust enforcement, see ch 6 below.

2. When enforcement of Community competition law is entrusted to national administrative and judicial authorities, the Member States may allocate different powers and functions to those different national authorities, whether administrative or judicial.

175. These provisions allow the Member States to fulfil their obligations under the Regulation, in particular under Article 11 of the Regulation, while remaining free to organise their system of public antitrust enforcement in conformity with the case law of their courts under Article 6 ECHR, their national constitutional provisions and their legislative policy choices.[249] How this works specifically with regard to the provisions of Article 11(3) and (4) and Article 11(6) of the Regulation is explained in more detail immediately below.[250]

176. As explained above,[251] Article 11(3) of Regulation No 1/2003 imposes on national competition authorities the obligation to inform the Commission at the beginning of proceedings under Articles 81 or 82 EC.

177. This obligation will be fulfilled in all Member States by the national authority which conducts the investigation. Those national authorities that are independent and impartial tribunals within the meaning of Article 6 ECHR, or that are otherwise separate from the authority conducting the investigation, will not have to do anything under Article 11(3) of the Regulation.

178. As explained above,[252] Article 11(4) of the Regulation obliges national competition authorities to consult the Commission before adopting a negative decision. This provision has been drafted so as to allow, in those Member States where the adjudicative function is separated from the prosecutorial function, the information and consultation to be taken care of by the prosecuting authority.

179. Indeed, the text of Article 11(4) of the Regulation,[253] provides for an obligation to inform the Commission 'no later than 30 days before the adoption of a decision', thus leaving open the possibility to do so much more in advance. The national authority fulfilling the Article 11(4) obligations must provide the Commission 'with a summary of the case, the envisaged decision or, in the absence thereof, any other document indicating the proposed course of action'. This language allows for a consultation by the prosecuting authority on the basis of the document to be submitted to the adjudicating authority setting out the prosecutor's case.

180. In those Member States where the adjudicative function has been attributed to an independent and impartial tribunal within the meaning of Article 6 ECHR, or otherwise to an authority separate from the prosecuting authority, the adjudicative authority will thus not need to be involved in any consultations with

---

[249] See para 172 above.
[250] The following paras draw from C Gauer, 'Does the Effectiveness of the EU Network of Competition Authorities Require a Certain Degree of Harmonisation of National Procedures and Sanctions?' in CD Ehlermann and I Atanasiu (eds) *European Competition Law Annual 2002: Constructing the EU Network of Competition Authorities* (Hart Publishing, 2004).
[251] Para 106.
[252] Paras 142 and 143.
[253] See para 142 above.

the Commission. Neither the parties' right to adversarial proceedings before such adjudicative authorities, nor the independence and impartiality of those authorities will thus be put in jeopardy.[254]

181. As already discussed above,[255] Article 11(6) of the Regulation reads as follows:

> The initiation by the Commission of proceedings for the adoption of a decision under Chapter III shall relieve the competition authorities of the Member States of their competence to apply Articles 81 and 82 of the Treaty. If a competition authority of a Member State is already acting on a case, the Commission shall only initiate proceedings after consulting with that national competition authority.

This provision allows the Commission to withdraw a case from a national competition authority.[256]

182. The application of Article 11(6) of the Regulation is limited and modulated by Article 35(3) and (4) of the Regulation, which read as follows:

> 3. The effects of Article 11(6) apply to the authorities designated by the Member States including courts that exercise functions regarding the preparation and the adoption of the types of decisions foreseen in Article 5. The effects of Article 11(6) shall not extend to courts insofar as they act as review courts in respect of the types of decisions foreseen in Article 5.
>
> 4. Notwithstanding paragraph 3, in the Member States where, for the adoption of certain decisions foreseen in Article 5, an authority brings an action before a judicial authority that is separate and different from the prosecuting authority and provided that the terms of this paragraph are complied with, the effects of Article 11(6) shall be limited to the authority prosecuting the case which shall withdraw its claim before the judicial authority when the Commission opens proceedings and this withdrawal shall bring the national proceedings effectively to an end.

183. In those Member States where the prosecutorial and adjudicative functions are separated and the latter function has been attributed to an independent and impartial tribunal within the meaning of Article 6 ECHR, the initiation of proceedings by the Commission regarding a case which is already pending before the adjudicative authority thus obliges the prosecuting authority to withdraw its case from the adjudicative authority. The national law of the Member State concerned must ensure that this brings the national proceedings effectively to an end. It also follows that the consultation referred to in the last sentence of Article 11(6) of the Regulation[257] will take place between the Commission and the prosecuting

---

[254] As to the problems which would arguably have arisen under Article 6 ECHR if authorities that are independent and impartial tribunals within the meaning of that provision had been involved in consultations with the Commission, see sections 2.7.2 and 2.7.3 below.

[255] Paras 43, 110 and 143 above.

[256] It follows from Article 3(1) of the Regulation, that the national competition authority is simultaneously relieved of its competence to apply its national competition law in that case. See para 147 above.

[257] See para 181 above.

authority, not the adjudicative authority. Any (appearance of) interference with the independence of the adjudicative authority is thus avoided.

184. The second sentence of Article 35(3) of the Regulation makes it clear that Article 11(6) of the Regulation only applies to competition authorities at the level of first instance, not to courts reviewing the decisions taken by the competition authority in first instance. This limitation on the applicability of Articles 11(6) of the Regulation does not pose any problem from the perspective of the objective of ensuring consistent application of Articles 81 and 82 EC, given that such review courts (as well as all national competition authorities in first instance that qualify as a court or tribunal within the meaning of Article 234 EC) fall under the provisions of Article 15 of the Regulation and of Article 234 EC.[258]

1.2.11 Differences in Type and Level of Penalties

1.2.11.1 The Issue Put in Perspective

185. There exists a wide variation in the nature and the level of the penalties which can be imposed by the Commission and by the competition authorities of the various Member States for violations of Articles 81 and 82 EC.

186. The Commission can normally only impose fines on companies.[259] In all Member States, fines can be imposed on companies. The maximum amount of such fines varies between the Member States. In a number of Member States, fines can also be imposed on individuals within those companies. In some Member States, not only can individuals face fines, but also other penalties, in particular director disqualification and imprisonment.

187. For the same violation of Articles 81 or 82 EC, companies and individuals thus face very different penalties, depending on which competition authority (Commission or which national competition authority) deals with the case. According to Céline Gauer, 'this could be perceived as certain discrimination'.[260]

188. It could be argued that this is not a new situation created by Regulation No 1/2003. Indeed, this divergence already existed under Regulation No 17. It has only become more visible as a result of Regulation No 1/2003. On the other hand, it could be argued that Regulation No 17 did not deal with the enforcement of Articles 81 and 82 EC by national competition authorities, with the result that the Community legislator could not be held responsible for any perceived discrimination which resulted exclusively from national legislative choices, whereas

---

[258] See also n 158 and n 239 above. As to the risk of national bias discussed in paras 138–44 above, it is obvious that there is much less of such a risk with national competition authorities that are independent and impartial tribunals within the meaning of Article 6 ECHR than with other national competition authorities.

[259] It can impose fines on natural persons in those rare cases where natural persons are undertakings. See n 223 above.

[260] C Gauer, n 250 above.

Regulation No 1/2003, in particular through its Article 5, allows national competition authorities to impose whatever penalties their national law provides for.

189. However, it should be pointed out that the principles of case allocation set out in the Joint Statement on the functioning of the network and the Notice on cooperation within the network,[261] ensure a high degree of predictability as to which competition authority (Commission or which national competition authority) will deal with any given case, and the Commission can ensure respect for these principles of allocation through the possible use of Article 11(6) of the Regulation.[262] As already pointed out above,[263] there is thus for instance no risk that individuals would be jailed in Ireland in a case where the relevant market is Scandinavia.

1.2.11.2 Article 12 of the Regulation

190. The variety in the types of penalties which can be imposed by the different members of the network of competition authorities could raise concerns with regard to the exchange of evidence within the network.

191. Article 12(1) of the Regulation reads as follows:

> For the purpose of applying Articles 81 and 82 of the Treaty the Commission and the competition authorities of the Member States shall have the power to provide one another with and use in evidence any matter of fact or of law, including confidential information.[264]

192. However, the types of evidence admissible, or the guarantees which must be respected in the collection of such evidence, often vary with the nature of the penalty which may be imposed. The privilege against self-incrimination may provide an example.[265]

193. In a number of judgments,[266] concerning questioning of natural persons in investigations potentially leading to those persons being convicted to

---

[261] See paras 100–3 and 110 above.

[262] By ensuring that case allocation is a predictable process, the Notice on cooperation within the network has thus averted the danger pointed out by Denis Waelbroeck in his paper 'Twelve Feet All Dangling Down and Six Necks Exceeding Long: The EU Network of Competition Authorities and the European Convention on Fundamental Rights' in CD Ehlermann and I Atanasiu (eds) *European Competition Law Annual 2002: Constructing the EU Network of Competition Authorities* (Hart Publishing, 2004) of a possible violation of Articles 7 and 14 ECHR.

[263] Para 131.

[264] Article 12(2) of the Regulation adds: 'Information exchanged shall only be used for the purpose of applying Article 81 or Article 82 of the Treaty and in respect of the subject-matter for which it was collected by the transmitting authority. However, where national competition law is applied in the same case and in parallel to Community competition law and does not lead to a different outcome, information exchanged under this article may also be used for the application of national competition law'. See para 195 below as to Article 12(3) of the Regulation.

[265] See section 5.1.2 below.

[266] *Funke v France* (25 February 1993, A/256–A); *John Murray v United Kingdom* (8 February 1996, Reports 1996–I, p 49); *Saunders v United Kingdom* (17 December 1996, Reports 1996–VI, p 2064); *Servès v France* (20 October 1997, Reports 1997–VI, p 2173); *Condron v United Kingdom* (2 May 2000, Application 35718/97); *Averill v United Kingdom* (6 June 2000, Application 36408/97); *Coëme and*

imprisonment or other sanctions in criminal trials, the European Court of Human Rights has allowed the use of coercive powers to obtain existing documents or other objects, but has objected to the use in evidence of any answers obtained from the accused through compulsory questioning during a non-judicial investigation, including answers to purely factual questions. It is also apparent from these judgments that the complexity of antitrust investigations or the public interest in detecting and punishing antitrust violations would probably not constitute acceptable justifications.[267]

194. On the other hand, with regard to the rights of legal persons in proceedings under Regulation No 17, the Court of Justice has allowed the Commission to use its coercive powers not only to obtain existing documents from the undertaking being investigated, but also to ask questions of a factual nature which do not compel the undertaking to give directly incriminating answers.[268] The latter rule has been restated by the Council in recital 23 of the Regulation, which reads as follows:

> The Commission should be empowered throughout the Community to require such information to be supplied as is necessary to detect any agreement, decision or concerted practice prohibited by Article 81 of the Treaty or any abuse of a dominant position prohibited by Article 82 of the Treaty. When complying with a decision of the Commission, undertakings cannot be forced to admit that they have committed an infringement, but they are in any event obliged to answer factual questions and to provide documents, even if this information may be used to establish against them or against another undertaking the existence of an infringement.

195. The Council has taken into account such differences in applicable procedural rights and guarantees resulting from differences in the nature of the penalties which can be imposed, by limiting the rule laid down in Article 12(1) of the Regulation through the following exception in Article 12(3) of the Regulation:

> Information exchanged pursuant to paragraph 1 can only be used in evidence to impose sanctions on natural persons where:
>
> — the law of the transmitting authority foresees sanctions of a similar kind in relation to an infringement of Article 81 or Article 82 of the Treaty or, in the absence thereof,
> — the information has been collected in a way which respects the same level of protection of the rights of defence of natural persons as provided for under the national

Others v Belgium (22 June 2000, Applications nos 32492/96, 32547/96, 32548/96, 33209/96 and 33210/96); *IJL and Others v United Kingdom* (19 September 2000, Application nos. 29522/95, 30056/96 and 30574/96); *Heaney and McGuinness v Ireland* (21 December 2000, Application 34720/97); *Quinn v Ireland* (21 December 2000, Application 36887/97); *JB v Switzerland* (3 May 2001, Application 31827/96); *PG and JH v United Kingdom* (25 September 2001, Application 44787/98); *Beckles v United Kingdom* (8 October 2002, Application 44652/98); and *Allan v United Kingdom* (5 November 2002, Application 48539/99).

[267] *Saunders v United Kindom*, n 266 above, para 74; and *Heany and McGuinness v Ireland*, n 266 above, paras 57–58.

[268] Judgment of 18 October 1989 in Case 374/87 *Orkem v Commission* [1989] ECR 3343. See also Judgment of the Court of First Instance of 20 February 2001 in Case T–112/98 *Mannesmannröhren-Werke v Commission* [2001] ECR II–732.

rules of the receiving authority. However, in this case, the information exchanged cannot be used by the receiving authority to impose custodial sanctions.

196. This provision ensures that, to the extent that differences in procedural rights and guarantees result from differences in the kind of sanctions which can be imposed by the different members of the network, the exchange of information within the network cannot lead to any procedural right or guarantee being weakened or undermined.

1.2.11.3 Is Harmonisation Desirable and Possible?

197. The variety in the kind and the level of penalties which can be imposed by the different members of the network of competition authorities raises the question whether it would be desirable and possible to harmonize the sanctions for violations of Articles 81 and 82 EC.

198. The first question should be what types of sanctions are optimal from the perspective of effective antitrust enforcement. As I have argued in detail elsewhere,[269] I personally believe that the effective enforcement of Articles 81 and 82 EC requires a combination of, on the one hand, fines on companies and, on the other hand, for horizontal, secret price-fixing, bid-rigging and market-allocation schemes, imprisonment for the individuals responsible for these infringements.[270]

199. My personal impression is that, slowly but surely, the whole of Europe is moving towards this optimal set of sanctions. Indeed, it would seem that most jurisdictions are historically moving through similar phases in the same direction. In a first phase, abandoned by some Member States only very recently,[271] there was no real cartel prohibition, only a system of control of abuse, under which, once an abuse had been established, the undertakings concerned would have been ordered to put an end to this abuse for the future. Non-respect of this specific order for the future may have been punishable with criminal sanctions, including imprisonment. In a second phase, first reached by the European Coal and Steel Community in the early 1950s, and subsequently by Germany and by the European Economic Community in the late 1950s, cartels were prohibited, but the direct effect of this prohibition was softened through a notification system, which allowed temporary immunity from sanctions,[272] and violations of the prohibition

---

[269] The Optimal Enforcement of EC Antitrust Law, n 29 above, chs 8 and 9. See also OECD, Report on the nature and impact of hard core cartels and sanctions against cartels under national competition laws (DAFFE/COMP (2002) 7, 9 April 2002).

[270] Fines on individuals are unlikely to be effective, because of the problem of indemnification. See *The Optimal Enforcement of EC Antitrust Law*, n 29 above, section 8.6.2. Other non-pecuniary sanctions, such as director disqualification may be useful in addition to imprisonment, but cannot be a full substitute for it; idem, section 8.6.6. Private actions for damages are inefficient compared to the administratively cheaper and more reliable alternative of fines imposed by competition authorities. See ch 4 below and paras 66–68 above.

[271] The Netherlands for instance abandoned this first phase in 1997, and Luxembourg only in 2004.

[272] See para 56 above, and G Marenco, n 24 above, p 174–75.

were only punishable with fines on undertakings. In a third phase, reached at the Community level through Regulation No 1/2003, the deterrent effect of the cartel prohibition is enhanced through the abolition of the notification system. In a fourth phase, reached long since by the United States and Canada,[273] and recently entered into by the United Kingdom,[274] the threat of individual sanctions, in particular imprisonment, is added, so as to increase deterrence for those types of cartel infringements which are most profitable and most difficult to detect, namely secret price-fixing, bid-rigging and market-sharing arrangements.

200. Would it possible to speed this evolution up by providing through a Community act not only for fines on undertakings but also for imprisonment and possibly other sanctions on individuals at the level of the Community as well as in all Member States? Legally, Article 83 EC, possibly combined with Article 308 EC, would in my view provide a sufficient legal basis.[275] It will however take time before all Member States, in particular those which only recently left the first of the four historical phases just mentioned, will find such a move politically accept-able.[276]

1.2.12 Differences in Procedural Rights and Guarantees

201. The procedural rights and guarantees for companies or individuals being investigated or prosecuted in proceedings at the Community level and in the different Member States have not been harmonised by Regulation No 1/2003.

202. It should however be kept in mind that a common minimum level of protection applies both at the Community level and in all the Member States, namely the level guaranteed by the European Convention on Human Rights, as interpreted by the European Court of Human Rights, and by the Charter of Fundamental Rights of the European Union.[277] Recital 37 of the Regulation expressly mentions that 'this Regulation respects the fundamental rights and observes the principles recognised in particular by the Charter of Fundamental Rights of the European Union. Accordingly, this Regulation should be interpreted and applied with respect to those rights and principles'.

---

[273] On paper the Unites States have been in this fourth phase since the 1890 Sherman Act. It was not until 1959, however, that prison sentences were imposed against businessmen for price fixing without acts or threats of violence. See JC Gallo, *et al*, 'Criminal Penalties Under the Sherman Act: A Study of Law and Economics' (1994) 16 *Research in Law and Economics* 25, 40; *The Optimal Enforcement of EC Antitrust Law*, n 29 above, section 8.1.2.

[274] See Enterprise Act 2002, http://www.hmso.gov.uk/acts/acts2002/20020040.htm.

[275] See *The Optimal Enforcement of EC Antitrust Law*, n 29 above, sections 8.7.4.1–8.7.4.5, and n 91 and n 139 above. The need, if any, to add Article 308 EC as legal basis would result from the explicit reference to (only) fines and periodic penalty payments in Article 83(2)(a) EC.

[276] Idem, sections 8.6.7 and 9.5. See also C Harding, n 201 above; C Harding and J Joshua, *Regulating Cartels in Europe* (OUP, 2003); PF Kunzlik, 'Globalization and Hybridization in Antitrust Enforcement: European "Borrowings" from the US Approach' (Summer 2003) *The Antitrust Bulletin* 319–53.

[277] See ch 2 below.

203. It should also be recalled that Article 12(3) of the Regulation ensures that, to the extent that differences in procedural rights and guarantees result from differences in the kind of sanctions which can be imposed by the different members of the network, the exchange of information within the network cannot lead to any procedural right or guarantee being weakened or undermined.[278]

204. It is however a fact that, as a result of national laws providing for more extensive protection that the minimum level required under the European Convention of Human Rights as interpreted by the European Court of Human Rights, there exist today some differences between Member States, or between Member States and the Community level, in procedural rights and guarantees, which do not result from differences in the type of sanctions, and which are thus not covered by Article 12(3) of the Regulation.

205. When the members of the network assist each other in collecting evidence, it could thus happen that one member of the network, either on its own initiative or at the second competition authority's request, collects, in accordance with the law governing the investigative powers of the first authority, evidence which the second authority could not have lawfully collected under its own law, and transfers this evidence to the second authority so as to allow it to use this evidence.

206. For instance, the Commission could lawfully collect and subsequently transmit to a UK competition authority information which under UK law would be protected by in-house counsel legal privilege, a privilege recognised neither in Community law, nor in the case law of the European Court of Human Rights.[279]

207. A second example would be where the Commission collects evidence through a request for information to which the undertaking concerned is obliged to respond under Community law as long as the questions are factual and do not compel the undertaking to give directly incriminating answers, which does not appear contrary to the case law of the European Court of Human Rights,[280] and transmits this information for use in evidence to the German competition authority, which might not have been able to collect this information itself, or at least not to use it if it had collected it itself, because of the right not to incriminate oneself as laid down in Paragraph 136(1) of the German code of criminal procedure.[281]

208. As the exception contained in Article 12(3) of the Regulation only covers differences in procedural rights and guarantees resulting from differences in the type of sanctions that can be imposed, the main rule of Article 12(1) of the Regulation appears to apply in such cases. In the above examples, this would mean that the UK or German competition authorities can use the evidence which was collected by the Commission and transmitted to them, even if they could not

---

[278] See paras 192–96 above.

[279] See Judgment of the Court of Justice of 18 May 1982 in Case 155/79 *AM&S v Commission* [1982] ECR 1575; and Order of the Court of First Instance of 4 April 1990 in Case T–30/89 *Hilti v Commission* [1990] *ECR* II–163. See also, however, Order of the President of the Court of First Instance of 30 October 2003 in Joined Cases T–125/03 R and T–253/03 R *Akzo Nobel Chemicals v Commission*, not yet published in ECR, currently on appeal before the Court of Justice, Case C–7/04 P(R).

[280] See paras 193 and 194 above, and ch 5 below.

[281] See *Mannesmannröhren-Werke v Commission*, n 268 above, paras 80–81.

themselves lawfully have collected this evidence, or could not have used it if they had collected it themselves.[282]

209. That this result was intended by the Council is clear from recital 16 of the Regulation, which states that 'the rights of defence enjoyed by undertakings in the various systems can be considered sufficiently equivalent' and which confirms that the rule laid down in Article 12 of the Regulation applies 'notwithstanding any national provision to the contrary'.

1.2.13 Limitation Periods for the Imposition of Penalties

210. Article 25 of Regulation No 1/2003 sets out the limitation periods applicable to the imposition of fines and periodic penalty payments by the Commission pursuant to Articles 23 and 24 of the Regulation. The main difference with the previously applicable rules, contained in Regulation No 2988/74,[283] is that the running of the limitation period is now interrupted not only by actions of the Commission but also by actions of the national competition authority.

211. Regulation No 1/2003 does not harmonize limitation periods for the imposition of penalties by national competition authorities, which remain a matter of national law.

212. There exist significant differences between the limitation periods applicable in different Member States, and between these limitation periods and those set out in Article 25 of the Regulation.

213. As with the differences in type and level of penalties, it could be argued that this is not a new situation created by Regulation No 1/2003.[284] On the other hand, the fact that Article 12 of the Regulation allows the transfer of entire cases between members of the network of competition authorities adds a new dimension. It could be feared that a case would be transferred from one authority to another at a late stage of the proceedings for the sole purpose of avoiding the proceedings becoming time barred. However, paragraph 19 of the Notice on cooperation within the network appears to exclude such transfers, where it states that 're-allocation of a case after the initial allocation period of two months should only occur where the facts known about the case change materially during the course of the proceedings'.[285]

---

[282] Unless of course, as a reaction to this effect of Article 12 of Regulation No 1/2003, the legislators or the courts in the jurisdictions with the lower standard of protection of the defendant increase their standard to the higher level. Seen from this perspective, Article 12(3) of the Regulation not only serves to protect the higher standards of protection of the defendant in proceedings where sanctions can be imposed on natural persons, but also to prevent that the free circulation of evidence as provided for in Article 12(1) of the Regulation would result in such higher standards becoming also applicable in proceedings where only sanctions on legal persons can be imposed.

[283] See Recital 31 and Article 37 of Regulation No 1/2003.

[284] See para 188 above.

[285] See para 109 above.

214. It would be possible to harmonize, on the basis of Article 83 EC, the limitation periods for the imposition of penalties for violation of Articles 81 and 82 EC by all members of the network of competition authorities. I would, however, personally take the view that such harmonization would only make sense as part of a wider harmonization of the types and level of penalties that can be imposed by the different competition authorities.[286]

1.2.14 Leniency

215. The Commission and a number of national competition authorities have leniency programmes, under which they offer, under varying conditions, full immunity or a significant reduction in the penalties which they would otherwise impose or seek to have imposed on participants in secret cartels, in exchange for the freely volunteered disclosure of information on the cartel which satisfies specific criteria prior to or during the investigative stage of proceedings.[287]

216. Not all national competition authorities have a leniency programme, but the number of those that have one is increasing, as it becomes more widely recognised that leniency is a particularly effective instrument in the fight against hard core cartels.[288]

217. Regulation No 1/2003 does not impose on the Member States the obligation to provide for leniency programmes, and it does not harmonise the conditions of national leniency programmes either.

218. It could be feared that the information obligations contained in Article 11 of the Regulation,[289] as well as the possibility of exchanging information under Article 12 of the Regulation,[290] might undermine the trust of potential leniency applicants, and thus undermine the effectiveness of the leniency programmes of the Commission and of those national competition authorities that have such programmes.

219. This problem has been solved in paragraphs 37 and following of the Notice on cooperation within the network,[291] which provide for the necessary guarantees that a second member of the network will not undermine the effectiveness of the leniency programme of a first authority by prosecuting a leniency applicant on the basis of information received from the first authority that had been voluntarily provided to that first authority by the leniency applicant, unless

---

[286] See paras 197–200 above.

[287] See para 37 and n 14 of the Notice on cooperation within the network, n 7 above. The Commission's current leniency programme is contained in its Notice on immunity from fines and reduction of fines in cartel cases, [2002] OJ C45/3.

[288] See OECD, *Fighting Hard-Core Cartels: Harm, Effective Sanctions and Leniency Programs* (2002), accessible at http://www.oecd.org/pdf/M00036000/M00036562.pdf, and ch 5 below.

[289] See paras 106 and 142 above.

[290] See para 191 above.

[291] See n 7 above.

the leniency applicant has also applied for leniency with the second authority or unless the leniency applicant consents.[292]

220. Another possible solution would be to provide, on the basis of Article 83 EC, for a harmonised leniency programme covering the Commission and all national competition authorities. Again I would personally take the view that this would only make sense as part of a wider harmonisation of the types and level of penalties that can be imposed by the different competition authorities.[293]

1.2.15 Languages

221. When the Commission deals with a case under Articles 81 or 82 EC, the companies being investigated have the right to have any requests for information, statements of objections or decisions addressed to them in the language of their Member State.[294] Complainants can address themselves to the Commission in any of the 20 official languages, and have the right to be answered in the same language.[295] Final decisions adopted by the Commission are normally published in the Official Journal of the European Union, which appears in the 20 official languages.[296]

222. Neither the Treaty nor Regulation No 1/2003 contains any explicit provisions determining the languages to be used by national competition authorities or national courts when they apply Articles 81 and 82 EC pursuant to the Regulation.

223. Indeed the fact that national competition authorities work in only one or two languages, which makes their functioning much cheaper than that of the Commission, constitutes one of the reasons why it is in the interest of efficient enforcement of Articles 81 and 82 EC that more cases should be dealt with by national competition authorities rather than by the Commission.[297]

224. However, all Member States must respect the fundamental right to a fair trial as recognised in the European Convention on Human Rights and the Charter of Fundamental Rights of the European Union, including in particular the rights, explicitly provided for in Article 6(3) (a) and (e) ECHR, for anyone charged with

---

[292] See also para 26 of the Notice on the co-operation between the Commission and the courts of the EU Member States in the application of Articles 81 and 82 EC, n 9 above, where the Commission states that it will not transmit to national courts information voluntarily submitted by a leniency applicant without the consent of that applicant.

[293] See paras 197–200 and 214 above.

[294] See Article 3 of Regulation No 1 [1958] OJ B17/385 (Special English Edition 1952–58, p 59), last modified by Annex II, ch 22, para 1, of the Accession Act [2003] OJ L236/791.

[295] See the third sentence of Article 21 EC, Article 2 of Regulation No 1, n 294 above, and Article 5(4) of the Commission Regulation relating to proceedings by the Commission pursuant to Articles 81 and 82 of the EC Treaty, n 6 above.

[296] See Article 30(1) of Regulation No 1/2003, which imposes publication, but not necessarily in the Official Journal, and Article 5 of Regulation No 1, note 294 above, which provides that the Official Journal shall be published in the 20 official languages. See, however, Council Regulation (EC) No 930/2004 of 1 May 2004 on temporary derogation measures relating to the drafting in Maltese of the acts of the institutions of the European Union, [2004] OJ L169/1.

[297] See para 53 above.

a 'criminal offence' within the meaning of the Convention 'to be informed promptly, in a language which he understands and in detail, of the nature and the cause of the accusation against him' and 'to have the assistance of an interpreter if he cannot understand or speak the language used in court'.

225. Finally, it should be kept in mind that the principles of allocation set out in the Notice on cooperation within the network indicate that a material link between the infringement and the territory of a Member State must exist in order for that Member State's competition authority to be considered well placed to deal with a case, and that the Commission can ensure respect for these principles through the use of its powers under Article 11(6) of the Regulation.[298] This means that there is no risk of a Finnish company that only does business on a Scandinavian market being prosecuted in Spanish in Spain.

[298] See paras 102 and 110 above.

2

The European Competition Network, the European Convention on Human Rights and the Charter of Fundamental Rights of the EU

2.1 INTRODUCTION

226. This chapter addresses the question of the compatibility of the European Competition Network as created by Regulation No 1/2003[1] (hereafter also: 'the network' and 'the Regulation') with the Convention for the Protection of Human Rights and Fundamental Freedoms[2] (hereafter also: 'the European Convention on Human Rights', 'the Convention' or 'ECHR') and with the Charter of Fundamental Rights of the European Union[3] (hereafter also: 'the Charter of Fundamental Rights', 'the Charter' or 'CFR').

227. The chapter is structured as follows: Section 2.2 describes the European Competition Network as set up under Regulation No 1/2003, pointing out the three objectives or functions of the network (efficient allocation of cases, assistance in respect of fact-finding and coordination to ensure the consistent application of Articles 81 and 82 EC) and the regulatory provisions designed to achieve these objectives. Sections 2.3 and 2.4 introduce respectively the European Convention on Human Rights and the Charter of Fundamental Rights, pointing out their relevant provisions in the present context, and describing briefly their legal status. Sections 2.5, 2.6 and 2.7 analyse, respectively with regard to the three objectives or functions of the network, possible problems under the European Convention on Human Rights and the Charter of Fundamental Rights, followed by a brief conclusion in Section 2.8.

---

[1] Council Regulation (EC) No 1/2003 of 16 December 2002 on the implementation of the rules on competition laid down in Articles 81 and 82 of the Treaty [2003] OJ L1/1.

[2] Convention for the Protection of Human Rights and Fundamental Freedoms as amended by Protocol No 11 with Protocol Nos 1, 4, 6 and 7, available at http://www.echr.coe.int/Eng/basic Texts.htm.

[3] [2000] OJ C364/1.

2.2 THE EUROPEAN COMPETITION NETWORK

2.2.1 General Provisions

228. Article 11(1) of Regulation No 1/2003 provides generally:

> The Commission and the competition authorities of the Member States shall apply the Community competition rules in close cooperation.[4]

Recital 15 of the Regulation adds that the Commission and the national competition authorities should thus 'form together a network of public authorities'.

229. At the time of the adoption of the Regulation, the Council and the Commission adopted a Joint Statement on the functioning of the network of competition authorities (hereafter: 'the Joint Statement'), entered in the Council Minutes.[5]

230. As announced in recital 15 of the Regulation and in point 4 of the Joint Statement, the Commission adopted a Notice on cooperation within the Network of Competition Authorities (hereafter: 'the Notice'),[6] which contains further modalities for the cooperation within the network. Paragraph 72 of the Notice states that 'the principles set out in this notice will also be abided by those Member States' competition authorities which have signed a statement in the form of the Annex to this notice'. A list of these authorities is published on the website of the Commission.[7]

231. According to paragraph 1 of the Notice:

> The network is a forum for discussion and cooperation in the application and enforcement of EC competition policy. It provides a framework for the cooperation of European competition authorities in cases where Articles 81 and 82 of the Treaty are applied and is the basis for the creation and maintenance of a common competition culture in Europe. The network is called 'European Competition Network' (ECN).

232. Three objectives or functions of the cooperation within the network can be distinguished: (1) efficient allocation of cases between the members of the network, (2) assistance between the members of the network in respect of fact-finding, and (3) coordination within the network so as to ensure consistent application of Articles 81 and 82 EC by all its members.

---

[4] As the Regulation has Article 83 EC as its sole legal basis, 'the Community competition rules' can here only mean Articles 81 and 82 EC and their implementing rules.

[5] Council Document 15435/02 ADD 1, of 10 December 2002, available at http://register.consilium.eu.int. According to its point 3, 'this Joint Statement is political in nature and does therefore not create any legal rights or obligations. It is limited to setting out common political understanding shared by all Member States and the Commission on the principles of the functioning of the Network'.

[6] [2004] OJ C101/43.

[7] http://europa.eu.int/comm/competition/antitrust/legislation/list_of_authorities_joint_statement.pdf.

2.2.2 Efficient Allocation of Cases Between the Members of the Network

233. According to paragraph 5 of the Notice, all the competition authorities belonging to the network 'are responsible for an efficient division of work with respect to those cases where an investigation is deemend necessary'. Recital 18 of the Regulation indicates that 'the objective [is] that each case should be handled by a single authority'.

234. A number of provisions of the Regulation are instrumental to achieve this objective of allocating each case to the single best placed authority.

235. First, Article 35 requires the Member States to designate the competition authority or authorities responsible for the application of Articles 81 and 82 EC, and to take the measures necessary to empower those authorities to apply those Articles. According to the explanatory memorandum of the Commission's proposal which led to the Regulation, the full empowerment of the national competition authorities is—

the precondition for the proper functioning of the network of competition authorities. Without it, case allocation could not take place as envisaged, and the Commission might be forced to take a disproportionate share of cases concerning the markets of a Member State whose authority is unable to apply Articles 81 and 82.[8]

236. Second, Article 11(3) provides:

The competition authorities of the Member States shall, when acting under Article 81 or Article 82 of the Treaty, inform the Commission in writing before or without delay after commencing the first formal investigative measure. This information may also be made available to the competition authorities of the other Member States.

Similarly, Article 11(2) provides that 'the Commission shall transmit to the competition authorities of the Member States copies of the most important documents it has collected [...]'. Article 12 further provides that 'for the purpose of applying Articles 81 and 82 of the Treaty the Commission and the competition authorities of the Member States shall have the power to provide one another with and use in evidence any matter of fact or of law, including confidential information'. As pointed out in the explanatory memorandum of the Commission's proposal, 'effective case allocation [...] makes it necessary that the members of the network should inform each other of all new cases and exchange relevant case-related information'.[9] Article 12 'also allows the transfer of entire case files [...], the objective being to render possible the transfer of a case from one authority to another in the interest of effective case allocation'.[10]

237. Third, Article 13 of the Regulation empowers national competition authorities and the Commission to suspend or terminate proceedings on the

---

[8] COM (2000) 582, p 30.
[9] Idem, p 12.
[10] Idem, p 21.

ground that another member of the network is or has been dealing with the same case. As stated in the explanatory memorandum of the Commission's proposal, this Article 'removes risks of duplication of work and incentives for multiple complaints'.[11] The provision empowers national competition authorities and the Commission to suspend or terminate duplicative proceedings, but it does not oblige them to do so. According to the explanatory memorandum, it is 'neither necessary nor appropriate to oblige other competition authorities to suspend or terminate their proceedings. It is the task of the network to ensure in practice that resources are used efficiently'.[12] Indeed, in the absence of a rule determining which authority is the single best placed to deal with the case, a mandatory rule would not make sense, as only those authorities which are not the best placed should suspend or terminate their proceedings.

238. Fourth, Article 11(6) provides that the competition authorities of the Member States are automatically relieved of their competence if the Commission initiates its own proceedings. As pointed out in the explanatory memorandum of the Commission's proposal, this provision 'serves to ensure efficient case allocation [...]'.[13]

239. Whereas all these provisions are instrumental to achieve the objective of allocating each case to the single best placed authority, the Regulation does not contain any rules or criteria identifying which authority is the best placed to deal with a case.

240. The Joint Statement and the Notice do not either contain a set of rules identifying which authority is the *best* placed to deal with a case. They do, however, contain a set of conditions determining which authorities can be considered to be *well* placed to deal with a case.

241. Paragraph 8 of the Notice reads as follows:

An authority can be considered to be well placed to deal with a case if the following three cumulative conditions are met:

(1) the agreement or practice has substantial direct actual or foreseeable effects on competition within its territory, is implemented within or originates from its territory;

(2) the authority is able to effectively bring to an end the entire infringement ie it can adopt a cease and desist order the effect of which will be sufficient to bring an end to the infringement and it can, where appropriate, sanction the infringement adequately;

(3) it can gather, possibly with the assistance of other authorities, the evidence required to prove the infringement.

242. Paragraph 9 of the Notice adds that 'the above criteria indicate that a material link between the infringement and the territory of a Member State must exist in order for that Member State's competition authority to be considered well placed'.

---

[11] Idem, p 21.
[12] Idem, pp 12 and 13.
[13] Idem, p 21.

243. Whereas the Notice, in line with recital 18 of the Regulation,[14] states that the network members will endeavour to allocate cases 'to a single well placed competition authority as often as possible',[15] the possibility of parallel action by the competition authorities of two or three Member States appears not to be excluded.[16]

244. As to the Commission, it considers itself:

> particularly well placed if one or several agreement(s) or practice(s), including networks of similar agreements or practices, have effects on competition in more than three Member States (cross-border markets covering more than three Member States or several national markets). Moreover, the Commission is particularly well placed to deal with a case if it is closely linked to other Community provisions which may be exclusively or more effectively applied by the Commission, if the Community interest requires the adoption of a Commission decision to develop Community competition policy when a new competition issue arises or to ensure effective enforcement.[17]

2.2.3 Assistance Between Members of the Network in Respect of Fact-Finding

245. Article 22(2) of the Regulation provides that 'at the request of the Commission, the competition authorities of the Member States shall undertake the inspections which the Commission [has decided]'. Article 22(1) reads as follows:

> The competition authority of a Member State may in its own territory carry out any inspection or other fact-finding measure under its national law on behalf and for the account of the competition authority of another Member State in order to establish whether there has been an infringement of Article 81 or Article 82 of the Treaty. Any exchange and use of the information collected shall be carried out in accordance with Article 12.

According to the explanatory memorandum of the Commission's proposal which led to the Regulation, 'such cooperation enables national competition authorities to deal with cases where some evidence is to be found in other Member States. Without such mechanisms a real decentralisation of the application of Community competition rules would be seriously hampered'.[18]

246. As already indicated above, Article 12 of the Regulation allows more generally for the transfer of information between the members of the network, and its subsequent use as evidence by the receiving authority.

---

[14] See para 233 above.
[15] Para 7 of the Notice.
[16] See paras 5, 12, 13 and 14 of the Notice.
[17] Paras 14 and 15 of the Notice.
[18] COM (2000) 582, p 26.

2.2.4 Coordination to Ensure the Consistent Application of Articles 81 and 82 EC

247. According to the explanatory memorandum of the Commission's proposal which led to the Regulation:

> Maintaining consistent application is essential in an enforcement system in which parallel powers to apply Articles 81 and 82 are exercised by the Commission, national competition authorities and national courts. If significant differences in the application of these provisions were to develop the consistency of Community competition law and the proper functioning of the single market would be put at risk. It is therefore necessary to adopt measures addressing the danger of inconsistent application effectively.[19]

248. A number of provisions in the Regulation allow coordination within the network so as to ensure consistent application of Articles 81 and 82 EC by all its members, by providing for (1) exchange of information between the members of the network, (2) consultation within the network and (3) supervision by the Commission over the competition authorities of the Member States.

2.2.4.1 Exchange of Information Between the Members of the Network

249. As already indicated above, Article 11 (2) and (3) and Article 12 of the Regulation provide for information to be exchanged between the members of the network.

2.2.4.2 Consultations Within the Network

250. Article 11(4) and (5) and Article 14 of the Regulation provide for consultations within the network.

251. As to cases dealt with by the Commission, Article 14 provides for the consultation of the Advisory Committee on Restrictive Practices and Dominant Positions, composed of representatives of the competition authorities of the Member States, prior to the taking of a final decision by the Commission.

252. As to cases dealt with by competition authorities of the Member States, Article 11(4) reads as follows:

> No later than 30 days before the adoption of a decision requiring that an infringement be brought to an end, accepting commitments or withdrawing the benefit of a block exemption Regulation, the competition authorities of the Member States shall inform the Commission. To that effect, they shall provide the Commission with a summary of the case, the envisaged decision or, in the absence thereof, any other document indicating the proposed course of action. This information may also be made available to the competition authorities of the other Member States. At the request of the Commission, the acting competition authority shall make available to the Commission other

---

[19] Idem, p 23.

documents it holds which are necessary for the assessment of the case. The information supplied to the Commission may be made available to the competition authorities of the other Member States. National competition authorities may also exchange between themselves information necessary for the assessment of a case that they are dealing with under Article 81 or Article 82 of the Treaty.

253. Furthermore, Article 11(5) states that 'the competition authorities of the Member States may consult the Commission on any case involving the application of Community law'.

254. Article 14(7) further provides that, 'at the request of a competition authority of a Member State, the Commission shall include on the agenda of the Advisory Committee cases that are being dealt with by a competition authority of a Member State under Article 81 or Article 82 of the Treaty. The Commission may also do so on its own initiative'. According to the explanatory memorandum of the Commission's proposal, the purpose of this provision 'is to allow the Committee to serve as a forum for discussion of all cases that may be of common interest, in particular cases raising issues of consistent application of Articles 81 and 82'.[20]

2.2.4.3 The Commission's Powers of Control

255. Article 11(6) of the Regulation provides that 'the initiation by the Commission of proceedings for the adoption of a decision under Chapter III shall relieve the competition authorities of the Member States of their competence to apply Articles 81 and 82 of the Treaty'.

256. As explained in the explanatory memorandum of the Commission's proposal, this provision serves to ensure consistent application of Articles 81 and 82 EC: 'In case of substantial disagreement within the network, the Commission retains the power to withdraw a case from a national competition authority by itself initiating proceedings in the case'.[21]

257. Article 16(2) further provides:

When competition authorities of the Member States rule on agreements, decisions or practices under Article 81 or Article 82 of the Treaty which are already the subject of a Commission decision, they cannot take decisions which would run counter to the decision adopted by the Commission.

258. As pointed out in the explanatory memorandum of the Commission's proposal, 'national competition authorities can avoid taking conflicting decisions by consulting the Commission and—in cases where a Commission decision is pending before the Community courts—by suspending their own proceedings'.[22]

---

[20] Idem, p 22.
[21] Idem, p 10. See also p 21.
[22] Idem, p 24.

2.3 THE EUROPEAN CONVENTION ON HUMAN RIGHTS

2.3.1 Relevant Provisions

259. In the context of competition law enforcement, two sets of provisions in the European Convention on Human Rights appear relevant: (1) the right to a fair trial and the other guarantees protecting defendants in criminal proceedings, and (2) the protection of private life and of property.

2.3.1.1 Right to a Fair Trial and Other Guarantees Protecting Defendants in Criminal Proceedings

2.3.1.1.1 Right to a Fair Trial (Article 6 ECHR)

260. The first sentence of Article 6(1) ECHR reads as follows:

> In the determination of his civil rights and obligations or of any criminal charge against him, everyone is entitled to a fair and public hearing within a reasonable time by an independent and impartial tribunal established by law.

261. The remaining provisions of Article 6 ECHR list some further guarantees protecting defendants in criminal proceedings, as does Article 7 ECHR.

2.3.1.1.2 Right Not to be Tried or Punished Twice (Article 4 Protocol No 7)

262. Article 4 of Protocol No 7 to the Convention states:

> 1. No one shall be liable to be tried or punished again in criminal proceedings under the jurisdiction of the same State for an offence for which he has already been finally acquitted or convicted in accordance with the law and penal procedure of that State.
>
> The provisions of the preceding paragraph shall not prevent the reopening of the case in accordance with the law and penal procedure of the State concerned, if there is evidence of new or newly discovered facts, or if there has been a fundamental defect in the previous proceedings, which could affect the outcome of the case.

2.3.1.2 Protection of Private Life and of Property

2.3.1.2.1 Right to Respect for Private Life (Article 8 ECHR)

263. Article 8 ECHR reads as follows:

> 1. Everyone has the right to respect for his private and family life, his home and his correspondence.
>
> 2. There shall be no interference by a public authority with the exercise of this right except such as is in accordance with the law and is necessary in a democratic society in the interests of national security, public safety or the economic well-being of the country, for the prevention of disorder or crime, for the protection of health or morals, or for the protection of the rights and freedoms of others.

2.3.1.2.2 *Protection of Property (Article 1 Protocol No 1)*

264. Article 1 of Protocol No 1 to the Convention provides:

> Every natural or legal person is entitled to the peaceful enjoyment of his possessions. No one shall be deprived of his possessions except in the public interest and subject to the conditions provided for by law and by the general principles of international law.
>
> The preceding provisions shall not, however, in any way impair the right of a State to enforce such laws as it deems necessary to control the use of property in accordance with the general interest or to secure the payment of taxes or other contributions or penalties.

2.3.2 Legal Status

265. Neither the European Community nor the European Union are parties to the European Convention on Human Rights, which is not as such part of Community law. According to the case law of the Court of Justice, however, fundamental rights are part of the general principles of Community law, and the Court of Justice and the Court of First Instance thus ensure respect of these rights on the basis of Article 220 EC.[23] In defining and applying fundamental rights, the Community Courts draw from the constitutional traditions common to the Member States and from international treaties on which Member States have collaborated and to which they are signatories. In that respect the Community Courts have accorded particular significance to the Convention.[24]

266. The core of this case law is now enshrined in what is now Article 6(2) EU:

> The Union shall respect fundamental rights, as guaranteed by the European Convention for the Protection of Human Rights and Fundamental Freedoms signed in Rome on 4 November 1950 and as they result from the constitutional traditions common to the Member States, as general principles of Community law.

By virtue of Article 46(d) EU, the 'powers' of the Court of Justice with respect to Article 6(2) EU are confined to 'action of the institutions, insofar as the Court has jurisdiction under the Treaties establishing the European Communities and under this Treaty'.

---

[23] Judgment of 12 November 1969 in Case 29/69 *Stauder v Stadt Ulm* [1969] ECR 419, para 7.

[24] See for example Judgements of the Court of justice of 18 December 1997 in Case C–309/96 *Annibaldi* [1997] ECR I–7493; and of 17 December 1998 in Case C–185/95 P *Baustahlgewebe* [1998] ECR I–8417; and Judgment of the Court of First Instance of 20 February 2001 in Case T–112/98 *Mannesmannröhren-Werke* [2001] ECR II–732. All 25 Member States of the EU are parties to the Convention as amended by its Protocol No 11, as well as to Protocol No 1 thereto. However, only 19 of the 25 Member States have ratified Protocol No 7 (Germany, the Netherlands, Portugal and Spain have signed the Protocol, without ratification; Belgium and the United Kingdom have not signed. See http://conventions.coe.int). Insofar as this situation might have raised doubts as to the status as general principle of Community law of the right not to be tried or punished twice as laid down in Article 4 of Protocol No 7, this doubt has been removed by the proclamation of the Charter of Fundamental Rights, given that Article 50 of the Charter contains the corresponding right.

2.4 THE CHARTER OF FUNDAMENTAL RIGHTS

2.4.1 Introduction: The Charter and its Relationship with the European Convention on Human Rights

267. The Charter of Fundamental Rights of the European Union was solemnly proclaimed by the European Parliament, the Council and the Commission on 7 December 2000.[25]

268. According to its preamble,

this Charter reaffirms [...] the rights as they result, in particular, from the constitutional traditions and international obligations common to the Member States, the Treaty on European Union, the Community Treaties, the European Convention for the Protection of Human Rights and Fundamental Freedoms, the Social Charters adopted by the Community and by the Council of Europe and the case-law of the Court of Justice of the European Communities and the European Court of Human Rights.

269. As to the scope of the Charter, its Article 51(1) provides:

The provisions of this Charter are addressed to the institutions and bodies of the Union with due regard for the principle of subsidiarity and to the Member States only when they are implementing Union law. They shall therefore respect the rights, observe the principles and promote the application thereof in accordance with their respective powers.

270. Article 52(3) of the Charter provides:

In so far as this Charter contains rights which correspond to rights guaranteed by the Convention for the Protection of Human Rights and Fundamental Freedoms, the meaning and scope of those rights shall be the same as those laid down by the said Convention. This provision shall not prevent Union law providing more extensive protection.

271. It follows that, if a fundamental right enshrined in the Charter corresponds to a right guaranteed by the Convention, the latter serves as a minimum in determining the scope and meaning of the right in question. The Charter, which is part of Union law, may however provide more extensive protection.[26]

---

[25] See n 3 above. See also K Lenaerts and E De Smijter, 'A "Bill of Rights" for the European Union' (2001) 38 *Common Market Law Review* 273.

[26] K Lenaerts and E De Smijter, n 25 above, p 293.

2.4.2 Relevant Provisions

2.4.2.1 Right to a Fair Trial and Other Guarantees Protecting Defendants in Criminal Proceedings

2.4.2.1.1 Right to a Fair Trial (Article 47 CFR)

272. The first sentence of the second alinea of Article 47 of the Charter reads as follows:

> Everyone is entitled to a fair and public hearing within a reasonable time by an independent and impartial tribunal established by law.

273. According to the explanatory memorandum provided by the Secretariat of the body which drafted the Charter,[27] this provision,

> corresponds to Article 6(1) ECHR. […] In Community law, the right to a fair hearing is not confined to disputes relating to civil law rights and obligations. That is one of the consequences of the fact that the Community is a community based on the rule of law […]. Nevertheless, in all respects other than their scope, the guarantees afforded by the ECHR apply in a similar way in the Union.[28]

2.4.2.1.2 Right Not to be Tried or Punished Twice (Article 50 CFR)

274. Article 50 of the Charter reads as follows:

> No one shall be liable to be tried or punished again in criminal proceedings for an offence for which he or she has already been finally acquitted or convicted within the Union in accordance with the law.

275. According to the explanatory memorandum, this provision 'corresponds to Article 4 of Protocol No 7 to the ECHR, but its scope is extended to European Union level between the Courts of the Member States'.[29]

2.4.2.2 Protection of Private Life and of Property

2.4.2.2.1 Respect for Private Life (Article 7 CFR)

276. Article 7 of the Charter provides:

> Everyone has the right to respect for his or her private and family life, home and communications.

277. According to the explanatory memorandum, 'the rights guaranteed in Article 7 correspond to those guaranteed by Article 8 of the ECHR. To take

---

[27] Council of the EU, Charter of Fundamental Rights of the European Union—Explanations relating to the complete text of the Charter (December 2000), available at http://ue.eu.int/df/docs/en/EN_2001_1023.pdf.

[28] Idem, pp 65–66.

[29] Idem, p 76.

account of developments in technology the word "correspondence" has been replaced by "communications" '.[30]

2.4.2.2.2 Right to Property (Article 17 CFR)

278. Article 17 of the Charter reads as follows:

1. Everyone has the right to own, use, dispose of and bequeath his or her lawfully acquired possessions. No one may be deprived of his or her possessions, except in the public interest and in the cases and under the conditions provided for by law, subject to fair compensation being paid in good time for their loss. The use of property may be regulated by law in so far as is necessary for the general interest.

2. Intellectual property shall be protected.

279. According to the explanatory memorandum, 'Article 17 corresponds to Article 1 of the Protocol to the ECHR'.[31]

2.4.2.3 Limitations (Article 52 CFR)

280. Article 52(1) of the Charter reads as follows:

Any limitation on the exercise of the rights and freedoms recognised by this Charter must be provided for by law and respect the essence of those rights and freedoms. Subject to the principle of proportionality, limitations may be made only if they are necessary and genuinely meet objectives of general interest recognised by the Union or the need to protect the rights and freedoms of others.

281. As already indicated above, Article 52(3) CFR provides that, if a fundamental right enshrined in the Charter corresponds to a right guaranteed by the Convention, the latter serves as a minimum in determining the scope and meaning of the right in question.

2.4.3 Legal Status

282. The inter-governmental conference which was meeting at the time when the Charter was drafted could have decided to insert the Charter into the Treaties on which the Union is founded or to add a reference to it in Article 6(2) EU. Instead, the Charter was merely the subject of a solemn proclamation by the European Parliament, the Council and the Commission. As Lenaerts and De Smijter have pointed out that:

In practice, however, the legal effect of the solemn proclamation of the Charter of Fundamental Rights of the European Union will tend to be similar to that of insertion into the Treaties on which the Union is founded. Indeed, to the extent that the charter is

---

[30] Idem, p 25.
[31] Idem, p 75. See also p 35.

to be regarded as an expression of the constitutional traditions common to the Member States, the Court will be required to enforce it by virtue of Article 6(2) juncto Article 46(d) EU 'as general principles of Community law'. The holistic interpretation given by the Court to the term 'common constitutional traditions', the composition and the functioning of the Convention which drafted the Charter as well as the unanimous acceptance of the text of the Charter by the three EU institutions with legislative powers, may reasonably lead to the conclusion that the Charter is to be regarded as an emanation of those common constitutional traditions, in the substantive sense of the term 'constitutional traditions'. The Charter is thus part of the *acquis communautaire*, even if it is not part yet of the Treaties on which the Union is founded.[32]

283. The Charter has since been included as Part II in the draft Treaty establishing a Constitution for Europe, adopted by the European Convention on 13 June and 10 July 2003,[33] and has been maintained in the text of the Constitution as agreed by the Heads of State or Government at their meeting on 18 June 2004.[34]

284. Recital 37 of Regulation No 1/2003 states that 'this Regulation respects the fundamental rights and observes the principles recognised in particular by the Charter of Fundamental Rights of the European Union. Accordingly, this Regulation should be interpreted and applied with respect to those rights and principles'.

2.5 POSSIBLE PROBLEMS RELATED TO CASE ALLOCATION

285. As to the allocation of cases between the members of the network, two possible problems can be identified: (A) possible differences in applicability of the Convention or the Charter to the different members of the network and (B) double jeopardy.

2.5.1 Differences in Applicability of the Convention and the Charter

286. Under Regulation No 1/2003, a case will be allocated either to the competition authority of a Member State or to the Commission, depending on which authority is the best placed to deal with the case.

287. Given that all 25 Member States are parties to the Convention,[35] whereas the European Community and the European Union are not, the allocation of the

---

[32] K Lenaerts and E De Smijter, n 25 above, p 298–99. See 'European Union Law and National Constitutions', FIDE XX Congress (London, 30 October–2 November 2002) and its reports: J Dutheil de la Rochère and I Pernice, 'General Report: European Union Law and National Constitutions, FIDE XX Congress (London, 2002); P Oliver, Community Report: European Union Law and National Constitutions, FIDE XX Congress (London, 2002), both available at http://www.fide2002.org.

[33] [2003] OJ C169/1.

[34] Conference of the Representatives of the Governments of the Member States, documents CIG 85/04 of 18 June 2004 and CIG 81/04 of 16 June 2004.

[35] See n 24 above as to the Protocols to the Convention.

case to a national authority or to the Commission will determine whether or not the Convention applies to the treatment of the case. It could be argued that the Member States would be in breach of their obligations under the Convention whenever they allow a case to be transferred from their national competition authorities, which are bound by the Convention, to the Commission, which is not.

288. This problem does however not appear to be a real one. Under Article 1 of the Convention, Member States 'shall secure to everyone within their jurisdiction the rights and freedoms defined in [the] Convention'. This obligation is fulfilled as long as an equivalent level of protection of fundamental rights as required under the Convention is also guaranteed when the case is dealt with by the Commission.[36] As explained above,[37] the case law of the Court of Justice, and the provisions of the EU Treaty, provide for an equivalent protection via the general principles of Community law.

289. As to the Charter, according to Article 51(1) thereof, its provisions are addressed not only to the institutions of the Union, such as the Commission, but also 'to the Member States [...] when they are implementing Union law'. The Charter thus applies equally when a case is dealt with under Articles 81 or 82 EC by the Commission or by the competition authority of a Member State.

2.5.2 Double Jeopardy

290. As explained above, the objective of the Regulation is that each case should be handled by a single authority.[38] If this objective were not achieved and some cases were dealt with by several authorities within the network, problems could arise under the *ne bis in idem* principle.

2.5.2.1 The Old Situation Under Regulation No 17

291. Under Regulation No 17 the competition authorities of the Member States have only rarely applied Articles 81 and 82 EC.[39] Instead they normally applied their national competition laws.

---

[36] See Decision of the European Commission of Human Rights of 9 February 1990, *M & Co v Germany*, Case 13258/87, *YECHR*, 1990, p 46. See also Judgment of the European Court of Human Rights of 18 February 1999, *Matthews v United Kingdom*, Application 24833/94.

[37] Paras 265 and 266.

[38] See para 233 above.

[39] As to the reasons for this lack of application, see G Marenco, 'The Uneasy Enforcement of Article 81 EEC as Between Community and National Levels' in BE Hawk (ed), *Annual Proceedings of the Fordham Corporate Law Institute 1993* (Kluwer, 1994) 605; H-P von Stoephasius, 'Enforcement of EC Competition Law by National Authorities' in PJ Slot and A McDonnell (eds), *Procedure and Enforcement in EC and US Competition Law* (Sweet and Maxwell, 1993) 32; Editorial Comments, 'Subsidiarity in EC Competition Law Enforcement' (1995) 32 *Common Market Law Review* 1; and my book *The Optimal Enforcement of EC Antitrust Law* (Kluwer, 2002) 140–41.

2.5.2.1.1 *The Case Law of the Court of Justice*

292. In *Wilhelm v Bundeskartellamt*, the Court of Justice held that the possibility of one and the same agreement being the object of two sets of parallel proceedings, one before the Commission under Article 81 EC, the other before the national authorities under national law, was not contrary to the *ne bis in idem* principle, given the differences between the two laws, notably because Community law focuses on the effect on trade between Member States.[40]

293. The Court did however add that,

> if [...] the possibility of two procedures being conducted seperately were to lead to the imposition of consecutive sanctions, a general requirement of natural justice, such as that expressed at the end of the second paragraph of Article 90 of the ECSC Treaty, demands that any previous punitive decision must be taken into account in determining any sanction which is to be imposed.[41]

2.5.2.1.2 *The Convention*

294. It can be doubted whether the judgment in *Wilhelm v Bundeskartellamt* is entirely compatible with Article 4 of Protocol No 7 to the European Convention of Human Rights. Indeed, the European Court of Human Right has ruled that Article 4 of Protocol No 7 is breached not only when a person is tried or punished twice for nominally the same offence but also when he or she is prosecuted twice for two offences the essential elements of which overlap.[42] Articles 81 and 82 EC, on the one hand, and national competition laws, on the other hand, may very well constitute an example of such overlap. Indeed, whereas Articles 81 and 82 EC contain an element not embraced by national competition laws, namely the effect on trade between Member States, the essential elements of national competition laws would often appear to cover the same ground as Articles 81 and 82 EC. However, Article 4 of Protocol No 7 ECHR only applies to double prosecution 'under the jurisdiction of the same State'.[43]

2.5.2.1.3 *The Charter*

295. The situation under the Charter appears much clearer. Whereas Article 4 of Protocol No 7 ECHR only applies to double prosecution 'under the jurisdiction of

---

[40] Judgment of 13 February 1969 in Case 14/68 *Wilhelm v Bundeskartellamt* [1969] ECR 3, paras 3 and 11.

[41] Idem, para 11.

[42] Judgment of the European Court of Human Rights of 29 August 2001, *Fischer v Austria*, Application 37950/97, discussing earlier Judgments of 23 October 1995, *Gradinger v Austria*, A/328–C, and of 30 July 1998, *Oliveira v Swizerland*, Application 25711/94. In the United States, the Supreme Court has similarly held in *Blockburger v US* 284 US 299 (1932) that punishment for two statutory offences arising out of the same criminal act or transaction does not violate the double jeopardy clause in the 5th Amendment to the US Constitution only if 'each provision requires proof of an additional fact which the other does not'. See also more recently *US v Dixon* 113 SCt 2849, 2856 (1993).

[43] Similarly, in the United States, the courts have held that the state and federal governments are separate sovereigns and that successive prosecutions based on the same underlying conduct do not violate the double jeopardy clause if the prosecutions are brought by separate sovereigns. See *US v Lanza* 260 US 377, 382 (1922) and more recently *US v Koon* 34 F3d 1416, 1438 (9th Cir 1994).

the same State', Article 50 CFR prohibits double prosecution 'within the Union'. It thus clearly also covers the situation of parallel prosecutions by the Commission and a national competition authority, or by the competition authorities of several Member States.

2.5.2.2 The Situation Under Regulation No 1/2003

296. Article 3(1) of the Regulation provides:

Where the competition authorities of the Member States or national courts apply national competition law to agreements, decisions by associations of undertakings or concerted practices within the meaning of Article 81(1) of the Treaty which may affect trade between Member States within the meaning of that provision, they shall also apply Article 81 of the Treaty to such agreements, decisions or concerted practices. Where the competition authorities of the Member States or national courts apply national competition law to any abuse prohibited by Article 82 of the Treaty, they shall also apply Article 82 of the Treaty.

297. This means that under Regulation No 1/2003 the competition authorities of the Member States will be obliged to apply Articles 81 and 82 EC to any case affecting trade between Member States, either in combination with national competition law or in isolation. Whenever the same case is dealt with by the Commission and a national competition authority, or by the authorities of several Member States, these authorities will thus be applying nominally the same law, and the applicability of the *ne bis in idem* principle becomes all the more obvious.

298. Like under Regulation No 17, multiple proceedings by the Commission and a national competition authority, or by the authorities of several Member States, may not be contrary to Article 4 of Protocol No 7 ECHR, which only applies to double prosecution 'under the jurisdiction of the same State', but there would a problem under Article 50 CFR, which prohibits double prosecution 'within the Union'.

2.5.2.3 The Application of Articles 81 and 82 EC
is of a Criminal Law Nature

299. The above conclusion that multiple proceedings under Articles 81 or 82 EC by the Commission and a national competition authority, or by the authorities of several Member States, concerning the same agreement or practice would raise a problem under Article 50 CFR is dependent on such proceedings being qualified as 'criminal'. Indeed, Article 50 CFR only contains a right not to be tried or punished twice 'in criminal proceedings'.

300. The Charter does not contain any definition of what is 'criminal'. Given the close relationship between the Charter and the Convention, the obvious

approach would be to give 'criminal' in the Charter the same meaning as this term has in the Convention.[44]

301. Article 23(5) of the Regulation No 1/2003 provides, like Article 15(4) of Regulation No 17, that decisions by which the Commission imposes fines on undertakings pursuant to that regulation 'shall not be of a criminal law nature'. This provision is however not decisive in determining whether proceedings based on that regulation are of a criminal law nature within the meaning of the Convention. Indeed, according to the case law of the European Court of Human Rights, the indications furnished by domestic law as to the criminal nature of the offence 'have only a relative value', the term 'criminal' within the meaning of Article 6 ECHR being 'autonomous'.[45]

302. For Article 6 to apply by virtue of the words 'criminal charge', 'it suffices that the offence in question should by its nature be "criminal" from the point of view of the Convention', because it relates to 'a general rule, whose purpose is both deterrent and punitive', 'or should have made the person concerned liable to a sanction which, in its nature and degree of severity, belongs in general to the "criminal" sphere'.[46] As I have argued in detail elsewhere,[47] it appears difficult, if not impossible, to deny that the application of the criteria set out in the case law of the European Court of Human Rights leads to the conclusion that proceedings based on Regulation No 17 or now Regulation No 1/2003, leading or possibly leading to decisions in which the Commission finds a violation of Articles 81 or 82 EC, orders its termination and imposes fines relate to 'the determination of a criminal charge' within the meaning of Article 6 ECHR.[48] The same would hold true for national proceedings leading to or possibly leading to findings of violations of Articles 81 and 82 EC and imposing penalties for such violations.

---

[44] In the Convention, the term appears in several articles. The case law of the European Court of Human Rights on the concept of 'criminal' focuses on Article 6 ECHR, but there are no reasons to assume that the concept would not be exactly the same in other provisions of the Convention and its Protocols. *Gradinger v Austria* and *Fischer v Austria*, n 42 above, appear to confirm that the term 'criminal' has the same meaning in Article 4 of Protocol No 7 ECHR as in Article 6 ECHR, as one of the two Austrian proceedings in both of these cases was of an administrative nature according to Austrian law, but nevertheless considered 'criminal' for the purposes of Article 4 of Protocol No 7 ECHR.

[45] *Öztürk v Germany* judgment of 21 February 1984, A/73, paras 50 and 52. See also above, ch 1, n 88.

[46] *Lutz v Germany* judgment of 25 August 1987, A/123, para 55; and *Bendenoun v France* judgment of 24 February 1994, A/284, para 47.

[47] See WPJ Wils 'La Compatibilité des Procédures Communautaires en Matière de Concurrence Avec la Convention Européenne des Droits de l'Homme' (1996) 32 *Cahiers de Droit Européen* 329.

[48] See also Opinion of Judge Vesterdorf acting as Advocate General in Case T–1/89 *Rhône- Poulenc v Commission* [1991] ECR II–867, 885; Opinion of Advocate General Léger in Case C–185/95 P *Baustahlgewebe v Commission* [1998] ECR I–8422 para 31; and Judgment of the Court of Justice of 8 July 1999 in Case C–199/92 P *Hüls v Commission* [1999] ECR I–4383 paras 149–50; as well as K Lenaerts and J Vanhamme, 'Procedural Rights of Private Parties in the Community Administrative Process' (1997) 34 *Common Market Law Review* 531, 557.

2.5.2.4 Some Further Issues Concerning the Scope of the Prohibition on Multiple Prosecutions and Punishments

2.5.2.4.1 Parallel Proceedings are Temporarily Possible

303. According to the terms of Article 50 CFR, 'no one shall be liable to be tried or punished again in criminal proceedings for an offence for which he or she has already been finally acquitted or convicted within the Union in, accordance with the law'.

304. The prohibition of double prosecution and punishment does thus not exclude the possibility of parallel proceedings being conducted by several members of the network of competition authorities at the same time, as long as none of these proceedings has already reached the stage of final acquittal or conviction. This means that at a preliminary stage, when it may not yet be clear which member of the network is the best placed to deal with the case, several competition authorities may investigate the same agreement or practice. However, at the latest at the moment when the first proceeding is closed by a final acquittal or conviction, the other authorities have to discontinue their proceedings.

2.5.2.4.2 The Types of Decision Precluding a Second Prosecution or Punishment

305. Article 50 CFR precludes further prosecution or punishment for an offence for which the person concerned 'has already been finally acquitted or convicted within the Union in accordance with the law'. This raises the question as to what types of decision qualify as 'final acquittal or conviction'.

2.5.2.4.2.1 Prohibition and Fining Decisions

306. There can be no doubt that decisions pursuant to Article 7 of the Regulation No 1/2003, under which the Commission may find infringements of Articles 81 or 82 EC, and decisions pursuant to Article 23(2)(a) of the Regulation, under which the Commission may impose fines for such infringements, constitute 'convictions' within the meaning of Article 50 CFR. If the addressees of these decisions bring an application for annulment before the Community Courts, these decisions will however only be 'final' when confirmed by the Community Courts. Similarly, decisions of competition authorities of the Member States requiring that infringements of Articles 81 or 82 EC be brought to an end or imposing fines, pursuant to Article 5 of the Regulation, constitute 'convictions'. Again, they would only become 'final' at the end of possible applications for judicial review or appeals.

2.5.2.4.2.2 Non-Infringement Decisions

307. Equally, there can be no doubt that decisions taken pursuant to Article 10 of the Regulation, under which the Commission may find that Articles 81 or 82 EC are not applicable to an agreement or practice, constitute 'acquittals' within the meaning of Article 50 CFR.

308. As to the competition authorities of the Member States, the last sentence of Article 5 of the Regulation provides that 'where on the basis of the information

in their possession the conditions for prohibition are not met they may likewise decide that there are no grounds for action on their part'. Such a decision can probably not be qualified as a 'final acquittal' within the meaning of Article 50 CFR.

2.5.2.4.2.3 Commitment Decisions

309. Article 9 of the Regulation reads as follows:

1. Where the Commission intends to adopt a decision requiring that an infringement be brought to an end and the undertakings concerned offer commitments to meet the concerns expressed to them by the Commission, the Commission may by decision make those commitments binding on the undertakings. Such a decision may be adopted for a specified period and shall conclude that there are no longer grounds for action by the Commission.

2. The Commission may, upon request or on its own initiative, reopen the proceedings:

(a) where there has been a material change in any of the facts on which the decision was based;
(b) where the undertakings concerned act contrary to their commitments; or
(c) where the decision was based on incomplete, incorrect or misleading information provided by the parties.

310. Recital 13 of the Regulation adds:

Commitment decisions should find that there are no longer grounds for action by the Commission without concluding whether or not there has been or still is an infringement. Commitment decisions are without prejudice to the powers of the competition authorities and courts of the Member States to make such a finding and decide upon the case.[49]

311. On the one hand, Recital 13 expressly states that the question of whether there has been or still is an infringement is left open. This would suggest that a consent decision is not to be regarded as an acquittal or conviction. On the other hand, Article 9 makes it clear that the decision shall terminate the Commission's proceedings, subject only to the possibility of reopening proceedings pursuant to the third paragraph. This rather suggests that a decision pursuant to Article 9 should preclude further prosecutions or punishments by other authorities. The latter view could arguably draw support from the judgment of the Court of Justice in *Hüseyin Gözütok and Klaus Brügge*.[50]

---

[49] See also the last sentence of Recital 22 of the Regulation.
[50] Judgment of 11 February 2003 in Joined Cases C–187/01 and C–385/01 *Hüseyin Gözütok and Klaus Brügge*, [2003] ECR I–1378, in which the Court held that the *ne bis in idem* principle as laid down in Article 54 of the Convention of 19 June 1990 applying the Schengen Agreement precludes a second prosecution where the first prosecution has been terminated in the form of a settlement by the public prosecutor before the case is brought to court. See also annotation by JAE Vervaele in (2004) 41 *Common Market Law Review* 795–812.

2.5.2.4.3 *Deducting the First Penalty from a Second One Will Not Suffice*

312. Article 50 CFR clearly establishes the right for any person not 'to be tried or punished again' in criminal proceedings for an offence for which he or she has already been finally acquited or convicted. A first acquittal or conviction thus precludes any subsequent proceedings. Thus it does not suffice to deduct from the penalty imposed in the second proceeding any penalty imposed in the first proceeding. The second proceedings are precluded as such.

313. This has also been held by the European Court of Human Rights with regard to Article 4 of Protocol No 7 ECHR in *Fischer v Austria*:

> The Court is not convinced by the Government's argument that the case was resolved due to the reduction of the applicant's prison term by one month, being equivalent to the fine paid in the administrative proceedings. The reduction of the prison term [...] cannot alter the above finding that the applicant was tried twice for essentially the same offence, and the fact that both his convictions stand.[51]

2.5.2.4.4 *Limitations Under Article 52 CFR*

314. Article 4 of Protocol No 7 ECHR does not provide for any possible derogation or limitation to the right not to be tried or punished twice. By extending this right to situations where the prosecutions take place in different jurisdictions within the Union, Article 50 CFR extends the scope of Article 4 of Protocol No 7 ECHR. It could thus be argued that limitations would still be possible under Article 52 CFR in multi-jurisdictional cases. On the other hand, it could be argued that, by extending Article 4 of Protocol No 7 ECHR to multi-jurisdictional cases, Article 52 CFR has extended the scope of application but not altered the substance of the Article 4 of Protocol No 7 ECHR, including the impossibility of derogations. In any event, it is difficult to see what objectives of general interest that do not apply within a single jurisdiction could justify limitations to the right not to be tried or punished twice in multi-jurisdictional cases, particularly in the context of the European Competition Network, as envisaged by Regulation No 1/2003, given the close cooperation which characterises the functioning of this network.[52]

2.6 POSSIBLE PROBLEMS RELATED TO ASSISTANCE IN FACT-FINDING

315. Two problems may arise as to the assistance between members of the network in respect of fact-finding: (A) the extension of the possible use of evidence to members of the network other than the one collecting the evidence and (B) different levels of protection of the rights of defence in the jurisdictions concerned.

---

[51] See n 42 above, para 30.
[52] See also para 430 below.

2.6.1 Extension of the Possible Use of Evidence to Members of the Network Other Than the One Collecting the Evidence

2.6.1.1 The Old Situation Under Regulation No 17

316. Article 20(1) of Regulation No 17 provided that information acquired as a result of requests for information or verifications pursuant to Regulation No 17 'shall be used only for the purpose of the relevant request or investigation'.

317. In *Spanish Banks* the Court of Justice had made it clear that in consequence the competition authorities of the Member States, which could receive this information pursuant to Article 10 of Regulation No 17, which provided for the involvement of the Member States in the Commission's proceedings, could not use themselves this information in evidence in their own proceedings applying Community or national competition law.[53]

318. As to information collected by national competition authorities, it depended on the applicable national law whether or not this information could be transferred to and subsequently used in evidence by the competition authorities of other Member States. The Commission could always request the national authority pursuant to Article 11 of Regulation No 17 to hand over the information, and subsequently use it in evidence.

2.6.1.2 The Situation Under Regulation No 1/2003

319. Article 12 of Regulation No 1/2003 provides that 'for the purpose of applying Articles 81 and 82 of the Treaty the Commission and the competition authorities of the Member States shall have the power to provide one another with and use in evidence any matter of fact or of law, including confidential information'. Article 22 further provides for the possibility for one member of the network to carry out fact-finding measures at the request and on behalf of another member of the network.

320. Each member of the network will thus be able to use in evidence information collected by any member of the network.

2.6.1.3 Assessment Under the Charter and the Convention

321. Restrictions on the possible use of evidence collected by a competition authority, such as the restriction laid down in Article 20(1) of Regulation No 17 as interpreted by the Court of Justice, could be considered as responding to two kinds of concern relating to fundamental rights.[54]

---

[53] Judgment of 16 July 1992 in Case C–67/91 *Asociación Española de Banca Privada and Others* ('*Spanish banks*') [1992] ECR I–4820. National authorities may however use the information as intelligence, prompting their own investigations.

[54] Compare with the *Spanish Banks* judgment, n 53 above, paras 36–37, with the Opinion of Advocate General Mischo in Joined Cases 46/87 and 227/88 *Hoechst v Commission* [1989] ECR 2909

322. First, to the extent that the investigative measures used interfere with privacy, use restrictions serve to prevent unnecessary or abusive interference, in that they preclude the investigating authority from using its investigative powers for purposes unrelated to those for which the investigative powers have been granted.

323. Second, use restrictions could also contribute to guaranteeing a fair trial in that the undertakings or persons being investigated know, when subjected to investigative measures, by whom and for what type of offences they are being prosecuted.

324. Restrictions on the possible use of evidence collected by a competition authority could thus be valuable with respect both to the right to respect for private life, as guaranteed by Article 8 ECHR and Article 7 CFR, and to the right to a fair trial, as guaranteed by Article 6 ECHR and Article 47 CFR.

325. It would not appear, however, that the extension to all members of the network of the possible use in evidence of information collected by any member of the network would lead to a breach of any of those fundamental rights.

326. Indeed, as long as the possible use of the information collected remains limited to the application of Articles 81 and 82 EC—as guaranteed by Articles 12(2) and 28(1) of Regulation No 1/2003, the guarantee against the use of investigative powers for purposes unrelated to those for which the investigative powers have been granted remains in place.

327. As to the second concern underlying use restrictions, the extension does not appear problematic either. It is true that the undertakings or persons being investigated, when subjected to investigative measures, face somewhat more uncertainty as to the question by whom they are being prosecuted, in that the prosecuting authority may later turn out to be another member of the network than the one investigating initially, but this uncertainty would appear to remain within acceptable limits, given the closed number of members of the network.

328. As an additional guarantee, it could be considered to provide that, when members of the network make requests for information and carry out investigations, they would indicate to the undertakings or persons being investigated the possibility of the information collected being transferred and subsequently used by other members of the network. It could also be provided that the undertakings or persons concerned would be informed when information is transferred to another member of the network for use in evidence.

paras 206–8, and with the Opinion of Advocate General Mischo of 25 October 2001 in Case C–244/99 P *DSM v Commission* [1992] *ECR* I–8398 para 317.

2.6.2 Different Levels of Protection of the Rights of Defence in the Jurisdictions Concerned

2.6.2.1 The Problem

329. Community law, which governs the collection and use of evidence by the Commission, and the 25 national laws, which—in the absence of applicable Community law rules—govern the collection and use of evidence by the competition authorities of the Member States, may differ with respect to the type of evidence which can be legally collected, or the way in which it can be collected, or with respect to what evidence can be adduced. When the members of the network assist each other in collecting evidence, it could happen that one member of the network, either on its own initiative or at the second competition authority's request, collects, in accordance with the law governing the investigating powers of the first authority, evidence which the second authority could not have lawfully collected under its own law, and hands over this evidence to the second authority so as to allow it to use this evidence. For instance, the Commission could lawfully collect and subsequently transmit to the Belgian competition authority information which under Belgian law would be protected by in-house counsel legal privilege, a privilege not recognised in Community law.[55] A second example would be where the Commission collects evidence through a request for information to which the undertaking concerned is obliged to respond under Community law,[56] and transmits this information for use in evidence to the German competition authority, which might not have been able to collect this information itself because of the right not to incriminate oneself as laid down in Paragraph 136(1) of the German code of criminal procedure.[57]

330. To analyse this problem, it may be helpful to draw a distinction according to the source of the difference in protection levels in the two jurisdictions concerned, namely whether the difference reflects a requirement to respect fundamental rights as guaranteed in the Convention or the Charter, or whether the difference is due to a national law or Community law providing for a level of protection exceeding the requirements of the Convention and the Charter.

---

[55] See Judgment of the Court of Justice of 18 May 1982 in Case 155/79 *AM&S v Commission* [1982] ECR 1575; and Order of the Court of First Instance of 4 April 1990 in Case T–30/89 *Hilti v Commission* [1990] *ECR* II–163. See however also Order of the President of the Court of First Instance of 30 October 2003 in Joined Cases T–125/03 R and T–253/03 R *Akzo Nobel Chemicals v Commission*, not yet published in ECR, currently on appeal before the Court of Justice, Case C–7/04 P(R).

[56] See Judgment of the Court of First Instance of 20 February 2001 in Case T–112/98 *Mannesmannröheren-Werke v Commission* [2001] ECR II–732.

[57] See idem, paras 80–81.

2.6.2.2 Where the Difference Reflects a Requirement to Respect Fundamental Rights as Guaranteed in the Convention or the Charter

331. As explained above, the Charter equally applies to the Commission and to the competition authorities of the Member States when the latter are implementing Community competition law. The fundamental rights laid down in the Convention also have to be respected by the competition authorities of the Member States, since they are parties to the Convention, as well as by the Commission, as general principles of Community law.

332. The Convention and the Charter may nevertheless impose different requirements on different members of the network, reflecting relevant differences between the various national laws and Community law.

333. For instance, whereas Community law only provides for fines on undertakings for violations of Articles 81 or 82 EC, national law may provide for individual decision-makers within those companies being sentenced to prison. It appears that Article 6 ECHR grants natural persons faced with the risk of a prison sentence a broad right of silence, allowing them to refuse to answer requests for information.[58] At present, there is no case law of the European Court of Human Rights indicating that Article 6 ECHR would also imply a similarly broad right of silence for legal persons faced with the risk of being fined.[59]

334. In this example, a problem under the Convention would arise if the competition authority of a Member State in which prison sanctions lie for violation of Articles 81 or 82 EC were to use in evidence information collected by another member of the network which itself could have obtained and used this evidence without violating Article 6 ECHR given that under its law no prison sanctions lie. The rather obvious solution to this problem is that the competition authority of the Member State in which prison sanctions lie should abstain from using this evidence, or preferably even avoid receiving it.

335. This solution appears to be achieved indeed through Article 12(3) of the Regulation, which reads as follows:

Information exchanged pursuant to paragraph 1 can only be used in evidence to impose sanctions on natural persons where:

— the law of the transmitting authority foresees sanctions of a similar kind in relation to an infringement of Article 81 or Article 82 of the Treaty or, in the absence thereof,
— the information has been collected in a way which respects the same level of protection of the rights of defence of natural persons as provided for under the national rules of the receiving authority. However, in this case, the information exchanged cannot be used by the receiving authority to impose custodial sanctions.

---

[58] See the following judgments of the European Court of Human Rights: *Funke v France*, 25 February 1993, A/256–A; *John Murray v United Kingdom*, 8 February 1996, Reports 1996–I, p 49; *Saunders v United Kingdom*, 17 December 1996, Reports 1996–VI, p 2064; *Servès v France*, 20 October 1997, Reports 1997–VI, p 2173; and *JB v Switzerland*, 3 May 2001, Application 31827/96.

[59] See further section 5.2 below.

2.6.2.3 Where the Difference is Due to a National Law or Community Law Providing for a Level of Protection Exceeding the Requirements of the Convention and the Charter

336. A national law or Community law may provide for some protection not required by the Convention or the Charter. For instance, legal privilege for in-house counsel provided for in some national laws such as Belgian law does not appear to correspond to any right guaranteed by the Convention or the Charter. It logically follows that the Convention and the Charter do not stand in the way of the Belgian competition authority using in evidence information which it could not have collected itself under Belgian law because of the in-house counsel legal privilege but which it obtained under the Regulation from the Commission or from another member of the network under whose national law a similar privilege is not recognised.[60]

2.7 POSSIBLE PROBLEMS RELATED TO COORDINATION TO ENSURE CONSISTENCY

337. Three possible problems may arise in relation to the coordination within the network: (A) different levels of protection of the confidentiality of information exchanged, (B) the consultations within the network and the right to adversarial proceedings and (C) the Commission's powers of control and the independence of national competition authorities.

2.7.1 Different Levels of Protection of the Confidentiality of Information Exchanged

338. When information is exchanged within the network, the confidentiality of this information may be protected to varying degrees by the different members of the network.

339. As to the protection of business secrets and other confidential information, two sets of provisions of the Convention and the Charter may come into play.

340. First, the right to respect for private life and for correspondence or communications, as guaranteed by Article 8 ECHR and Article 7 CFR, could be relevant. Indeed, according to the case law of the European Court of Human Rights, 'private life is a broad term not susceptible to exhaustive definition. […] It may include activities of a professional or business nature'.[61]

---

[60] See also paras 204–9 above.

[61] Judgment of 25 September 2001, *PG and JH v United Kingdom*, Application 44787/98, para 56, referring to the judgments in *Niemitz v Germany*, 16 December 1992, A/251–B, para 29, and *Halford v United Kingdom*, 25 June 1997, Reports 1997–III, para 44.

341. Second, business secrets may benefit from protection under the right to property, as guaranteed by Article 1 Protocol 1 ECHR and Article 17 CFR. According to the case law of the European Court of Human Rights, 'the concept of "possessions" in Article 1 of Protocol No 1 has an autonomous meaning which is certainly not limited to ownership of physical goods: certain other rights and interests constituting assets can also be regarded as "property rights", and thus as "possessions" for the purposes of this provision'.[62]

342. Article 28(2) of the Regulation provides that, without prejudice to the provisions on cooperation within the network and with national courts and to the provisions on the hearing of parties, complainants and other interested parties,

> the Commission and the competition authorities of the Member States, their officials, servants and other persons working under the supervision of these authorities as well as officials and civil servants of other authorities of the Member States shall not disclose information acquired or exchanged by them pursuant to this Regulation and of the kind covered by the obligation of professional secrecy.

343. As pointed out in the explanatory memorandum of the Commission's proposal which led to the Regulation, this provision 'makes the obligation of professional secrecy laid down in Article 20(2) of the existing Regulation No 17 applicable to all confidential information exchanged by the national competition authorities under the proposed Regulation'.[63]

344. There are no reasons to believe that this level of protection, which will apply as a uniform minimum standard to all members of the network, would be insufficient in the light of the Convention and the Charter.[64] The possibility that some national law may provide an even higher level of protection does not raise any problem under the Convention or the Charter.

2.7.2 Consultations Within the Network and the Right to Adversarial Proceedings

2.7.2.1 The Problem

345. Under the Regulation, when a competition authority intends to adopt a decision finding an infringement of Articles 81 or 82 EC, ordering its termination or

---

[62] *Gasus Dosier- und Fördertechnik GmbH v the Netherlands*, 23 February 1995, A/ 306–B, para 53; and *Iatridis v Greece*, 25 March 1999, Application 31107/96, para 54. See also *Tre Traktörer AB v Sweden*, 7 July 1989, A/159, para 53; and *Fredin v Sweden*, 18 February 1991, A/192, para 40. Article 17 (2) CFR explicitly protects intellectual property, which could arguably include business secrets.

[63] See n 8 above, p 28.

[64] According to the case law of the European Court of Human Rights, neither the right to respect for private life and correspondence nor the right to property are absolute. A fair balance must be struck between the demands of the general interest and the requirements of the protection of the individual's fundamental rights. See *Sporrong and Lönnroth v Sweden*, 23 September 1982, A/52, para 69; *Brumarescu v Romania*, 28 October 1999, Application 28342/95; and *Z v Finland*, 25 February 1997, Reports 1997–I, para 99.

imposing penalties, it first has to consult other members of the network. According to Articles 11(4) and 14 of the Regulation, the Commission is required to consult the Advisory Committee, composed of representatives of the competition authorities of the Member States, whereas the competition authorities of the Member States are obliged to consult the Commission, which will associate the other members of the network in the consultation process.

346. The question arises whether the undertakings or persons concerned should be entitled to have knowledge of and comment on the opinions given by other members of the network.[65]

2.7.2.2 The Case Law of the European Court of Human Rights

347. According to the case law of the European Court of Human Rights, the right to a fair trial, as guaranteed by Article 6 ECHR, includes the fundamental right that proceedings should be adversarial.[66]

348. In several cases concerning the role of the Advocate General or similar officers at the Court of Cassation or Supreme Court in Belgium, Portugal, the Netherlands and France,[67] and at the *Conseil d'Etat* in France,[68] the European Court of Human Rights has held that this right to adversarial proceedings 'means in principle the opportunity for the parties to a criminal or civil trial to have knowledge of and comment on all evidence adduced or observations filed, even by an independent member of the national legal service, with a view to influencing the court's decision'.[69]

349. In reaching the conclusion that parties should be entitled to have knowledge of and comment on the opinion of the Advocate General or similar officer, the European Court of Human Rights has regard to what is at stake for the person being tried and to the nature of the opinion. For instance, in the case concerning the procedures before the Portuguese Supreme Court, the following relevant elements were identified:

> [T]he duty of the Attorney-General's department at the Supreme Court is mainly to assist the court and to help ensure that its case-law is consistent. [...], the department's intervention in the proceedings was more particularly justified for the purposes of upholding the public interest. [...]

---

[65] The third and fourth sentences of Article 27(2) of the Regulation appear to exclude such a right, at least in the context of access to the file in proceedings conducted by the Commission: 'The right of access to the file shall not extend to confidential information and internal documents of the Commission or the competition authorities of the Member States. In particular, the right of access shall not extend to correspondence between the Commission and the competition authorities of the Member States, or between the latter, including documents drawn up pursuant to Articles 11 and 14.'

[66] *Ruiz-Mateos v Spain*, 23 June 1993, A/262, para 63.

[67] *Borgers v Belgium*, 30 October 1991, A/214–B; *Vermeulen v Belgium* and *Lobo Machado v Portugal*, 20 February 1996, Reports 1996–I; *Van Orshoven v Belgium*, 25 June 1997, Reports 1997–III; *JJ v the Netherlands* and *KDB v the Netherlands*, 27 March 1998, Reports 1998–II; and *Reinhardt and Slimane-Kaïd v France*, 31 March 1998, Reports 1998–II.

[68] *Kress v France*, 7 June 2001, Application 39594/98.

[69] Lobo Machado v Portugal, n 59 above, para 31.

[...] great importance must be attached to the part actually played in the proceedings by the member of the Attorney-General's department, and more particularly to the content and effects of his observations. These contain an opinion which derives its authority from that of the Attorney-General's department itself. Although it is objective and reasoned in law, the opinion is nevertheless intended to advise and accordingly influence the Supreme Court.[70]

350. Opinions of the Commission (in association with the network) to a national competition authority pursuant to Article 11(4) of the Regulation and opinions of the Advisory Committee pursuant to Article 14 of the Regulation would appear to be comparable in nature to the observations of the Advocate Generals or similar officers considered by the European Court of Human Rights.

351. Before jumping to the conclusion that Article 6 ECHR and Article 47 CFR thus appear to give the undertakings or persons concerned the right to have knowledge of and comment on the opinions pursuant to Articles 11(4) and 14 of the Regulation, we should however draw a distinction between the members of the network that constitute and those that do not constitute 'independent and impartial tribunals' within the meaning of Article 6 ECHR and Article 47 CFR.[71]

2.7.2.3 Administrative Authorities Versus Independent and Impartial Tribunals

352. Article 6(1) ECHR provides that 'in the determination of [...] any criminal charge against him, everyone is entitled to a fair and public hearing [...] by an independent and impartial tribunal [...]'.

353. The European Court of Human Rights has however ruled that, for reasons of efficiency, the prosecution and punishment of offences which are 'criminal' within the wider meaning of Article 6 ECHR can be entrusted to administrative authorities which do not or not entirely meet the requirements of independence and impartiality, provided that the persons concerned are enabled to take any decision thus made before a judicial body that has full jurisdiction and does provide the full guarantees of Article 6(1) ECHR.[72]

354. Since it combines the functions of prosecutor and judge when applying Articles 81 and 82 EC, the Commission can manifestly not be regarded as an independent and impartial tribunal, but its decisions can be challenged before the Court of First Instance, which provides the full guarantees of Article 6(1) ECHR and which undertakes a comprehensive review of the Commission's decisions.[73]

---

[70] Idem, paras 28–29.

[71] See also section 1.2.10 above.

[72] *Öztürk v Germany*, 21 February 1984, A/73, para 56; and *Bendenoun v France*, 24 February 1994, A/284, para 46. This possibility does however not exist for 'serious charges classified as "criminal" under both domestic and Convetiuon law', which should be dealt with already in first instance by a tribunal fully meeting the requirements of Article 6(1) ECHR: *De Cubber v Belgium*, 26 October 1984, A/86, paras 31–32 and *Findlay v United Kingdom*, 25 February 1997, Reports 1997–I, para 79.

[73] See WPJ Wils, referred to in n 47 above, p 337–38; K Lenaerts and J Vanhamme, n 48 above, p 559–62.

355. The same applies to those national competition authorities, such as the German *Bundeskartellamt* or the Italian *Autorità garante della Concorrenza e del Mercato*, which combine the functions of prosecutor and judge, but whose decisions can be challenged before a court fulfilling the requirements of Article 6(1) ECHR.

356. In some other Member States, decisions finding violations of Articles 81 or 82 EC or imposing penalties for such violations are taken by independent and impartial tribunals. For instance, in Sweden, the Stockholm City Court is the body which has the power to impose fines for violations of Articles 81 and 82 EC, in proceedings brought by the Competition Authority. In Ireland, Articles 81 and 82 EC are enforced through criminal procedures. The Competition Authority refers the case to the Director of Public Prosecutions, which decides whether or not to take proceedings before the criminal courts.

2.7.2.4 Administrative Authorities

357. In the case of the Commission and of those national competition authorities which are not independent and impartial tribunals within the meaning of Article 6(1) ECHR but whose decisions are subject to full review by a judicial body meeting all requirements of the said provision, it can be argued that the right to adversarial proceedings, and the resulting right to have knowledge of and comment on all observations filed with a view to influencing the court's decision, does not apply at the level of the decision by the competition authority, but only at the level of the court reviewing the decision.

358. The fact that, in proceedings before the Commission, undertakings do not have the right to comment on the opinion of the Advisory Committee is thus not incompatible with Article 6 ECHR and Article 47 CFR. For the same reason, national competition authorities such as those in Germany and Italy would thus not be obliged under Article 6 ECHR and Article 47 CFR to give the undertakings concerned the possibility to comment upon the opinion of the Commission received pursuant to the consultation under Article 11(4) of the Regulation.

2.7.2.5 Independent and Impartial Tribunals

359. Where decisions are taken by independent and impartial tribunals, such as the Stockholm City Court or the Irish criminal courts, it would appear to follow from the case law of the European Court of Human Rights on Article 6 ECHR discussed above[74] that, if such tribunals were to receive observations from the Commission (or from other members of the network) pursuant to Article 11 of the Regulation, the undertakings or persons being prosecuted should be entitled to have knowledge of and to comment on these observations.

---

[74] See paras 347–50 above.

360. There are several possible means of ensuring that the consulations within the network do not lead to violations of the right to adversarial proceedings as guaranteed by Article 6 ECHR and Article 47 CFR:

361. The first possibility would have been to exclude independent and impartial tribunals from the obligation of consultation provided for in Article 11(4) of the Regulation. This could have been done either through a specific exclusion added to this provision, or more generally by specifying in the Regulation that the notion of 'competition authorities of the Member States' in the Regulation does not include independent and impartial tribunals. This first possibility has not been chosen by the legislator. Indeed, Article 35(1) of the Regulation expressly provides that the designated competition authorities 'may include courts'.

362. The second possibility is for the independent and impartial tribunals which receive observations from the Commission (or from other members of the network) following consultation pursuant to Article 11(4) of the Regulation to provide the undertakings or persons being prosecuted the opportunity to comment on these observations.

363. The third possibility is for the information and consultation under Article 11(4) of the Regulation to be taken care of by the prosecuting authority rather than by the independent and impartial tribunal. Indeed, the text of Article 11(4) of the Regulation provides for an obligation to inform the Commission 'no later than 30 days before the adoption of a decision', thus leaving open the possibility to do so much more in advance. The national authority fulfilling the Article 11(4) obligations must provide the Commission 'with a summary of the case, the envisaged decision or, in the absence thereof, any other document indicating the proposed course of action'. This language allows for a consultation by the prosecuting authority on the basis of the document to be submitted to the independent court setting out the prosecutor's case.[75]

2.7.3 The Commission's Powers of Control and the Independence of National Competition Authorities

364. It has been argued, notably by Fourgoux,[76] that the obligation for the competition authorities to consult the Commission provided for in Article 11(4) of the Regulation together with the Commission's power pursuant to Article 11(6) of the Regulation to withdraw the case from the national competition authority removes the independence of national competition authorities and thus raises a problem under Article 6 ECHR.

---

[75] See also section 1.2.10.2 above.

[76] JC Fourgoux, 'Un Nouvel Antitrust Européen: Espoirs et Craintes', conference held at the *Tribunal de Commerce de Paris*, 22 October 2001.

365. According to the case law of the European Court of Human Rights:

Only an institution that has full jurisdiction and satisfies a number of requirements, such as independence of the executive and also of the parties, merits the designation "tribunal" within the meaning of [Article 6(1) ECHR].[77]

366. In *Beaumartin v France*, for instance, the European Court of Human Rights found that the French Conseil d'Etat did not meet these requirements under a practice, discontinued in 1990, which 'meant that, when the administrative court encountered serious difficulties in interpreting an international treaty, it was obliged to request the Minister for Foreign Affairs to clarify the meaning of the impugned provision and it then had to abide by his interpretation in all circumstances'.[78]

367. When applying this case law to the members of the EU network of competition authorities, a distinction should again be made between those authorities that do and those that do not qualify as independent and impartial tribunals within the meaning of Article 6(1) ECHR.

368. In the case of those national competition authorities, such as those in Germany and Italy, which are not independent and impartial tribunals but whose decisions are subject to full review by a judicial body meeting all the requirements of Article 6(1) ECHR, the requirements of full jurisdiction and independence only apply at the level of the reviewing court. The application of Article 11 of Regulation to national competition authorities of the German and Italian type is thus unproblematic.

369. As to the application of Article 11 of the Regulation to independent and impartial tribunals, such as the Stockholm City Court or the Irish criminal courts, it has already be pointed out above that the information and consultation under Article 11(4) can be done by the prosecuting authority.[79] As to the application of Article 11(6), Article 35(4) of the Regulation provides that,

in the Member States where, for the adoption of certain types of decisions foreseen in Article 5, an authority brings an action before a judicial authority that is separate and different from the prosecuting authority and provided that the terms of this paragraph are complied with, the effects of Article 11(6) shall be limited to the authority prosecuting the case which shall withdraw its claim before the judicial authority when the Commission opens proceedings and this withdrawal shall bring the national proceedings effectively to an end.

The risk of incompatibility with Article 6 ECHR and Article 47 CFR can thus be avoided.

---

[77] *Beaumartin v France*, 24 November 1994, A/296–B, para 38, referring to *Ringei v Austria*, 16 July 1971, A/13, para 9, *Le Compte, Van Leuven and De Meyere v Belgium*, 23 June 1981, A/43, para 55 and *Belilos v Switzerland*, 29 April 1988, A/132, para 64.

[78] Idem, para 38.

[79] See para 363 above.

2.8 CONCLUSION

370. Provided that the stated objective that each case should be dealt with by a single authority is achieved, and provided that Article 11(4) of the Regulation is not applied by independent and impartial tribunals within the meaning of Article 6 ECHR and Article 47 CFR, but rather by the prosecuting authorities, the structure and functioning of the European Competition Network as set up under Regulation No 1/2003 does not appear, in the current state of the case law of the European Court of Human Rights, incompatible with the requirements of the European Convention on Human Rights and of the Charter of Fundamental Rights of the EU.

3

The Principle of Ne Bis In Idem

3.1 INTRODUCTION

371. The principle of *ne bis in idem* (or *non bis in idem*), which is the European equivalent of the double jeopardy clause in the US, restricts the possibility of a same defendant being prosecuted or punished several times for the same offence.

372. The purpose of this chapter is to study the application of this principle to EC antitrust enforcement. The chapter will focus more specifically on the prosecution and punishment of hard-core violations of Articles 81 or 82 EC, such as price cartels.

373. Enforcement with regard to such violations takes place essentially through the imposition of fines on companies. Indeed, the European Commission (hereafter also: 'the Commission') lacks the power to impose or to seek the imposition of other types of sanctions.[1] According to Article 5 of Regulation No 1/2003,[2] Member States can provide in their national law for other types of sanctions to be imposed by national authorities, but at the moment most Member States do not use or intend to use this possibility.[3] This chapter will therefore focus on the imposition of fines on companies.

374. Following this first, introductory section, this chapter is structured as follows: Section 3.2 presents the principle of *ne bis in idem* as enshrined in Article 4 of protocol 7 to the European Convention on Human Rights and Article 50 of the Charter of Fundamental Rights of the European Union. Section 3.3 examines from an economic perspective the rationale underlying the principle of *ne bis in idem*. In sections 3.4 and 3.5 the insights from the sections 4.2 and 4.3 are applied to EC antitrust enforcement. Section 3.4 considers only the European Commission and deals in particular with the question under what circumstances

---

[1] I have argued elsewhere that the effective enforcement of Articles 81 and 82 EC would require not only fines on undertakings but also penalties for individuals, in particular imprisonment. See my book *The Optimal Enforcement of EC Antitrust Law: Essays in Law and Economics* (Kluwer, 2002) chs 8 and 9. The Commission can already today impose fines on natural persons in the rare situation where a violation of Articles 81 or 82 EC is committed by an unincorporated business. See idem, 188–90.

[2] Council Regulation (EC) No 1/2003 of 16 December 2002 on the implementation of the rules on competition laid down in Articles 81 and 82 of the Treaty, [2003] OJ L1/1. According to its Articles 43 and 45, this regulation has replaced Council Regulation No 17, [1962] OJ 13/204 (Special English Edition 1959–62, p 87) last amended by Council Regulation (EC) No 1216/1999, [1999] OJ L148/5, from 1 May 2004. Regulation No 17 did not regulate the choice of sanctions at national level.

[3] Before 1 May 2004, not all Member States provided for sanctions at the national level for violations of Articles 81 and 82 EC, but under Article 35 of Regulation No 1/2003 they must do so since 1 May 2004.

the Commission can try a second time to impose a fine on a company for violation of Articles 81 or 82 EC if a first decision to that effect has been annulled by the Community judicature. Section 3.5 concerns the network of competition authorities, as set up under Regulation No 1/2003, and examines whether or under what circumstances a company can be prosecuted or fined simultaneously or consecutively by several members of the network.

3.2 THE PRINCIPLE OF *NE BIS IN IDEM* IN THE EUROPEAN CONVENTION ON HUMAN RIGHTS AND IN THE CHARTER OF FUNDAMENTAL RIGHTS OF THE EUROPEAN UNION

3.2.1 Article 4 of Protocol No 7 to the European Convention on Human Rights

375. Article 4 of Protocol No 7 to the Convention for the Protection of Human Rights and Fundamental Freedoms[4] (hereafter also: 'the European Convention on Human Rights' or 'ECHR') reads as follows:

> 1. No one shall be liable to be tried or punished again in criminal proceedings under the jurisdiction of the same State for an offence for which he has already been finally acquitted or convicted in accordance with the law and penal procedure of that State.

> 2. The provisions of the preceding paragraph shall not prevent the reopening of the case in accordance with the law and penal procedure of the State concerned, if there is evidence of new or newly discovered facts, or if there has been a fundamental defect in the previous proceedings, which could affect the outcome of the case.

376. All 25 Member States of the EU are parties to the Convention as amended by its Protocol No 11. However, only 19 of the 25 Member States have ratified Protocol No 7.[5] Insofar as this situation might have raised doubts as to the status as general principle of Community law of the right not to be tried or punished twice as laid down in Article 4 of Protocol No 7, this doubt has been removed by the proclamation of the Charter of Fundamental Rights of the European Union, given that its Article 50 contains the corresponding right.[6] In *PVC II*, the Court of Justice has confirmed that 'the principle of *non bis in idem* [...] is a fundamental principle of Community law also enshrined in Article 4(1) of Protocol No 7 to the ECHR'.[7]

---

[4] Convention for the Protection of Human Rights and Fundamental Freedoms as amended by Protocol No 11 with Protocol Nos 1, 4, 6 and 7, available at: http://www.echr.coe.int/Eng/BasicTexts.htm.

[5] Germany, the Netherlands, Portugal and Spain have signed the Protocol, without ratification; Belgium and the United Kingdom have not signed. See http://conventions.coe.int.

[6] See paras 384–88 below.

[7] Judgment of 15 October 2002 in Joined Cases C–238/99 P etc, *Limburgse Vinyl Maatschappij (LVM) and Others v Commission* [2002] ECR I–8618 para 59.

377. Article 4 of Protocol No 7 ECHR only confers a right not be tried or punished twice 'in criminal proceedings'.

378. Article 23(5) of Regulation No 1/2003, like Article 15(4) of Regulation No 17, states that decisions by which the Commission imposes fines on undertakings pursuant to that regulation 'shall not be of a criminal law nature'. This provision is however not decisive in determining whether proceedings based on that regulation are of a criminal law nature within the meaning of the Convention. Indeed, according to the case law of the European Court of Human Rights, the indications furnished by domestic law as to the criminal nature of the offence 'have only a relative value', the term 'criminal' within the meaning of Article 6 ECHR being 'autonomous'.[8]

379. For Article 6 ECHR to apply by virtue of the words 'criminal charge', 'it suffices that the offence in question should by its nature be "criminal" from the point of view of the Convention', because it relates to 'a general rule, whose purpose is both deterrent and punitive', 'or should have made the person concerned liable to a sanction which, in its nature and degree of severity, belongs in general to the "criminal" sphere'.[9] As I have argued in detail elsewhere,[10] it appears difficult, if not impossible, to deny that the application of the criteria set out in the case law of the European Court of Human Rights leads to the conclusion that proceedings based on Regulation No 17 or now Regulation No 1/2003, leading or possibly leading to the imposition of fines for violation of Articles 81 or 82 EC relate to 'the determination of a criminal charge' within the meaning of Article 6 ECHR.[11] The same would hold true for national proceedings leading to or possibly leading to fines for violations of Articles 81 and 82 EC.

380. The European Court of Human Rights has so far rendered five judgments interpreting Article 4 of Protocol No 7 ECHR.[12] All five cases concerned road traffic accidents which had led to both a conviction by a criminal court and the imposition of an administrative sanction. While the issue of what constitutes a 'criminal proceeding' was not debated before the Court, these cases thus appear to confirm that the notion of 'criminal' under Article 4 Protocol No 7 ECHR has the same wide meaning as under Article 6 ECHR.

---

[8] *Öztürk v Germany*, 21 February 1984, A/73, paras 52 and 50. See also n 88 of ch 1 above.

[9] *Lutz v Germany*, 25 August 1987, A/123, para 55; and *Bendenoun v France*, 24 February 1994, A/284, para 47.

[10] See WPJ Wils, 'La Compatibilité des Procédures Communautaires en Matière de Concurrence Avec la Convention Européenne des Droits de l'Homme' (1996) 32 *Cahiers de Droit Européen* 329.

[11] See also Opinion of Judge Vesterdorf acting as Advocate General in Case T–1/89 *Rhône- Poulenc v Commission* [1991] ECR II–867, 885; Opinion of Advocate General Léger in Case C–185/95 P *Baustahlgewebe v Commission* [1998] ECR I–8422 para 31; and Judgment of the Court of Justice of 8 July 1999 in Case C–199/92 P *Hüls v Commission* [1999] ECR I–4383 paras 149–50; as well as K Lenaerts and J Vanhamme, 'Procedural Rights of Private Parties in the Community Administrative Process' (1997) 34 *Common Market Law Review* 531, 557.

[12] *Gradinger v Austria*, 23 October 1995, A/328–C; *Oliveira v Switzerland*, 30 July 1998, Application 25711/94; *Franz Fischer v Austria*, 29 May 2001, Application 37950/97; *WF v Austria*, 30 May 2002, Application 38275/97; *Sailer v Austria*, 6 June 2002, Application 38237/97. It has also rendered a number of admissibility decisions regarding this provision.

381. Of these five judgments only the *Franz Fischer v Austria* judgment appears of interest,[13] in particular with respect to two issues:

382. First, it follows from this judgment that Article 4 of Protocol No 7 is breached not only when a person is tried or punished twice for nominally the same offence but also when he or she is prosecuted twice for two offences the essential elements of which overlap.[14] In the United States, the Supreme Court has similarly held in *Blockburger v US*[15] that punishment for two statutory offences arising out of the same criminal act or transaction violates the double jeopardy clause in the 5th Amendment to the US Constitution unless 'each provision requires proof of an additional fact which the other does not'.[16]

383. Second, the judgment in *Franz Fischer v Austria* confirms that a violation of the principle of *ne bis in idem* as laid down in Article 4 of Protocol No 7 ECHR cannot be avoided by reducing the amount of the second punishment by the amount of the first punishment, as this principle prohibits not only double punishment but also double prosecution.[17]

3.2.2 Article 50 of the Charter of Fundamental Rights of the European Union

384. The Charter of Fundamental Rights of the European Union (hereafter also: 'the Charter of Fundamental Rights', 'the Charter' or 'CFR') was solemnly pro-

---

[13] The only issue discussed in the *Gradinger v Austria* and *Oliveira v Switzerland* is the question whether Article 4(1) of Protocol No 7 ECHR prohibits double prosecution for nominally different offences based on the same act. As the Court itself pointed out in para 23 of its judgment in *Franz Fischer v Austria*, 'the Court's approach in the Gradinger and Oliveira judgments [...] appears somewhat contradictory'. The Court resolved this contradiction in *Franz Fischer v Austria*. The later judgments in *WF v Austria* and *Sailer v Austria* merely repeat that judgment.

[14] Para 25 of the judgment reads as follows:

> The Court observes that the wording of Article 4 of Protocol No 7 does not refer to 'the same offence' but rather to trial and punishment 'again' for an offence for which the applicant has already been finally acquitted or convicted. Thus, while it is true that the mere fact that a single act constitutes more than one offence is not contrary to this Article, the Court must not limit itself to finding that the applicant was, on the basis of one act, tried or punished for nominally different offences. The Court [...] notes that there are cases where one act, at first sight, appears to constitute more than one offence, whereas a closer examination shows that only one offence should be prosecuted because it encompasses all the wrongs contained in the others [...]. An obvious example would be an act which constitutes two offences, one of which contains precisely the same elements as the other plus an additional one. There may be other cases where the offences only slightly overlap. Thus, where different offences based on the same act are prosecuted consecutively, one after the final decision of the other, the Court has to examine whether or not such offences have the same essential elements.

In para 29 the Court added that 'the question whether or not the *non bis in idem* principle is violated concerns the relationship between the two offences and can, therefore, not depend on the order in which the respective proceedings are conducted'.

[15] 284 US 299 (1932).

[16] See also more recently *US v Dixon* 113 SCt 2849, 2856 (1993).

[17] Para 30 of the judgment.

claimed by the European Parliament, the Council of the European Union and the European Commission on 7 December 2000.[18]

385. According to its preamble,

[t]his Charter reaffirms [...] the rights as they result, in particular, from the constitutional traditions and international obligations common to the Member States, the Treaty on European Union, the Community Treaties, the European Convention for the Protection of Human Rights and Fundamental Freedoms, the Social Charters adopted by the Community and by the Council of Europe and the case-law of the Court of Justice of the European Communities and the European Court of Human Rights.

As to the scope of the Charter, its Article 51(1) provides that,

[t]he provisions of this Charter are addressed to the institutions and bodies of the Union with due regard for the principle of subsidiarity and to the Member States only when they are implementing Union law. They shall therefore respect the rights, observe the principles and promote the application thereof in accordance with their respective powers.

386. Article 50 of the Charter restates the principle of *ne bis in idem* as follows:

No one shall be liable to be tried or punished again in criminal proceedings for an offence for which he or she has already been finally acquitted or convicted within the Union in accordance with the law.

387. According to the explanatory memorandum provided by the Secretariat of the body which drafted the Charter,[19] this provision 'corresponds to Article 4 of Protocol No 7 to the ECHR, but its scope is extended to European Union level between the Courts of the Member States'.[20]

In accordance with Article 50, the 'non bis in idem' principle applies not only within the jurisdiction of one State but also between the jurisdictions of several Member States. That corresponds to the acquis in Union law; see Articles 54 to 58 of the Schengen Convention, Article 7 of the Convention on the Protection of the European Communities' Financial Interests and Article 10 of the Convention on the Fight Against Corruption.[21]

388. As to the scope of the guaranteed right, Article 52 of the Charter provides generally:

1. Any limitation on the exercise of the rights and freedoms recognised by this Charter must be provided for by law and respect the essence of those rights and freedoms. Subject

---

[18] [2000] OJ C364/1, also available at http://ue.eu.int/df/docs/en/CharteENpdf.

[19] Council of the EU, Charter of Fundamental Rights of the European Union—Explanations relating to the complete text of the Charter (December 2000), available at http://ue.eu.int/df/docs/en/EN_2001_1023.pdf.

[20] Idem, p 76.

[21] Idem, p 69. Convention of 19 June 1990 implementing the Schengen Agreement, [2000] OJ L239/19; Convention of 26 July 1995 on the protection of the European Communities' financial interests, [1995] OJ C316/49; Convention of 26 May 1997 on the fight against corruption involving officials of the European Communities or officials of Member States of the European Union, [1997] OJ C195/2.

to the principle of proportionality, limitations may be made only if they are necessary and genuinely meet objectives of general interest recognised by the Union or the need to protect the rights and freedoms of others.

2. [...]

3. In so far as this Charter contains rights which correspond to rights guaranteed by the Convention for the Protection of Human Rights and Fundamental Freedoms, the meaning and scope of those rights shall be the same as those laid down by the said Convention. This provision shall not prevent Union law providing more extensive protection.

3.3 THE ECONOMICS OF *NE BIS IN IDEM*

389. In this section I examine from an economic perspective the rationale underlying the principle of *ne bis in idem*.[22] As explained hereafter, the principle of *ne bis in idem* contributes to efficient law enforcement in that it prevents over-punishment, creates incentives for efficient prosecution, prevents vexatious multiple prosecutions and creates incentives for efficient coordination between prosecutors.

3.3.1 The Problems of Over-Punishment and Under-Punishment

390. The ideal of optimal law enforcement is to achieve optimal deterrence (and/or retributive justice) at minimal cost. When considering the prosecution of an individual case, the double objective is thus to impose the optimal penalty at minimal cost. The optimal penalty is zero if the case does not involve a violation of the law. If there is a violation, it is the amount corresponding to the requirements of deterrence and/or retributive justice.[23]

391. As far as the objective of imposing the optimal penalty is concerned, multiple prosecutions are undesirable to the extent that they lead or risk leading to over-punishment. If for instance a first prosecution has correctly ended in an acquittal in a case where there is indeed no violation of the law, any additional prosecutions serve no useful purpose and risk leading to an erroneous conviction. If the optimal penalty for a violation is imposed in a first prosecution, additional prosecutions similarly serve no useful purpose but risk leading to over-punishment if further penalties are added. This provides a first economic rationale underlying the principle of *ne bis in idem*.

392. However, as far as the objective of imposing the optimal penalty is concerned, if a first prosecution has failed to secure the optimal penalty for a violation,

---

[22] My 'economic' approach is a wide one, potentially including as relevant to the analysis all aspects or considerations which may have an impact on human well-being; on my methodology, see *The Optimal Enforcement of EC Antitrust Law*, n 1 above, p 3–7.

[23] On optimal penalties in general and in particular in the context of EC competition law, see *The Optimal Enforcement of EC Antitrust Law*, n 1 above, in particular ch 2.

additional prosecutions are desirable up to the point where the optimal penalty is reached. If for instance a first prosecution has failed to secure any penalty for a violation of the law, further prosecutions are desirable. Similarly, if a first prosecution has led to the imposition of a penalty which is lower than the optimal penalty, a second prosecution is desirable so as to increase the punishment, but only up to the point where the optimal penalty is reached. To ensure that this point is not exceeded, the amount of the penalty already imposed in the first prosecution may have to be set against the amount imposed in the second prosecution.

393. Of course the objective of imposing the optimal penalty must be balanced against the other objectives and considerations discussed hereafter.

3.3.2 The Cost of Multiple Prosecutions

394. All prosecutions are costly. Relevant costs include not only the administrative cost for the authorities involved, but also the administrative and psychological or other costs borne by the defendant. From the perspective of minimizing cost, multiple prosecutions would thus always appear undesirable. This concern must however be balanced against the objective of securing the optimal penalty. If there is a strong need for a second prosecution, because a serious violation would otherwise remain unpunished or punished only by a penalty that is far below the optimal, and a second prosecution is likely to redress this situation, the cost concern will be outweighed.

395. In fact the balance between the likely benefit of the prosecution in terms of securing optimal punishment and the administrative cost of the prosecution is not necessarily different when the question is whether to engage in a second prosecution than when the first prosecution is to be decided. Indeed, at the time of the decision whether to start a second prosecution, the cost of the first prosecution is sunk and should thus no longer be taken into account. Cost would only be more of an obstacle for a second prosecution than for a first one if either the first prosecution had already led to some penalty being imposed, with the result that the possible benefit of a second prosecution would be reduced to the differential between that penalty and the optimal penalty, or the failure of the first prosecution had in some way revealed that a successful prosecution would be more costly than could be anticipated before the first prosecution was started. On the other hand, to the extent that the second prosecution can at least in part rely on the work already done in the first prosecution, cost may be less of a concern for starting second prosecutions than for starting first ones.[24]

---

[24] On the other hand the psychological cost for the defendant of a second prosecution might be larger than for a first prosecution. If this were true (I am unaware of any empirical evidence confirming or infirming this hypothesis), this would constitute a fifth economic rationale underlying the principle of *ne bis in idem*, in addition to the justifications relating to avoidance of over-punishment, incentives for efficient prosecution, risk of vexatious multiple prosecutions and incentives for efficient coordination between prosecutors.

3.3.3 Incentives for Efficient Prosecution

396. Imagine a prosecutor who is careless in preparing and conducting a first prosecution, with the result that no penalty or much too low a penalty is imposed for a serious violation. As explained above, the need to secure the punishment required by deterrence and/or distributive justice is likely to outweigh the cost of a second prosecution in such a situation. One should however also take into account the effect which the possibility of a second chance may have on the incentives of the prosecutor to take due care when preparing and conducting the first prosecution.

397. The optimal level of care which one would want a prosecutor to take when preparing and conducting a first prosecution is certainly not infinite. Indeed, additional care, for instance in collecting additional evidence, will consume scarce enforcement resources. At some point, it may be desirable for instance to have the prosecutor stop collecting additional evidence and proceed with the prosecution, at the risk of possibly having to start over again later if the evidence turns out to be insufficient. The reason why there is a risk that prosecutors would not always spontaneously strike this balance optimally is that part of the cost of multiple prosecutions, namely the cost borne by the defendant, may not enter into the prosecutor's calculations.

398. A ban on multiple prosecutions may thus be desirable to the extent that it induces prosecutors to take due care when preparing and conducting prosecutions. This constitutes a second economic rationale underlying the principle of *ne bis in idem*.

399. However, a blanket ban on multiple prosecutions, even in those cases where the prosecutor acted with due care in the first prosecution, risks inducing excessive care in preparing and conducting prosecutions. The solution may be to adopt a case-by-case approach, for instance allowing a second prosecution when based on additional evidence which the prosecutor could not reasonably be expected to have used at the time of the first prosecution, but not allowing it when the additional evidence could reasonably already have been used in the first prosecution.[25] Article 4(2) of Protocol No 7 ECHR indeed allows for such a case-by-case approach, if provided for in the law of the State concerned.

---

[25] An alternative solution may be to allow a second prosecution whenever a serious violation would otherwise remain unpunished or punished only by a penalty that is far below the optimal, but to condemn the prosecutor to compensate the defendant for the costs borne by the latter in the first prosecution. If this compensation is complete, in that it covers all the costs borne by the defendant, it will force the prosecutor to take these costs into account when calculating how much care to take in preparing and conducting the first prosecution. But in practice it may be difficult to ensure compensation of all costs borne by the defendant, including the psychological cost. This alternative solution risks thus either being very costly to administer (if all costs were to be measured) or leading to excessive multiple prosecutions (if the non-monetary costs were neglected).

3.3.4 The Risk of Vexatious Multiple Prosecutions

400. In the above discussion of the incentives for prosecutors to take due care in preparing and conducting prosecutions, I have assumed that prosecutors may be careless but do not act in bad faith. One can however not exclude the possibility that a prosecutor may abuse his or her powers and deliberately bring multiple prosecutions for the sole purpose of inflicting on the defendant the cost of having to defend him-or-herself.

401. A ban on multiple prosecutions would remove the possibility of such costly abuse. This constitutes a third economic rationale underlying the principle of *ne bis in idem*.

402. However, a blanket ban on all multiple prosecutions, whether they are vexatious or not, would again be undesirable in that it would prevent second prosecutions in cases where a serious violation would otherwise remain unpunished or punished only by a penalty that is far below the optimal. The solution may again be a case-by-case approach under which multiple prosecutions would not be allowed where the multiple prosecutions appear vexatious or cannot be justified otherwise.[26]

3.3.5 Incentives for Efficient Coordination Between Prosecutors

403. A fourth economic rationale underlying the principle of *ne bis in idem* is that, in a setting where the same violation of the law could possibly be prosecuted by several different prosecutors, a ban on multiple prosecutions may induce efficient coordination and distribution of work between these prosecutors. Indeed, depending on the violation and on the legal instruments and resources available to the different prosecutors, one prosecutor may be better placed than another to prosecute that violation. If multiple prosecutions are not allowed, there will be a stronger common interest in ensuring that the violation is being prosecuted from the beginning by the prosecutor best placed to secure the optimal penalty at minimal cost, because there will be no second chance if a first prosecution has been brought by a less well placed prosecutor and has failed.

404. However, if for legal or practical reasons coordination between the prosecutors is impossible or very costly, a ban on multiple prosecutions would not lead to any efficiency benefit; on the contrary it will prevent second prosecutions in cases where a serious violation will therefore remain unpunished or punished only by a penalty that is far below the optimal.

---

[26] Alternatively one could again imagine an obligation for the prosecutor to indemnify the defendant for the costs borne because of the multiplicity of proceedings, arguably to be combined with some additional punishment for the prosecutor in case of established abuse. See however n 25 above as to the practical difficulty of such alternative solution.

405. Moreover, a ban on multiple prosecutions might lead to prosecutors pre-emptively launching the first prosecution for reasons unrelated to efficient enforcement, such as the desire to secure the financial benefit of a monetary penalty to be imposed on the defendant or the desire to protect a favoured defendant from the harsher penalty it would receive if prosecuted by another prosecutor, if such strategic behaviour cannot be prevented for legal or practical reasons. Similarly, a ban on multiple prosecutions might lead to increased forum shopping by defendants trying to be prosecuted first by the most lenient prosecutor.

406. A ban on multiple prosecutions thus appears only desirable to the extent that it covers prosecutors between whom coordination is not for legal or practical reasons impossible or very costly. This may explain the fact that Article 4 of Protocol No 7 ECHR only applies to multiple prosecutions 'under the jurisdiction of the same State'. The extension of the principle of *ne bis in idem* to the European Union level by Article 50 CFR, and already before by Article 54 of the Convention implementing the Schengen Agreement,[27] can be understood as reflecting either the reality that coordination between prosecutors from different States is easier within the Union, or at least an integrationist objective to bring about such a situation.

3.4 MULTIPLE PROSECUTIONS BY THE EUROPEAN COMMISSION

407. With respect to multiple prosecutions by the European Commission, the main question is under what circumstances the Commission can try a second time to impose a fine on a company for violation of Articles 81 or 82 EC if a first decision to that effect has been annulled by the Community judicature.

408. It may be useful to distinguish two situations, depending on whether the first decision has been annulled for procedural reasons or for lack of evidence. This distinction makes economic sense in that the likelihood that there exists a violation, and consequently a need for a second prosecution to secure the optimal penalty, is lower in the case where the first decision has been annulled for lack of evidence than in the case where the first decision has been annulled for procedural reasons. One would thus expect the law to be more restrictive with regard to the possibility of a second prosecution in the case where the first decision has been annulled for lack of evidence than in the case where the first decision has been annulled for procedural reasons.

3.4.1 Adoption of a Second Decision Where a First Decision Has Been Annulled for Procedural Reasons

409. In the PVC case, the Commission had adopted in 1988 a first decision imposing fines on a number of PVC producers. This decision had been annulled by the

---

[27] See n 21 above.

Court of Justice in 1994 because the Commission had failed to authenticate its decision in the way provided for by its own Rules of Procedure.[28] Following this annulment, the Commission adopted a second decision, duly authenticated, in which it reimposed the same fines. In its *PVC II* judgment, the Court of Justice confirmed the legality of this readoption on the following grounds:

> [...], the principle of *non bis in idem* merely prohibits a fresh assessment in depth of the alleged commission of an offence which would result in the imposition of either a second penalty, in addition to the first, in the event that liability is established a second time, or a first penalty in the event that liability not established by the first decision is established by the second.
>
> On the other hand, it does not in itself preclude the resumption of proceedings in respect of the same anti-competitive conduct where the first decision was annulled for procedural reasons without any ruling being given on the substance of the facts alleged, since the annulment decision cannot in such circumstances be regarded as an 'acquittal' within the meaning given to that expression in penal matters. In such a case, the penalties imposed by the new decision are not added to those imposed by the annulled decision but replace them.[29]

410.   If one applies the economic criteria set out in section 3.3 above, the result in the PVC case appears entirely justified. Indeed, if the Commission had not been allowed to adopt a second decision, a very serious violation of Article 81 EC would have remained unpunished. Moreover, the administrative cost of adopting the second decision was limited, as the second decision was all but identical to the first one. It was also clear that the Commission had not had any vexatious motives when it had failed properly to authenticate its first decision and thus caused the need for a later second decision. The only doubt one could have would concern the need to create incentives for the Commission not negligently to fail to respect its own Rules of Procedure. However, such incentives adequately result from the fact that the Commission had to pay the costs incurred by the defendant companies in the Court proceedings leading to the annulment of the first decision,[30] from the fact that the fines imposed in the second decision were identical in nominal amounts to the fines in the first decision, and thus significantly lower in real terms, given the four and a half year interval between the two decisions, as well as from the reputational damage which the Commission undoubtedly suffered.

---

[28] Judgment of 15 June 1994 in Case C–137/94 P *Commission v BASF and Others* [1994] ECR I–2629.

[29] Judgment of 15 October 2002 in Joined Cases C–238/99 P, C–244/99 P, C–245/99 P, C–247/99 P, C–250/99 P to C–252/99 P and C–254/99 P, *Limburgse Vinyl Maatschappij (LVM) and Others v Commission* [2002] ECR I–8616, paras 61 and 62.

[30] Point 3 of the operative part of the judgment of 15 June 1994, n 28 above.

3.4.2 Adoption of a Second Decision Where a First Decision Has Been Annulled for Lack of Evidence

411. Could the Commission also adopt a second decision imposing fines for a violation of Articles 81 or 82 EC if its first decision to that effect had been annulled by the Community judicature not for procedural reasons but for lack of evidence? For instance, in the Wood Pulp case, the Commission had fined a number of companies for allegedly having concerted on prices for bleached sulphate pulp in violation of Article 81 EC. The Court of Justice annulled this decision because it considered that the Commission had no documents directly establishing the existence of the concertation, whereas the other evidence on which the Commission relied, namely a system of quarterly price announcements and the simultaneity and parallelism of these announcements, did not constitute a sufficiently firm, precise and consistent body of evidence of concertation.[31] Could the Commission subsequently have adopted a second decision if it had been able to produce documentary evidence directly establishing the existence of concertation?[32]

412. The language used by the Court of Justice in its *PVC II* judgment[33] suggests that the principle of *ne bis in idem* opposes a second decision if the first decision has been annulled for lack of evidence. Indeed, in such circumstances a second decision would appear to amount to a second 'trial' following an 'acquittal' within the meaning of Article 4(1) Protocol 7 ECHR and Article 50 CFR.

413. However, Article 4(2) Protocol 7 ECHR expressly provides as an admissible limitation on the right laid down in Article 4(1) the possibility of 'reopening of the case in accordance with the law and penal procedure of the State concerned, if there is evidence of new or newly discovered facts, [...], which could affect the outcome of the case'. Under the same conditions a restriction on the right not to be tried twice should be permissible under Article 52 CFR.

414. To allow a second prosecution if and only if there is evidence of new or newly discovered facts makes sense under the economic criteria set out in section 3.3 above. Indeed, the need to allow under-punishment to be corrected can be reconciled with the need to provide incentives for prosecutors to be efficient in preparing and conducting prosecutions and the need to prevent vexatious multiple prosecutions by allowing a second prosecution when based on additional evidence which the prosecutor could not with reasonable diligence have used at the time of the first prosecution, but not allowing it when the additional evidence could already reasonably have been used in the first prosecution.

415. It should however be noted that Article 4(2) Protocol 7 ECHR requires that the reopening must be 'in accordance with the law' or, in the terms of Article

---

[31] Judgment of 31 March 1993 in Joined Cases C–89/85 etc *Ahlström Osakeyhtiö and Others v Commission* [1993] ECR I–1575, paras 70–127.

[32] That the possibility of such evidence being produced is not unplausible can be deduced from the Court's judgment, n 31 above, paras 68 and 69.

[33] See para 409 above.

52(1) CFR, 'provided for by law'.[34] It could be argued that Article 25(6) of Regulation No 1/2003, according to which 'the limitation period for the imposition of fines [...] shall be suspended for as long as the decision of the Commission is the subject of proceedings pending before the Court of Justice', constitutes an admittedly indirect but still sufficiently precise provision to this effect.[35]

3.5 MULTIPLE PROSECUTIONS AND MULTIPLE FINES IN THE EU NETWORK OF COMPETITION AUTHORITIES

3.5.1   The Old Situation Under Regulation No 17

416.   Under Regulation No 17 the competition authorities of the Member States have only rarely prosecuted infringements under Articles 81 or 82 EC.[36] Instead they have usually applied only their national competition laws.

417.   As early as 1969 the Court of Justice held in *Wilhelm v Bundeskartellamt* that Regulation No 17 does not exclude the possibility of one and the same agreement being the object of two sets of parallel proceedings, one before the Commission under Article 81 EC, the other before the national authorities under national law, and that such double prosecutions are not contrary to the *ne bis in idem* principle, given the differences between the two laws, notably because Community law focuses on the effect on trade between Member States.[37]

418.   The Court did however add that,

> if [...] the possibility of two procedures being conducted seperately were to lead to the imposition of consecutive sanctions, a general requirement of natural justice, such as that expressed at the end of the second paragraph of Article 90 of the ECSC Treaty, demands that any previous punitive decision must be taken into account in determining any sanction which is to be imposed.[38]

419.   Following the 2001 judgment of the European Court of Human Rights in *Franz Fischer v Austria*,[39] it has become highly doubtful whether one can still con-

---

[34] The terms 'in accordance with the law' in Article 4 Protocol 7 ECHR and in various other provisions of the ECHR should indeed be understood as meaning 'provided for by law'. See i.a. judgment of the European Court of Human Rights of 25 March 1983 in *Silver and Others v United Kingdom*, A/61, paras 85–90.

[35] Article 9(2)(a) of Regulation No 1/2003 provides for a possibility of reopening proceedings 'where there has been a material change in any of the facts on which the decision was based', but this provision only concerns proceedings previously closed by way of a decision making commitments binding pursuant to Article 9(1) of that regulation.

[36] For an explanation of the reasons for this lack of application of Articles 81 and 82 EC, see *The Optimal Enforcement of EC Antitrust Law*, n 1 above, p 140–41.

[37] Judgment of 13 February 1969 in Case 14/68 *Wilhelm v Bundeskartellamt* [1969] ECR 3, paras 3 and 11.

[38] Idem, para 11. See also Judgment of 14 December 1972 in Case 7/72 *Boehringer v Commission* [1972] ECR 1281, para 3.

[39] See n 12 above.

sider that there is no violation of the *ne bis in idem* principle in case of double prosecutions under Article 81 EC and under national competition law because of
Community law's specific focus on the effect on trade between Member States.
Indeed, under the test laid down in *Franz Fischer v Austria*, the principle of *ne bis
in idem* is breached not only when a person is tried or punished twice for nominally the same offence but also when he or she is prosecuted twice for two offences
the essential elements of which overlap.[40] This appears to be the case with respect
to Articles 81 or 82 EC and national competition laws. Indeed, whereas Articles 81
and 82 EC contain an element not embraced by national competition laws, namely
the effect on trade between Member States, the essential elements of national competition laws would appear to cover the same ground as Articles 81 and 82 EC.[41]

420.   It also follows from *Franz Fischer v Austria* that a violation of the principle of *ne bis in idem* cannot be avoided by reducing the amount of the second
punishment by the amount of the first punishment, as this principle prohibits not
only double punishment but also double prosecution.[42]

421.   In any event, as from 1 May 2004, national competition authorities, when
applying national competition law to agreements or practices covered by Articles
81 or 82 EC, will be obliged under Article 3(1) of Regulation No 1/2003 to apply
also Articles 81 or 82 EC, making the applicability of the *ne bis in idem* principle
all the more obvious.

3.5.2   The New Situation Under Regulation No 1/2003

422.   Pursuant to Article 35 of Regulation No 1/2003, all Member States have
empowered their national competition authorities to apply Articles 81 and 82 EC
at the latest by 1 May 2004. From that date on, Article 3(1) of Regulation No
1/2003 obliges national competition authorities, when applying national competition law to agreements or practices also covered by Articles 81 or 82 EC, also to
apply those provisions.

423.   According to recital 15 of Regulation No 1/2003, '[t]he Commission and
the competition authorities of the Member State should form together a network
of public authorities applying the Community competition rules in close cooperation'.

424.   It follows from Article 11(6) of Regulation No 1/2003 that simultaneous
prosecutions by the European Commission, on the one hand, and one or more
national competition authorities, on the other hand, will not be possible, as the
initiation of proceedings by the Commission will relieve national competition

---

[40] See n 14 above.

[41] See also Opinion of 11 February 2003 of Advocate General Ruiz-Jarabo Colomer in Case
C–213/00 P *Italcementi v Commission*, not yet published in ECR, para 91.

[42] See n 17 above. See also Opinion of 11 February 2003 of Advocate General Ruiz-Jarabo Colomer
in Case C–213/00 P *Italcementi v Commission*, not yet published in ECR, para 96.

authorities of their competence.[43] However, the regulation does not exclude the possibility that the Commission may start a second prosecution after a national competition authority has completed a first one.

425.   As to the possibility of several national competition authorities prosecuting and punishing the same violation of Articles 81 or 82 EC either simultaneously or consecutively, Article 13 allows competition authorities to suspend or terminate proceedings on the ground that another competition authority is dealing or has dealt with the case. The corresponding recital 18 of the regulation explains that 'the objective [is] that each case should be handled by a single authority'. Article 13 empowers national competition authorities and the Commission to suspend or terminate duplicative proceedings, but it contains no obligation to this effect. According to the explanatory memorandum to the Commission's proposal which led to Regulation No 1/2003, it is 'neither necessary nor appropriate to oblige other competition authorities to suspend or terminate their proceedings. It is the task of the network to ensure in practice that resources are used efficiently'.[44] Indeed, in the absence of a rule determining which authority is the single best placed to deal with the case, a mandatory rule would not make sense, as only those authorities which are not the best placed should suspend or terminate their proceedings.[45]

426.   Would it be admissible under the principle of *ne bis in idem* as enshrined in Article 4 Protocol 7 ECHR and Article 50 CFR for the Commission to start a second prosecution after a national competition authority has completed a first prosecution, and would it be possible for several national competition authorities to bring prosecutions for the same violation of Articles 81 or 82 EC?

---

[43]   Article 11(6) of Regulation No 1/2003 provides that '[t]he initiation by the Commission of proceedings for the adoption of a decision under Chapter III shall relieve the competition authorities of the Member States of their competence to apply Articles 81 and 82 of the Treaty'. The decisions listed in Chapter III of the Regulation are decisions finding an infringement and/or ordering its termination, decisions ordering interim measures, decisions making commitments binding and decisions finding that Articles 81 or 82 EC are not applicable to an agreement or practice. It follows from the case law of the Court of Justice with regard to the similarly worded Article 9(3) of Regulation No 17 that the initiation of a procedure requires 'an authoritiative act of the Commission, evidencing its intention of taking a decision'. See Judgment of 6 February 1973 in Case 48/72 *Brasserie de Haecht v Wilkin-Janssen* [1972] ECR 88, para 16. The effect of Article 11(6) is amplified by Article 3 of Regulation No 1/2003 which obliges national competition authorities also to apply Articles 81 or 82 EC when they apply national competition law to agreements or practices covered by Articles 81 or 82 EC The initiation of proceedings by the Commission thus in fact relieves national competition authorities not only of their competence to apply Articles 81 and 82 EC but also of their competence to apply national competition law.

[44]   COM (2000) 582, pp 12–13. Article 13 of Regulation No 1/2003 is identical to the Commission's proposal.

[45]   Indicative criteria have however been set out in paras 15–19 of the Joint Statement of the Council and the Commission on the functioning of the network of competition authorities, entered in the Council Minutes at the time of the adoption of Regulation No 1/2003 (Council document 15435/02 ADD1 of 10 December 2002, available at http://register.consilium.eu.int) and in paras 5–15 of the Commission Notice on cooperation within the Network of Competition Authorities, [2004] OJ C101/43. See also paras 100–10 above.

427.   Imagine by way of example that the main producers of some product for which the relevant geographic market is Europe had held a meeting on a certain date during which they had decided a concerted price increase.[46] Suppose that this violation of Article 81 EC happens to be prosecuted first by the competition authority of a Member State. Imagine further that either the national law of that Member State or the practice of that competition authority lead that authority, when deciding on the amount of the fines, only to take into account the effects of the violation on its own national territory,[47] and/or that the national law of that Member State only provides for low fines for violations of Articles 81 EC. Could either the Commission or the competition authority of a second Member State bring a second prosecution?

428.   The problem is not with Article 4 Protocol 7 ECHR which only prohibits multiple trials or punishments 'under the jurisdiction of the same State',[48] but with Article 50 CFR which extends the scope of the right not to be tried or punished twice 'within the Union'.[49]

429.   I personally do not believe that the applicability of Article 50 CFR can be avoided by arguing that the second prosecution would not be for the same offence, given that the first prosecution only took into account the effects of the violation of Article 81 EC on the territory of the Member State of the national authority which prosecuted first. Indeed, the offence constituted by the main producers of some product for which the relevant geographic market is Europe having held a meeting on a certain date during which they have decided a concerted price increase constitutes a single violation of Article 81 EC, irrespective of any effects it may have had or not have had in any part of the Community. The principle of *ne bis in idem* prohibits multiple prosecution or punishments for the same offence, not merely for the same effects of an offence.[50]

430.   Could a second prosecution by the European Commission or by another national competition authority be accepted under Article 52(1) CFR? This would require first that the possibility of such second prosecution be 'provided for by law'.[51] Regulation No 1/2003 does not appear to contain a sufficiently precise provision to this effect.[52] Furthermore it would have to be established that such a

---

[46] Compare with Commission Decision 98/247/ECSC of 21 January 1998 relating to a proceeding under Article 65 of the ECSC Treaty (Case IV/35.814—*Alloy Surcharge*), [1998] OJ L100/55.

[47] On the territorial scope of decisions of national competition authorities, see section 1.2.6 above.

[48] Similarly, in the United States, the courts have held that the state and federal governments are separate sovereigns and that successive prosecutions based on the same underlying conduct do not violate the double jeopardy clause if the prosecutions are brought by separate sovereigns. See *US v Lanza* 260 US 377, 382 (1922); and more recently *US v Koon* 34 F3d 1416, 1438 (9th Cir 1994).

[49] See para 387 above.

[50] See also Opinion of 11 February 2003 of Advocate General Ruiz-Jarabo Colomer in Case C–213/00 P *Italcementi v Commission*, not yet published in ECR, paras 94–96.

[51] See para 415 above.

[52] The conferral of competence to prosecute infringements of Articles 81 and 82 EC to the national competition authorities in Article 5 and to the Commission in Articles 7 and 23 of Regulation No 1/2003 does not appear to indicate the possibility of multiple prosecutions in the same case, all the less in the light of Recital 18 of the regulation which refers to 'the objective [...] that each case should be dealt with by a single authority'.

limitation on the right enshrined in Article 50 CFR is 'necessary and genuinely meet[s] objectives of general interest recognised by the Union' and would 'respect the essence' of the protected right.[53]

431.   Applying the economic criteria set out in section 3.3 above, should we be worried by Article 50 CFR thus creating an obstacle to a second prosecution?

432.   In the example as described above, where the first prosecution was brought by the authority of a Member State which did only take into account the effects of the violation on its own national territory or which in any event imposed only low fines, it would appear desirable, at first sight, for a second prosecution to be taken either by the Commission or by another national competition authority with stronger fining powers, so as to avoid under-punishment, at least if the differential between the fines imposed in the first Member State and the optimal fines is sufficiently large to outweigh the cost of a second prosecution.

433.   However, the picture changes if one takes into account the incentives for the network of EU competition authorities to function efficiently. Indeed, the fact that in the above example the first prosecution was brought by a competition authority which was not able to impose optimal penalties, thus prompting the need for additional prosecutions, appears clearly inefficient. A ban on multiple prosecutions would have the desirable effect of forcing the Commission and the competition authorities of the Member States fully to use the coordination mechanisms provided for in Regulation No 1/2003 so as to ensure that each case is dealt with by an authority capable of imposing the required penalties.[54] It would also have the desirable effect of encouraging the harmonization of national laws with regard to penalties imposed by national competition authorities, so as to ensure that penalties are sufficiently high in all Member States and that all competition authorities, when setting the amount of penalties, take into account the full effect of violations of Articles 81 or 82 EC throughout the territory of the Community.[55]

434.   A ban on multiple prosecutions might however also increase the risks of preemptive prosecutions and forum shopping. Indeed, a ban on multiple prosecutions might tempt a competition authority preemptively to launch the first prosecution for reasons unrelated to efficient enforcement, be it the desire to secure the

---

[53] See also para 314 above.

[54] The main instruments provided for in Regulation No 1/2003 are the information and consultation provisions in Article 11, the possibility of assistance between competition authorities in respect of fact-finding provided for in Article 21, the possibility of transferring information and even entire case files from one authority to another under Article 12 and the ultimate possibility for the Commission to withdraw the case from a national authority under Article 11(6). See also sections 1.2.5 and 2.2.2 above.

[55] Such harmonization could either happen voluntarily or be imposed through a new Council Regulation based on Article 83 EC. See section 1.2.11.3 above. Indeed, it can be argued that it already follows from Regulation No 1/2003, in particular from its Article 35, which requires Member States to designate their competition authorities responsible for the application of Articles 81 and 82 EC 'in such a way that the provisions of this regulation are effectively complied with', read in conjunction with Article 10 EC and Article 50 CFR, that Member States are under an obligation to ensure that their competition authorities take into account the full effect of violations of Articles 81 and 82 EC throughout the territory of the Community: see section 1.2.6 above.

financial benefit of the fines to be imposed or the desire to protect a favoured company from the higher penalty it would receive if prosecuted by another member of the network. To remove the risk of preemptive prosecutions to secure the financial benefit of the fines, it may be necessary to set up a system in which part of the proceeds of fines are shared within the network. The risk of preemptive prosecutions to protect a favoured defendant can be addressed to some extent through the mechanisms provided for in Regulation No 1/2003.[56] As to the risks of forum shopping, a ban on multiple prosecutions would induce leniency applicants to go first to the competition authority which offers the most generous leniency conditions. This may not necessarily be undesirable, as the optimal leniency policy probably consists in granting complete immunity to the single first cartel participant denouncing the cartel to the authorities.[57] In any event, the risks of undesirable forum shopping can be removed by harmonizing leniency policies.[58]

435.   By limiting the possibility of multiple prosecutions, Article 50 CFR is thus likely to have the effect of inducing effective coordination between the Commission and the national competition authorities as well as harmonization of their laws and policies on fines and leniency, which appears desirable from the perspective of efficient antitrust enforcement. That Article 50 CFR pushes towards harmonization should not come as a surprise. The extension of the scope of the principle of *ne bis in idem* to all jurisdictions within the Union, as brought about by Article 50 CFR and already before by Article 54 of the Convention implementing the Schengen Agreement,[59] undoubtedly has an integrationist objective and effect.[60]

---

[56] Article 11(4) contains an obligation for national competition authorities to consult the Commission on certain types of decisions, including decisions requiring that an infringement be brought to an end, and Article 11(6) allows the Commission to withdraw the case from the national authority. See section 1.2.8.1 above. The risk that the European Commission would want unduly to favour a defendant company can be addressed through the consultation of the Advisory Committee, composed of respresentatives of the competition authorities of the Member States, and the publication of its opinion, pursuant to Article 14(1) and (6) of Regulation No 1/2003, combined with the possibility for Member States to bring before the Court of Justice an application for annulment of the Commission decision for misuse of powers, pursuant to Article 230 EC.

[57] It would however be problematic if for instance a competition authority were to offer very generous leniency terms to several cartel participants instead of only to the single first one to cooperate. On the economics of leniency, see *The Optimal Enforcement of EC Antitrust Law*, n 1 above, ch 3, as well as section 5.2.3 below.

[58] Again, such harmonization could either happen voluntarily or be imposed through a new Council Regulation based on Article 83 EC. See also para 220 above.

[59] See para 387 above. See also Judgment of the Court of Justice of 11 February 2003 in Joined Cases C–187/01 and C–385/01 *Hüseyin Gözütok and Klaus Brügge* [2003] ECR I–1378.

[60] Article 50 CFR does of course not apply to jurisdictions outside the Union. It does therefore not stand in the way of double prosecutions and double punishments for instance by the US antitrust authorities on the one hand and the European Commission or a national competition authority on the other hand. See Judgment of the Court of First Instance of 9 July 2003 in Case T–224/00 *Archer Daniels Midland v Commission*, not yet published in ECR, paras 85–112 and Judgment of the Court of First Instance of 29 April 2004 in Joined Cases T–236/01 etc *Tokai Carbon and Others v Commission*, not yet published in ECR, para 137. Applying the economic criteria set out in section 3.3 above, a ban on multiple prosecutions appears also undesirable because, in contrast with the situation inside the Union, full coordination between the different prosecutors would be impossible or very problematic within the existing legal frameworks.

4

Should Private Antitrust Enforcement Be Encouraged?

4.1.1 Overview

436. This chapter deals with the question whether private enforcement of EC antitrust law should be encouraged. The chapter focuses more specifically on the prohibitions of restrictive agreements and of abuse of a dominant position laid down in Articles 81 and 82 EC.[1] These prohibitions are today almost exclusively enforced through public enforcement by the European Commission (hereafter also: 'the Commission') and the competition authorities of the Member States (hereafter also: 'the national competition authorities'). In private litigation, Articles 81 and 82 EC are regularly invoked as a defence (or 'shield'), mainly in contractual disputes, but rarely are the EC antitrust rules used proactively (as a 'sword') to claim damages or injunctive relief in national courts. This raises the question whether it would be desirable for private enforcement to take on a larger role in the enforcement of Articles 81 and 82 EC.

437. The remainder of section 4.1 briefly describes the current situation with regard to private enforcement of EC antitrust law, the much bigger role of private antitrust enforcement in the United States and the calls which have been made to stimulate private antitrust enforcement in Europe. Section 4.2 sets out two possible goals of antitrust enforcement, namely ensuring (mainly through deterrence) that the antitrust prohibitions are not violated and pursuing corrective justice through compensation. Section 4.3 presents the reasons why public enforcement is inherently superior to private enforcement with regard to the first of these goals (ensuring that the antitrust prohibitions are not violated). Section 5.4 argues that from this perspective there is not even a case for a supplementary role for private EC antitrust enforcement, beyond the current use as a shield. Section 4.5 discusses the question whether the pursuit of corrective justice through compensation could justify an increased use of private enforcement. Section 4.6 summarises my conclusions.

---

[1] Merger control will not be discussed.

4.1.2 The Current Role of Private Enforcement in Europe

438. Articles 81 and 82 EC can be used in two ways in private litigation: as a 'shield' and as a 'sword'.[2] The antitrust prohibitions are used as a shield when they are invoked in defence against a contractual claim for performance or for damages because of non-performance or against some other claim, for instance in an intellectual property infringement action. The antitrust rules are used as a sword if they are used proactively by private parties as a basis for claiming damages or injunctive relief.

439. The use of Article 81 EC as a shield in contractual disputes has its basis directly in the EC Treaty. Indeed, Article 81(2) EC provides that 'any agreements [...] prohibited pursuant to this article shall be automatically void'. In *BRT v SABAM*, on a preliminary reference from a national court before which Article 82 EC was invoked in an intellectual property infringement case, the Court of Justice held more generally that 'as the prohibitions of Articles 81(1) and 82 tend by their very nature to produce direct effects in relations between individuals, these articles create direct rights in respect of the individuals concerned which the national courts must safeguard'.[3]

440. The voidness sanction provided for in Article 81(2) EC is undoubtedly a useful and effective instrument to enforce the prohibition of restrictive agreements contained in Article 81 EC. Indeed, by making restrictive agreements legally unenforceable, it reinforces the natural tendency of parties to cheat on their agreements, thus making the conclusion and maintenance of such agreements more difficult.

441. In practice it appears that Article 81(2) is regularly invoked in contractual disputes as a defence against actions for breach of contract. Under Regulation No 17,[4] the voidness defence could also be invoked with regard to agreements which fell under Article 81(1) EC, which were not covered by a block exemption and which had not been earlier notified to the Commission, even if they fulfilled the four conditions of Article 81(3) and did thus not fall under the material prohibition laid down in Article 81 EC. This aberration has come to an end as a result of Regulation No 1216/1999,[5] which modified Regulation No 17 with respect to vertical agreements, and Regulation No 1/2003,[6] which has replaced Regulation No 17 and entirely abolished the notification system.[7] For those cases where the agree-

---

[2] See FG Jacobs and T Deisenhofer, 'Procedural Aspects of the Effective Private Enforcement of EC Competition Rules: A Community Perspective' in CD Ehlermann and I Atanasiu (eds), *European Competition Law Annual 2001: Effective Private Enforcement of EC Antitrust Law* (Hart Publishing, 2003).

[3] Judgment of 30 January 1974 in Case 127/73 *BRT v SABAM* [1973] ECR 51, para 16.

[4] Council Regulation No 17 of 6 February 1962 [1962] OJ 13/204 (Special English Edition 1959–62, p 87).

[5] Council Regulation (EC) No 1216/1999 of 10 June 1999 amending Regulation No 17 [1999] OJ L148/5.

[6] Council Regulation (EC) No 1/2003 of 16 December 2002 on the implementation of the rules on competition laid down in Articles 81 and 82 of the Treaty [2003] OJ L1/1.

[7] See section 1.1.4.1 above.

ment is indeed contrary to Article 81, and the voidness sanction is thus justified, Regulation No 1/2003 has furthermore facilitated the invocation of the voidness defence, in that it has given national courts the power to apply themselves the four conditions of Article 81(3), instead of having to suspend their proceedings and wait for a decision of the Commission on whether or not the four conditions of Article 81(3) are met.[8]

442. As to the use of Articles 81 or 82 EC as a sword, the EC Treaty is silent. Regulation No 17 does not in any way hint at this possibility either. Only relatively recently, in *Courage v Crehan*, did the Court of Justice clearly hold that 'the full effectiveness of Article 81 of the Treaty and, in particular, the practical effect of the prohibition laid down in Article 81(1) would be put at risk if it were not open to any individual to claim damages for loss caused to him by a contract or by conduct liable to restrict or distort competition',[9] thereby confirming the possibility of actions for damages for violation of Article 81 EC before the national courts. As to Regulation No 1/2003, its Article 6 provides that 'national courts shall have the power to apply Articles 81 and 82 of the Treaty'. That this is meant to cover not only the use of the antitrust provisions as a shield but also their use as a sword, is apparent from recital 7 of the regulation according to which 'national courts have an essential part to play in applying the Community competition rules. When deciding disputes between private individuals, they protect the subjective rights under Community law, for example by awarding damages to the victims of infringements'.

443. In practice it appears that the use of Articles 81 and 82 EC as a sword in private litigation has been rare.[10] I do not expect Regulation No 1/2003 to bring about a major change in this respect. By abolishing the notification system and the exclusive competence of the Commission to apply Article 81(3), this regulation removes an obstacle for private enforcement of Article 81, as it will no longer be possible in practice to bring court proceedings to a halt by lodging a notification with the Commission. As the experience with Article 82 EC shows, however, the relative absence of private enforcement is mainly due to other factors.[11]

444. If private actions for damages or injunctive relief are very rare in Europe, it should however be noted that private complainants play an important role in the public enforcement of Articles 81 and 82 EC. Indeed, under Article 3 of Regulation No 17 and Article 7 of Regulation No 1/2003, any natural or legal person who can show a legitimate interest can lodge a complaint requesting the Commission to

---

[8] Idem, section 6.4.2.3. See also Article 2 of Regulation No 1/2003 concerning the burden of proof.

[9] Judgment of 20 September 2001 in Case C–453/99 *Courage v Crehan* [2001] ECR I–6314, para 26. In para 104 of his Opinion of 22 May 2003 in Joined Cases C–246/01, C–306/01, C–354/01 and C–355/01, *AOK Bundesverband*, not yet published in ECR, Advocate General Jacobs has expressed the view that the same analysis would apply equally to injunctive relief.

[10] See R Whish, *Competition Law*, 5th edn (Lexis-Nexis Butterworths, 2001) 281, for references to some of the few examples known of. It is difficult to estimate the exact amount of private litigation because cases may be settled without much publicity.

[11] See *The Optimal Enforcement of EC Antitrust Law*, n 7 above, section 6.4.2.1; FG Jacobs and T Deisenhofer, n 2 above.

take action against a violation of Articles 81 or 82 EC. Many Commission actions start this way. If the Commission does not intend to act upon the complaint, it has to take a reasoned decision rejecting the complaint, and this decision can be subjected to judicial review by the Court of First Instance.[12]

4.1.3 Private Enforcement in the United States

445. In marked contrast with the situation in Europe, private actions for damages and, to a much lesser extent, for injunctive relief, based on the antitrust provisions of the Sherman and Clayton Acts, are very common in the United States.

446. Already in 1890, Section 7 of the Sherman Act, since replaced by Section 4 of the Clayton Act, provided for private enforcement of the antitrust laws. Section 4 of the Clayton Act currently provides that 'any person who shall be injured in his business or property by reason of anything forbidden in the antitrust laws may sue therefor in [a] district court of the United States [...], and shall recover threefold damages by him sustained, and the cost of suit, including a reasonable attorney's fee'.[13] This provision thus not only creates the possibility to bring actions for damages, but specifically encourages such actions by providing in addition for treble damages[14] and, as an exception to the normal American rule that each party bears its own costs, irrespective of whether the suit is succesful, provides for a right for the successful plaintiff to recover its costs, including expert fees, and attorney's fees.[15] Private damage actions are further facilitated by Section 5 of the Clayton Act, which provides that 'a final judgment or decree [...] rendered in any civil or criminal proceeding brought by or on behalf of the United States under the antitrust laws to the effect that a defendant has violated said laws shall be prima facie evidence against such defendant in any action or proceeding brought by any other party', and that the four-year statute of limitations applicable to private damages actions is suspended during the pendency of 'any civil or criminal proceeding [...] instituted by the United States', and for one year thereafter.[16]

447. Section 16 of the Clayton Act also provides for a specific right for 'any person, firm, corporation, or association [...] to sue for and have injunctive relief [...] against threatened loss or damage by a violation of the antitrust laws'.[17]

---

[12] See Judgment of the Court of First instance of 18 September 1992 in Case T–24/90 *Automec II* [1992] ECR II–2250.

[13] § 4 Clayton Act, 15 USC § 15.

[14] The idea of treble damages comes from the now repealed English Statute of Monopolies of 1623, 21 Jac I, c 3 (1623), *repealed*, SL (Repeals) (1969).

[15] The cost rule is asymmetric, in that the successful defendant cannot claim recovery of his costs from the plaintiff. In Europe, cost rules are a matter of national law. The normal rule in most Member States is the symmetrical rule that the successful litigant (plaintiff or defendant) can recover costs from the other party.

[16] § 5 Clayton Act, 15 USC § 16 (Tunney Act).

[17] § 16 Clayton Act, 15 USC § 26.

448. In practice 90% of antitrust cases in the United States are private actions.[18] According to Professor Waller, private litigation consists of two general types: on the one hand suits between large competitors, comparable to ordinary business tort cases (but with the right to treble damages and recovery of attorney's fees), and on the other hand treble damage claims from direct purchasers who are victims of price fixing or similarly per se unlawful conduct. The latter frequently, but not necessarily, follow on government criminal prosecutions, are in the form of multiple class actions brought by counsel working on a contingent fee basis, and are eventually settled.[19]

4.1.4 Calls to Stimulate Private Enforcement in Europe

449. Given the very rare use of Articles 81 and 82 EC as a sword in private litigation, and the striking difference with the situation in the United States, calls to stimulate private enforcement in Europe have been made with some regularity.

450. As early as 1961, when it was consulted on the Commission's proposal for what became Regulation No 17, the European Parliament expressed its view that rules should be laid down not only for administrative sanctions for violation of articles 81 and 82 EC but also for the recovery of damages.[20] The Commission did however not propose such rules, and the Council did not include any in Regulation No 17.

451. Since 1973, when it first expressed this view in response to a parliamentary question,[21] the Commission has with some regularity expressed the view that private actions for damages could provide useful support for its own enforcement actions.[22] As already indicated above,[23] recital 7 of Regulation No 1/2003 also expresses this view. Apart from the abolition of the notification system and of the Commission's exclusive competence to apply Article 81(3), this regulation does however not contain any measures to stimulate the use of Articles 81 and 82 EC as a sword in private litigation. According to Joel Davidow: 'The European Union has no victim's compensation policy at all, [...]. Nor does it plan to establish one, any time soon'.[24]

452. As to the Court of Justice, its Advocate General Van Gerven expressed in 1993 the view that the Court should recognize a right to obtain damages for

---

[18] UK Department of Trade and Industry, 'Productivity and Enterprise—A World Class Competition Regime' (July 2001), available at http://www.dti.gov.uk, p 47.

[19] SW Waller, 'The Incoherence of Punishment in Antitrust' (22 August 2002), available at http://www.luc.edu/schools/law/antitrust/docs/pnnsment.pdf, p 4.

[20] OJ 1410/61 of 15 November 1961, point 11.

[21] Answer of 10 April 1973 to Written Question No 519/72 by Mr Vredeling, [1973] OJ C67/55.

[22] See list of statements from the Commission referred to in note 112 of the Opinion of Advocate General Van Gerven of 27 October 1993 in Case C–128/92 Banks [1994] ECR I–1251.

[23] See para 442 above.

[24] J Davidow, 'International Implications of US Antitrust in the George W Bush Era' (2002) 25 World Competition 493, 496.

violation of Articles 81 and 82 EC, arguing that such rule would be useful for the enforcement of these provisions.[25] As already indicated above, the Court indeed recognized a right to damages in *Courage v Crehan* in 2001, stating that 'actions for damages before national courts can make a significant contribution to the maintenance of effective competition in the Community'.[26]

453. Quite interestingly, as has been pointed out by Joel Davidow,[27] the US administration, which over the past years has been encouraging the EC to follow the US model with regard to other remaining differences between EC and US antitrust, has not advocated Europe following the American example of private antitrust enforcement.

4.2 THE GOALS OF ANTITRUST ENFORCEMENT

454. In order to provide criteria by which the desirability of increased private enforcement of Articles 81 and 82 EC can be judged, the objectives of antitrust enforcement should be identified.

455. The most obvious goal of antitrust enforcement is to ensure that the antitrust prohibitions are not violated and that the anticompetitive effects which the antitrust prohibitions aim to avoid are indeed avoided. This is done primarily through deterrence, ie by creating a credible threat of sanctions[28] in case of violation, so as to alter the potential antitrust violator's cost/benefit calculation, and thus make him refrain from committing violations.[29] Deterrence is probably particularly effective in the area of antitrust, since antitrust violations generally result from business decisions.[30] Deterrence is however not the only conceivable instrument to reduce the likelihood of antitrust violations taking place. Indeed, corporate managers are not necessarily just maximizers of profits for themselves and their principals. They may feel a moral responsibility to live within the law whether or not they are likely to be caught, and this normative commitment could trump their interest calculus.[31] Indeed, psychological research suggests that normative commitment is generally an important factor explaining compliance with the law.[32] To reduce the number of antitrust violations, one may thus, apart from

[25] Opinion of Advocate General Van Gerven of 27 October 1993 in Case C–128/92 *Banks* [1994] ECR I–1212, 1250–51.

[26] See n 9 above, para 27.

[27] See n 24 above, at 496.

[28] Including criminal penalties, civil or administrative penalties and private damages.

[29] See generally *The Optimal Enforcement of EC Antitrust Law*, n 7 above, in particular section 2.1.3. In general, prevention constitutes an alternative mechanism to deterrence. In the area of merger control, prevention is the most commonly used instrument, but it is inherently unsuited for the enforcement of articles 81 and 82 EC. See idem, sections 2.2.1 and 6.2.

[30] The results of a survey by Feinberg among the Brussels antitrust bar confirmed that disregard for the law in pursuit of corporate gain is a consistently important source of EC antitrust violations; RM Feinberg, 'The Enforcement and Effects of European Competition Policy: Results of a Survey of Legal Opinion' (1985) 23 *Journal of Common Market Studies* 373, 376.

[31] CD Stone, 'Sentencing the Corporation' (1991) 71 *Boston University Law Review* 383, 389.

[32] See TR Tyler, *Why People Obey the Law* (Yale University Press, 1990).

organizing deterrence, try to find ways to increase business people's normative commitment to the antitrust rules.[33] Finally, apart from deterrence and education (inculcation of norms), antitrust enforcement can help ensure that the antitrust prohibitions are not violated and the anticompetitive effects which the antitrust prohibitions aim to avoid are indeed avoided by clarifying or elaborating the law through interpretation and precedent setting.[34]

456. A possible second goal of antitrust enforcement is the pursuit of corrective justice through compensation. The idea here is not to prevent antitrust violations from happening—of course compensation awards can also act as a deterrent, but that falls under the first goal discussed above—but to correct for the consequences when a violation has taken place, by making the party which wrongfully committed the violation compensate other parties who innocently suffered the consequences of the violation.[35]

457. Whether the goal is deterrence (or the reduction of antitrust violations through other mechanisms) or compensation, the pursuit of these goals will always have a cost. Two types of costs could be distinguished. Firstly, the pursuit of deterrence or of compensation could have undesirable side-effects. For instance, errors or the risk of errors in the imposition of sanctions could lead to lawful and economically desirable conduct being deterred. Similarly, inaccurate compensation awards could actually create injustice. Secondly, the pursuit of deterrence or compensation will always have an administrative cost, which includes both the cost borne by the public sector (cost of antitrust agencies, prosecutors and courts) and the cost borne by the businesses or individuals concerned (cost of lawyers and experts, management time).

458. The presence of cost has two implications. Firstly, it raises the question how much deterrence or how much compensation is worth the cost of attaining it. The answer to this question depends on the one hand on how high the cost is and on the other hand on how much value society attaches to the avoidance of antitrust violations and to the pursuit of corrective justice through compensation.[36] In all likelihood something less than full deterrence or full compensation is

---

[33] See generally KG Dau-Schmidt, 'An Economic Analysis of the Criminal Law as a Preference—Shaping Policy' (1990) Duke law Journal 1; CR Sunstein, 'On the Expressive Function of the Law' (1996) 144 University of Pennsylvania Law Review 2021; DM Kahan, 'Social Influence, Social Meaning, and Deterrence' (1997) 83 Virginia Law Review 349; NK Katyal, 'Deterrence's Difficulty' (1997) 95 Michigan Law Review 2385; GE Lynch, 'The Role of Criminal Law in Policing Corporate Misconduct' (1997) 60 Law and Contemporary Problems 23; DM Kahan, 'Social Meaning and the Economic Analysis of Crime' (1998) 27 Journal of Legal Studies 609; and KG Dau-Schmidt, 'Preference shaping by the law' in P Newman (ed), The New Palgrave Dictionary of Economics and the Law (Macmillan, 1998) 84.

[34] See generally S Shavell, 'The Fundamental Divergence between the Private and the Social Motive to Use the Legal System' (1997) 26 Journal of Legal Studies 575, 579 and 595.

[35] See K Roach and MJ Trebilcock, 'Private Enforcement of Competition Laws' (1996) 34 Osgoode Hall Law Journal 461, 496.

[36] See generally, with regard to deterrence, GJ Stigler, 'The Optimum Enforcement of Laws' (1970) 78 Journal of Political Economy 526; KG Elzinga and W Breit, The Antitrust Penalties: A Study in Law and Economics (Yale University Press, 1976) 9–15.

optimal.[37] Secondly, and less controversially, whatever level of deterrence (or avoidance of antitrust violations) or corrective justice is aimed at, one should try to achieve that goal at the least possible cost.

4.3 THE INHERENT SUPERIORITY OF PUBLIC ENFORCEMENT

459. If the goal of antitrust enforcement is to ensure that the antitrust prohibitions are not violated,[38] public enforcement is inherently superior over private enforcement, for three sets of reasons, which are set out in this chapter: Firstly, public enforcement benefits from more effective investigative and sanctioning powers. Secondly, as private enforcement is driven by the private profit motive, it systematically diverges from the general interest. Thirdly, private enforcement is more costly than public enforcement.

4.3.1 Investigative and Sanctioning Powers

460. Competition authorities are better at discovering and proving antitrust infringement than private parties, because the authorities have wider investigative powers. This is true even in the US, where private plaintiffs benefit from liberal discovery rules.[39] It is certainly obvious in Continental Europe, where no such discovery rules exist. Introduction of American-style discovery would probably be undesirable because of its high cost and the risk of discovery being abused to obtain competitors' business secrets.[40] In Europe, private plaintiffs would have additional difficulties in gathering evidence on a transnational basis in several Member States, whereas the European Commission's investigatory powers cover the whole of the European Union,[41] and national competition authorities will be able to obtain the help of their colleagues from other Member States within the network set up under Regulation No 1/2003.[42]

461. Public enforcement is also superior in that more effective sanctions are available and that the level of the sanctions can be better controlled. As to the type of sanctions available, apart from injunctive relief, private enforcement can only lead to the imposition of monetary sanctions in the form of damages. Public enforcement allows not only for the imposition of monetary sanctions in the form

---

[37] For the reasons set out in section 4.5 below, I even believe that the costs of pursuing corrective justice through compensation are so high compared to the benefits that it would be optimal not to pursue this goal at all.

[38] The possible second goal of pursuing corrective justice through compensation is not considered in this ch, but will be discussed in section 4.5 below.

[39] KG Elzinga and W Breit, n 36 above, p 142–43.

[40] See FG Jacobs and T Deisenhofer, n 2 above; and JH Langbein, 'The German Advantage in Civil Procedure' (1985) 52 *University of Chicago Law Review* 823.

[41] As well as the European Economic Area, in cooperation with the EFTA Surveillance Authority.

[42] See n 6 above, in particular Article 22 of the regulation. See also FG Jacobs and T Deisenhofer, n 2 above; and chs 1 and 2 above.

of fines, but also other types of sanctions, such as director disqualifications and prison sanctions. The European Commission does not currently have the power to seek the imposition of the latter type of sanctions, but some national competition authorities do,[43] and the Commission may obtain this power in the future.[44] Indeed, as I have argued in detail elsewhere,[45] effective deterrence of price cartels and other antitrust violations of comparable profitability and ease of concealment requires a combination of monetary sanctions on companies and individual penalties, in particular imprisonment.

462. As to the level of the monetary sanctions (fines or damages), public enforcement has the additional advantage of allowing better control in setting the optimal amount of the sanction. In principle, the amount of monetary sanctions could be set either by reference to the gain obtained by the antitrust offender or by reference to the social loss, ie the harm caused to society. Under both approaches a multiplier should be applied in inverse proportion to the probability of detection and punishment.[46] Calculating the optimal amount of the sanction is always difficult in practice, but with public enforcement at least one can attempt to target the optimal amount as well as possible. When the sanction consists of damages awarded as a result of private litigation, it becomes virtually impossible to target the optimal amount. Indeed, damages will be calculated not by reference to the offender's gain or the social loss, but by reference to the losses which those plaintiffs who happen to bring claims manage to prove. An essential component of the social loss caused by antitrust violations, namely the welfare loss for those consumers who as a result of the supracompetitive pricing abstain from buying a good or service, will never be considered, as those customers will in practice not be able to prove their loss (assuming already that they are aware of it) and will thus not bring suit. Damages awarded to consumers who paid an overcharge as a result of the antitrust violation bear some relationship to the social loss, but lost profits, which would be the measure of damages in suits brought by nonconsumers (dealers or competitors), bear no relationship whatsoever with either the offender's gain or the social loss.[47] Furthermore, single damage awards fail to incorporate the necessary multiplier inversely reflecting the probability of detection and punishment. The trebling of damages in the US could be considered as trying to address this problem,[48] but it does so in a very crude way. Indeed, there is no reason to

---

[43] Most recently, the Enterprise Act 2002 introduced such sanctions in the UK. Legally they do not apply directly to Article 81 EC but to a separate cartel offence under national law. From a functional, economic perspective these are however additional sanctions for hard-core violations of Article 81 EC. See also para 157 above.

[44] On the legal possibility of such powers at the EC level, see *The Optimal Enforcement of EC Antitrust Law*, n 7 above, section 8.7.4.

[45] The Optimal Enforcement of EC Antitrust Law, n 7 above, ch 8.

[46] Idem, sections 2.3.1 and 2.3.2.

[47] FH Easterbrook, 'Detrebling Antitrust Damages' (1985) 28 *Journal of Law & Economics* 445, 462–63.

[48] It has been strongly argued that, in particular because of the absence of prejudgment interest, treble damages are in reality closer to single damages: RH Lande, 'Are Antitrust "Treble" Damages Really Single Damages?' (1993) 54 *Ohio State Law Journal* 115.

assume that trebling is the right multiplication, and it is certain that the multiplier should be variable, reflecting the fact that some types of antitrust violations are difficult to hide, thus necessitating a low multiplier or even no multiplier at all, whereas other types are easily concealable, thus requiring a high multiplier.[49]

4.3.2 Divergence Between the Private and the General Interest

463. Competition authorities are not perfect and they can and occasionally do make mistakes. But at least they try, or can be led (by the public scrutiny their behaviour is subjected to and by the finite budgets they are allocated) to try, to decide on case selection and priority setting with a view to maximizing respect for the antitrust prohibitions (through deterrence, education and clarification of the law), while minimizing the costs of antitrust enforcement.[50]

464. The same cannot be said about private plaintiffs. Indeed, there is no reason whatsoever why they would care about optimal enforcement. The only consideration which drives private enforcement is the private gains and expenses of the different potential plaintiffs. This leads to at least three problems: inadequate investment, unmeritorious suits and undesirable settlements.

465. The problem of inadequate investment results from the fact that, for many of the most meritorious antitrust enforcement actions, the social benefit (in terms of deterrence, education and clarification of the law) of succesfully bringing the action far exceeds the damages award a potential private plaintiff can hope for. Private plaintiffs will thus have insufficient incentives to invest in detecting and litigating meritorious cases.[51] It could be argued that the trebling of damages and the institution of class actions in the US to some extent address this problem. Trebling, however, is a inadequately indiscriminate measure, as it increases just as much the incentives to pursue meritorious cases as the perverse incentives to pursue unmeritorious cases. As to class actions, they generate huge administrative cost[52] and lead to a new set of incentive problems. Indeed, because of the weak

---

[49] FH Easterbrook, n 47 above, p 454–57; RA Posner, *Antitrust Law*, 2nd edn (Chicago University Press, 2001) 272.

[50] See, with regard to the US antitrust agencies, WH Page, 'Antitrust Damages and Economic Efficiency: An Approach to Antitrust Injury' (1980) 47 *University of Chicago Law Review* 467, 503 ('Although there are some random, even perverse, elements in the criteria for case selection by the Department of Justice and the Federal Trade Commission, those organizations have no clear incentive to bring anticompetitive cases, and seem to consider the efficiency consequences of their enforcement policies'); RA Posner, n 49 above, p 275–76 ('The tight budget constraint has forced the agencies to be selective in their choice of cases. Although they might select the silliest cases to bring, there is no reason in theory why they should and no evidence that they do.') See also KG Elzinga and W Breit, n 36 above, p 141.

[51] See generally S Shavell, n 34 above.

[52] See M Handler, 'The Shift from Substantive to Procedural Innovations in Antitrust Suits—The Twenty-Third Annual Antitrust Review' (1971) 71 *Columbia Law Review* 1, p 9–10, who concludes from his analysis that there is 'little doubt that massive class actions constitute a net liability for antitrust, for federal courts, and for society generally'. See also WM Landes and RA Posner, 'Should Indirect Purchasers Have Standing To Sue Under the Antitrust Laws? An Economic Analysis of the

control of clients on attorneys in class actions, such actions are driven by the attorneys' pursuit of fees, and there is even less reason to assume that the attorneys' interests will coincide with the general interest than that their clients' interests would.[53]

466. The problem of unmeritorious actions results primarily[54] from the difficulty of drawing the borderline between anticompetitive and procompetitive behaviour, especially in cases of alleged exclusionary practices, combined with the fact that competitor plaintiffs have as strong or arguably even stronger an incentive to bring actions against strong legitimate competition by their rivals as against anticompetitive behaviour.[55] In the US experience, the problem of unmeritorious actions appears to have been identified as a major problem by all observers not linked to the private antitrust bar.[56]

467. Just as private cost/benefit calculations drive the bringing of suits, they also determine their eventual settlement. Settlements may be desirable in that they save administrative cost,[57] but the private incentive to settle risks again fundamentally diverging from the general interest. Especially in the context of class actions, there is a serious risk of inadequate or even collusive settlements because of the attorneys' risk aversion and their interest in fees rather than damages.[58] In competitor suits there may be an incentive for cases to be settled in the form of a violation of Article 81 EC in that the defendant agrees to share the monopoly benefits with the plaintiff.[59] More generally, as Advocate General Jacobs and Thomas Deisenhofer have pointed out: 'it must be borne in mind that settlements are based on considerations of convenience and not necessarily on considerations

Rule of *Illinois Brick*' (1979) 46 *University of Chicago Law Review* 602, 607–8; JC Coffee, 'Rescuing the Private Attorney General: Why the Model of the Lawyer as Bounty Hunter is Not Working' (1983) 42 *Maryland Law Review* 215, 232–34.

[53] On the incentive problems in class actions, see JC Coffee, n 52 above; JR Macey and GP Miller, 'The Plaintiff's Attorney's Role in Class Action and Derivative Litigation: Economic Analysis and Recommendations for Reform' (1991) 58 *University of Chicago Law Review* 1.

[54] Another possible cause of unmeritorious litigation is the fact that, even if the action is rejected, the defendant may suffer unrecoverable costs, thus creating the potential for extortionate suits which defendants settle merely in order to avoid incurring defence costs. It could however be argued that this risk is not great, as defendants would not want to create a reputation for being a soft target for extortionate lawsuits.

[55] The reason why the incentive appears even stronger is that anticompetitive behaviour tends toward raising prices, which also benefits competitors, whereas legitimate competitive behaviour reduces the price level.

[56] See ie EA Snyder and TE Kauper, 'Misuse of the Antitrust Laws: The Competitor Plaintiff' (1991) 90 *Michigan Law Review* 551; SC Salop and LJ White, 'Economic Analysis of Private Antitrust Litigation' (1986) 74 *Georgetown Law Journal* 1001; WJ Baumol and JA Ordover, 'Use of Antitrust to Subvert Competition' (1985) 28 *Journal of Law & Economics* 247; and Posner, n 49 above, p 275.

[57] Article 9 of Regulation No 1/2003 provides for a possibility of settlement of cases initiated by the European Commission, modeled on the Amercian consent decrees. See *The Optimal Enforcement of EC Antitrust Law*, n 7 above, section 6.5.2.2, as well as section 2.5.2.4.2.3 above.

[58] JC Coffee, n 52 above, p 230–33.

[59] K Roach and MJ Trebilcock, n 35 above, p 488. A Brussels based private antitrust lawyer once told me the story of one of his clients who, upon having received legal advice that its dominant competitor was acting in violation of Article 82 EC, had used this legal opinion to negotiate a market-sharing agreement with the dominant competitor.

of legality. They are moreover rarely publicised. Settlements cannot therefore contribute to the same extent as judgments to the clarification and a better understanding of the competition rules'.[60]

4.3.3 Cost

468. Private enforcement appears more costly than public enforcement for two reasons. Firstly, in private enforcement many resources have to be spent in the determination and allocation of the damages,[61] more than those which would be spent in the setting of the sanction in public enforcement. Secondly, public enforcement may generally be cheaper because of the higher degree of specialisation of the actors involved and the generally lower cost of administrative procedures as compared with civil litigation. This double disadvantage of private enforcement is all the more pronounced in the case of class actions, which tend to be hugely expensive.[62]

4.4 NO NEED FOR SUPPLEMENTARY PRIVATE ENFORCEMENT

469. The preceding chapter sets out the reasons why, assuming that the goal of antitrust enforcement is to ensure that the antitrust prohibitions are not violated—the possible goal of compensation will be considered later in chapter V—public enforcement is inherently superior over private enforcement. It does not automatically follow that private enforcement could not play a useful supplementary role. However, for the reasons set out in this chapter, there does not appear to be a case either for a supplementary role for private enforcement of Articles 81 and 82 EC.

4.4.1 No Need for Private Enforcement to Provide Additional Sanctions

470. It is sometimes argued that private damages actions following prosecutions by the European Commission or by national authorities could provide useful additional sanctions. The fatal problem with this argument is that, if additional monetary sanctions were indeed required, these could be provided for in a much cheaper and more reliable way by increasing the fines imposed in the public enforcement proceeding.[63]

471. In the US, damages may have constituted a useful supplement before 1974, when the statutory ceiling for fines was very low, but this problem has since

---

[60] FG Jacobs and T Deisenhofer, n 2 above.
[61] KG Elzinga and W Breit, n 36 above, p 95.
[62] See n 52 above.
[63] See also M Handler, n 52 above, p 9.

disappeared.[64] In Europe, the Commission and the Council do not appear to consider that the ceiling of 10% of total turnover in Article 15(2) of Regulation No 17 and Article 23(2) of Regulation No 1/2003 is too low.[65] In any event, if it were too low, it could be raised.

472. As I have argued in detail elsewhere, I believe that there is a problem in Europe of inadequate sanctions for price cartels and other antitrust violations of comparable profitability and ease of concealment, because of the absence of individual penalties, in particular imprisonment.[66] But this problem cannot be solved by private enforcement.

4.4.2 No Need for Private Enforcement to Bring Additional Cases

473. It has also been argued that private enforcement could be useful in that it could result in additional antitrust enforcement cases being brought. The idea here is that private enforcement can deal with those antitrust violations public enforcement does not deal with. This argument seems to consist of three variations.

474. The first variation of the argument is that there would be such a mass of cases to be dealt with that public enforcement could not possibly deal with all of them. I find this argument unconvincing for several reasons. Firstly, it is in all likelihood not in the general interest that all antitrust violations are prosecuted. Indeed, as explained above,[67] antitrust enforcement always has a cost. How much antitrust enforcement is desirable depends of course on how much value society attaches to the avoidance of antitrust violations, but that value is certainly not infinite, given the multitude of other societal concerns. Secondly, it is not my impression that there is currently a problem of insufficient resources for the European Commission and national competition authorities which is not already being solved or could not realistically be solved.[68] Thanks to the abolition of the notification system by Regulation No 1/2003, the Commission will be able to better use the resources previously spent on unproductive notification work. Moreover, the staff of the Commission's Directorate-General for Competition has significantly increased in the last few years. As a result of Regulation No 1/2003, the Commission will from now on work together in a network with competition authorities in all the Member States. Several of these are well staffed and quite efficient. Those lagging behind will no doubt come under peer pressure to reach the

---

[64] See S Calkins, 'An Enforcement Official's Reflections on Antitrust Class Actions' (1997) 39 *Arizona Law Review* 413, 427–30, 440.

[65] Otherwise they would have followed the suggestion of the OECD Competition Law and Policy Division, made in response to the Commission's White Paper preceding the proposal for what became Regulation No 1/2003, to increase this ceiling. See *The Optimal Enforcement of EC Antitrust Law*, n 7 above, at n 132.

[66] The Optimal Enforcement of EC Antitrust Law, n 7 above, ch 8.

[67] See para 462 above.

[68] I do believe there is a problem of insufficient sanctioning powers, in particular the absence of criminal sanctions, and probably also insufficiently strong investigative powers, but these problems can only be solved by strengthening public enforcement, not by adding private enforcement.

same level. In any event, even if I were wrong, it would, because of all the reasons set out in section 4.3 above, be better to call for more resources for public enforcement, whenever needed, than to call for supplemental private enforcement.

475. The second variation on the argument that private enforcement could deal with cases not dealt with by public enforcement is that there would be certain types of meritorious cases which public enforcement does not deal with and which should thus be dealt with by private enforcement. I can see the origin of this argument in the US context, where public enforcement appears to be essentially limited to criminal prosecution of hard-core price fixing, bid rigging and market allocation cases,[69] but the situation in Europe is different. Even if the prosecution of hard-core cartels has received increased priority in the last years—it had in reality not much priority before—the fact remains that the European Commission and the national competition authorities deal with all kinds of violations of Articles 81 and 82 EC, and there are no signs that they would not intend to continue doing so.[70] Moreover, the other types of cases which are supposed to be brought by private enforcement risk being the unmeritorious ones discussed above.[71] As Judge Posner summarized the US experience: 'the influence of the private action on the development of antitrust doctrine has been on the whole a pernicious one'.[72]

476. The third variation on the argument that private enforcement could deal with cases not dealt with by public enforcement is that private enforcement has a failsafe function. There are two aspects to this argument. The first aspect has its origin in the US experience of ideological swings in antitrust enforcement depending on the administration in power.[73] I do not have the impression that the same problem exists in the different political, institutional and cultural context of EC antitrust enforcement. The second aspect of the argument relates to the fact that competition authorities may, for whatever unfortunate reasons, occasionally fail to bring certain prosecutions which clearly merit to be brought. In the case of the European Commission, however, this risk is already being addressed through another mechanism, namely the possibility for private parties to bring a complaint before the Commission, the obligation for the Commission to take a reasoned decision if it decides not to act upon the complaint, and the right for the complainant to have this decision reviewed by the Court of First Instance.[74]

[69] SW Waller, n 19 above, p 4.

[70] Evidence that the Commission intends to continue, together with the national competition authorities, to deal not only with hard-core violations but also with other types of violations of Articles 81 and 82 EC, can be found in the White Paper and the Explanatory Memorandum preceding Regulation No 1/2003; [1999] OJ C132/1, in particular paras 83–98, and COM (2000) 582 final, in particular explanations of proposed Articles 7 and 10.

[71] Para 470 above.

[72] RA Posner, n 49 above, p 275.

[73] CA Jones, Private Enforcement of Antitrust Law in the EU, UK and USA (OUP 1999) 15.

[74] See para 448 above. On private enforcement and private rights to initiate public enforcement as alternative mechanisms to control public enforcement monopolies, see generally RB Stewart and CR Sunstein, 'Public Programs and Private Rights' (1982) 95 Harvard Law Review 1195; and, proposing for the US Department of Justice a mechanism similar to the one existing for the European Commission, M Handler and MD Blechmann, 'Antitrust and the Consumer Interest: The Fallacy of Parens Patriae and A Suggested New Approach' (1976) 85 Yale Law Journal 626, 675.

4.5 THE PURSUIT OF CORRECTIVE JUSTICE THROUGH COMPENSATION

477. If, as argued in the two preceding chapters, there is no need for more private antitrust enforcement in Europe from the perspective of deterring or otherwise avoiding antitrust infringements, could the pursuit of corrective justice through compensation nevertheless justify an increased use of private actions for damages? The goal is then not to prevent antitrust violations from taking place—for the reasons set out in the two preceding chapters, public enforcement is better suited for pursuing that goal—but to correct for the consequences when antitrust violations have taken place, by making the party who wrongfully committed the violation compensate other parties who innocently suffered losses as a result of the violation.[75] Whether private enforcement should be encouraged for this purpose depends on how difficult or costly it is to achieve corrective justice in this area, and on how much value society attaches to this objective.

478. As to the value which society attaches to the pursuit of corrective justice in the antitrust context, I am not aware of any evidence that the citizens of Europe, outside the narrow circle of antitrust professionals, are seriously disturbed by the current absence of compensation for antitrust offences. As Professor Schwarz has pointed out in the US:

> The losses from antitrust violations are widely dispersed, do not represent the disappointment of strongly held expectations, and can in many cases be adapted to without severe dislocation in the lives of the persons affected. Moreover, existing welfare laws, unemployment compensation, bankruptcy laws, and a number of provisions in the tax laws provide relief from any catastrophic losses, including those that might result from an antitrust violation.[76]

479. As to the difficulty and hence the cost of truly achieving corrective justice through actions for damages, it would appear very high. Indeed, identifying the real victims of anticompetitive behaviour and the true extent of their loss is a very difficult task. The victims most deserving of compensation would be those consumers who have been priced out of the market as a result of the antitrust violation. But determining who would have purchased the good or service if its price had been lower, is exceedingly difficult. If the good or service is an input rather than a final product, it will also be necessary to trace the indirect effects produced by this substitution. In the US system of private enforcement, no attempt is even made to identify these victims.[77] As to those purchasers who paid an overcharge, unless they are final consumers, they are most likely to have passed on at least part

---

[75] See para 460 above.

[76] WF Schwarz, Private Enforcement of the Antitrust Laws: An Economic Critique (American Enterprise Institute, 1981) 32.

[77] WF Schwartz, 'An Overview of the Economics of Antitrust Enforcement' (1980) 68 *Georgetown Law Journal* 1075, 1091; WF Schwarz, n 76 above, p 29; and S Calkins, n 64 above, p 442–43.

of the overcharge to other, indirect purchasers.[78] In the US, direct purchasers can recover the whole overcharge, even if they have entirely passed it on to their customers, and indirect customers cannot sue, at least not under federal law.[79] If corrective justice is the objective, this simplifying rule appears undefendable, as it grants direct purchasers unjustified windfalls. Factually determining how much of an overcharge has been passed on, is however a very difficult task. On the side of the antitrust offender, equally complex problems arise. Indeed, the companies which committed the antitrust violations are unlikely to have retained their gains. It is more likely that the profits have been paid out in taxes, dividends, salaries and wages. In the US, empirical studies have estimated that unions are able to capture most of the monopoly profits earned by manufacturing firms.[80] The shareholders who received the dividends or the benefit of the increased share prices may very well have sold on their shares by the time damages are imposed. For all these reasons, in the antitrust context, attempts to achieve corrective justice through damages actions are likely to be very costly or to lead to results which do not really serve corrective justice.[81]

4.6 CONCLUSIONS

480. The EC antitrust prohibitions are regularly invoked in private litigation as a shield. Private parties also play an important role in public antitrust enforcement through complaints to the competition authorities. In marked contrast with the situation in the US, private actions for damages or for injunctive relief are rare.

481. In this chapter I have argued that this situation is a desirable one. Indeed, from the perspective of ensuring that the antitrust prohibitions are not violated, public antitrust enforcement is inherently superior to private enforcement, because of more effective investigative and sanctioning powers, because private antitrust enforcement is driven by private profit motives which fundamentally diverge from the general interest in this area, and because of the high cost of private antitrust enforcement. There is not even a case for a supplementary role for

---

[78] Idem. See also WM Landes and RA Posner, n 52 above; RG Harris and LA Sullivan, 'Passing On the Monopoly Overcharge: A Comprehensive Policy Analysis' (1979) 128 *University of Pennsylvania Law Review* 269.

[79] *Hanover Shoe v United Shoe Machinery* 392 US 481 (1968); *Illinois Brick v Illinois* 431 US 720 (1977). A number of states allow however for indirect purchasers to sue under state law. In *California v ARC America* 490 US 93 (1989) the US Supreme Court held that such state laws are not preempted by Section 4 of the Clayton Act.

[80] GJ Werden and MJ Simon, 'Why Price Fixers Should Go to Prison' [1987] *Antitrust Bulletin* 917 at note 35.

[81] As the whole of my reasoning in this ch focuses specifically on EC antitrust enforcement, my conclusion that actions for damages are not a useful instrument does not, or at least not necessarily, apply outside this context. In other areas of the law, identifying the victims of illegal behaviour and the true extent of their losses may be much less costly, or there may be a much stronger social need for compensation to achieve corrective justice. In the absence of public enforcement, private tort actions may also be indispensable to achieve deterrence.

private enforcement, as the adequate level of sanctions and the adequate number and variety of prosecutions can be ensured more effectively and at a lower cost through public enforcement. It also seems difficult to justify an increased role for private antitrust enforcement in Europe by the pursuit of corrective justice, as there does not appear to be a clear social need for such action, and because truly achieving corrective justice in the antitrust context is in practice a very difficult task. Any attempts to do so are likely to be very costly or to lead to results which do not really serve corrective justice.

5

The Collection of Intelligence and Evidence from Antitrust Violators

482. This chapter analyses, from a legal and economic perspective, the ways in which the European Commission and the competition authorities of the Member States can obtain intelligence and evidence of violations of Articles 81 or 82 EC from the undertakings that committed these violations or from their staff.

483. Under Regulation No 1/2003,[1] the European Commission (hereafter: 'the Commission') and the competition authorities of the Member States (hereafter also: 'the national competition authorities'), forming together a network of competition authorities (hereafter also: 'the competition authorities' and 'the European Competition Network'),[2] have the task of detecting and punishing violations of Articles 81 and 82 EC.[3] The competition authorities could collect the necessary intelligence and evidence from various sources. Information could be obtained in particular from complainants or other third parties. The best information will however usually be in the hands of the undertakings that have committed the violations and their staff. For certain types of violations, in particular secret price cartels, the undertakings that have committed the violations and their staff may be the only ones holding the information which the competition authorities need to detect and punish the violations.

484. Section 5.1 gives an overview of the legal instruments which are available to the European Commission and the competition authorities of the Member States in order to collect intelligence and evidence of violations of Articles 81 or 82 EC from the undertakings that have committed these violations (or are suspected of having committed them)[4] or from their staff.[5] On the one hand, the competition authorities have a number of powers of investigation which allow them either to take certain information by force or to coerce undertakings or members of their

---

[1] Council Regulation (EC) No 1/2003 of 16 December 2002 on the implementation of the rules on competition laid down in Articles 81 and 82 of the Treaty, [2003] OJ L1/1. According to its Articles 43 and 45, this regulation replaces Council Regulation No 17, [1962] OJ 13/204 (Special English Edition 1959–62, p 87) last amended by Council Regulation (EC) No 1216/1999, [1999] OJ L148/5, from 1 May 2004.

[2] See Recital 15 and Article 11 of Regulation No 1/2003.

[3] The authorities also have other tasks, but those are not considered here. As to the role of private enforcement, see ch 4 above, and n 62 and n 79 below.

[4] I will not repeat this qualification throughout this ch, the legal presumption of innocence being of course fully recognized.

[5] The same instruments may also be used to collect information from third parties, but that aspect is not further considered here.

staff to provide certain information. These powers are however subject to a number of limitations, including in particular those flowing from the privilege against self-incrimination. On the other hand, the European Commission and a number of national competition authorities also use the instrument of leniency, under which they can induce undertakings, and in the case of some Member States also individual members of their staff, to come forward and voluntarily provide information in exchange for immunity from punishment or reduced punishment. Section 5.2 contains an economic analysis of these mechanisms to collect intelligence and evidence from the undertakings that have committed antitrust violations and their staff, including an economic interpretation of the privilege against self-incrimination.

5.1 THE LAW

5.1.1 Powers of Investigation

485. The powers of investigation of the Commission and the competition authorities of the different Member States are not, or not necessarily, the same. Indeed, whereas Regulation No 1/2003 regulates the powers of investigation of the Commission, and also contains some provisions on cooperation within the European Competition Network, it does not regulate the powers of investigation of the competition authorities of the Member States, which are set out in their respective national laws.[6]

486. As to the European Commission, its powers of investigation are set out in Chapter V of Regulation No 1/2003, the two main instruments being requests for information (Article 18) and inspections (Articles 20 and 21).[7]

487. Under Article 18 of Regulation No 1/2003, the Commission can require undertakings and associations of undertakings to provide all necessary information (ie either to hand over existing documents or to provide answers to questions) specified in the request within the time-limit fixed in the request. When sending the request, the Commission is required to state the purpose of the request, meaning that it must identify, 'with reasonable precision', the suspected infringement of Articles 81 or 82 EC.[8] A request can be made if 'the Commission could

---

[6] Article 35 of Regulation No 1/2003 only contains the general obligation for Member States to designate their competition authorities 'in such a way that the provisions of this regulation are effectively complied with'.

[7] 'Inspections' is the new term in Regulation No 1/2003 for what the English-language version of Regulation No 17 called 'investigations'. Under Article 19 of Regulation No 1/2003, the Commission may also interview any natural or legal person who consents to be interviewed for the purpose of collecting information relating to the subject-matter of the investigation, but this 'power to take statements' is not much of a power, in the absence of any obligation or any penalties, even for providing misleading information.

[8] Opinion of Advocate General Jacobs of 15 December 1993 in Case C–36/92 P *SEP v Commission* [1994] ECR I–1914 (explicitly endorsed by the Court of Justice in its judgment of 19 May 1994 in the same case, [1994] ECR I–1932, para 21), para 30.

reasonably suppose, at the time of the request, that the document [or other information requested] would help it to determine whether the alleged infringement had taken place'.[9]

488. The Commission can choose either of two forms for its request: a simple request or a decision.[10] An undertaking or association of undertakings is not obliged to respond to a simple request. Only if the undertaking or association, intentionally or negligently, provides incorrect or misleading information can it be penalised by the Commission under Article 23(1)(a) of Regulation No 1/2003 with a fine of up to 1% of its total turnover in the preceding business year. On the contrary, requests made by decision are binding. Under Article 23(1)(b) of Regulation No 1/2003, the Commission can impose a fine of up to 1% of their total turnover in the preceding business year on undertakings or associations which, intentionally or negligently, supply incorrect, incomplete or misleading information or do not supply information within the required time-limit, and under Article 24(1)(d) of Regulation No 1/2003, the Commission can impose periodic penalty payments of up to 5% of the average daily turnover in the preceding business year per day in order to compel undertakings or associations to supply complete and correct information which it has requested by decision.

489. The addressees of requests for information made by decision can bring an application for judicial review of this decision before the Community Courts.[11]

490. Requests for information under Article 18 of Regulation No 1/2003 can only be addressed to undertakings or associations of undertakings. Article 18(4) provides that:

> The owners of undertakings or their representatives and, in the case of legal persons, companies or firms, or associations having no legal personality, the persons authorised to represent them by law or by their constitution shall supply the information requested on behalf of the undertaking or the association of undertakings concerned. Lawyers duly authorised to act may supply the information on behalf of their clients. The latter shall remain fully responsible if the information supplied is incomplete, incorrect or misleading.

The fines and periodic penalty payments provided for in Articles 23 and 24 of Regulation No 1/2003 can only be imposed on the undertakings or associations of undertakings.

491. Under Article 20 of Regulation No 1/2003, the Commission may conduct 'all necessary inspections of undertakings and associations of undertakings'. The officials and other persons authorised by the Commission to conduct the inspection have the power to enter any premises of the undertaking or association of undertakings, to examine all business-related records and to take or obtain copies

---

[9] Idem, para 21.

[10] Under Article 11 of Regulation No 17, the Commission could only use a decision after the undertaking had refused to answer a simple request. This limitation on the Commission's choice of instrument has been removed in Regulation No 1/2003.

[11] Pursuant to Article 18(3) of Regulation No 1/2003, this right to have the decision reviewed must be indicated in the decision.

or extracts. Under Article 20(2)(e) of Regulation No 1/2003, they are also empowered 'to ask any representative or member of staff of the undertaking or association of undertakings for explanations on facts or documents relating to the subject-matter and purpose of the inspection and to record the answers'.[12]

492. The Commission can again choose either of two forms of inspection: on the basis of a simple authorisation or on the basis of a decision. If the inspection is based on a simple authorisation, the undertaking or association of undertakings is not obliged to submit to it. However, under Article 23(1)(c) and (d) of Regulation No 1/2003, the Commission can impose on the undertaking or association a fine of up to 1% of the total turnover in the preceding business year where, intentionally or negligently, it produces the required business-related records in incomplete form or where, in response to a question asked under Article 20(2)(e), it gives an incorrect or misleading answer, or fails to correct within a time-limit set by the Commission an incorrect, incomplete or misleading answer given by a member of staff. If the inspection is based on a decision, the undertaking or association is required to submit to it. In addition to the penalties which can be imposed in case of an inspection based on a simple authorisation, the Commission can also impose, under Article 23(1)(c) and (d) of Regulation No 1/2003, fines of the same amount where the undertaking or association refuses to submit to the inspection, or where, in response to a question asked under Article 20(2)(e), it fails or refuses to provide a complete answer on facts relating to the subject-matter and purpose of the inspection. Under Article 24(1)(e) of Regulation No 1/2003, the Commission can also impose periodic penalty payments of up to 5% of the average daily turnover in the preceding business year per day in order to compel undertakings or associations to submit to an inspection ordered by decision. Moreover, Article 20(6) of Regulation No 1/2003 provides that, where the Commission officials conducting the inspection find that an undertaking opposes an inspection ordered by decision, the Member State concerned shall afford them the necessary assistance of the police or of an equivalent enforcement authority, so as to enable them to conduct their inspection.

493. The decision ordering the inspection must state the subject matter and purpose of the inspection.[13] This requirement is designed 'to show that the proposed entry onto the premises of the undertakings concerned is justified but also to enable those undertakings to assess the scope of their duty to cooperate'.[14] The Commission is obliged to state in the decision, 'as precisely as possible, what it is looking for and the matters to which the [inspection] must relate'.[15] If coercive measures are required under Article 20(6) of Regulation No 1/2003, the national

---

[12] Under Regulation No 17, the Commission officials could only seek explanations relating to the books and records under examination. See Judgment of the Court of Justice of 26 June 1980 in Case 136/79 *National Panasonic v Commission* [1980] ECR 2056, para 15; and Order of the Court of First Instance of 9 June 1997 in Case T–9/97 *Elf Atochem v Commission* [1997] *ECR* II–919, para 23.

[13] Article 20(4) of Regulation No 1/2003. A similar obligation exists for simple authorisations under Article 20(3).

[14] Judgment of 22 October 2002 in Case C–94/00 *Roquette Frères* [2002] ECR I–9039, para 47.

[15] Idem, para 48.

court with jurisdiction to authorise such measures has the obligation 'to ensure, in the specific circumstances of each individual case, that the coercive measure envisaged is not arbitrary or disproportionate to the subject-matter of the investigation ordered'.[16] The national court is thus required 'to satisfy itself that there exist reasonable grounds for suspecting an infringement of the competition rules by the undertaking concerned', and 'to verify that the coercive measures are proportionate to the subject-matter of the investigation ordered', ie 'that such measures are appropriate to ensure that the investigation can be carried out' and 'that such measures do not constitute, in relation to the aim pursued by the investigation in question, a disproportionate and intolerable interference'.[17]

494. The undertaking or association under inspection has the right to legal representation,[18] but the exercise of the right to consult a legal advisor must not unduly delay or impede the investigation.[19]

495. The addressees of a decision ordering an inspection can bring an application for judicial review of this decision before the Community Courts.[20]

496. Under Article 21 of Regulation No 1/2003, the Commission also has the power to order by decision an inspection of 'any other premises [...], including the homes of directors, managers and other members of staff of the undertakings and associations of undertakings concerned', if 'a reasonable suspicion exists that books or other records related to the business and to the subject-matter of the inspection, which may be relevant to prove a serious violation of Article 81 or Article 82 of the Treaty, are being kept in [those premises]'.[21] The decision must in particular state the reasons that have led the Commission to conclude that such a suspicion exists, and it cannot be executed without prior authorisation from the national judicial authority of the Member State concerned.[22] The provisions of Article 20(6) of Regulation No 1/2003, which provide for assistance by the national authorities, including the police, in case of opposition, also apply to inspections under Article 21 of Regulation No 1/2003, but the powers of the Commission to impose fines or periodic penalty payments under Articles 23 and 24 of Regulation No 1/2003 are not applicable.

497. The Commission's mandatory powers of investigation are subject to two sets of general limitations, flowing from legal professional privilege and the privilege against self-incrimination. It follows from legal professional privilege, as

---

[16] Idem, para 52. Article 20(7) of Regulation No 1/2003 leaves it to national law whether or not to require a judicial authorisation. Member States may however be under an obligation to require such an authorisation under Article 8 of the European Convention on Human Rights, as interpreted by the European Court of Human Rights in its judgment of 16 April 2002 in *Colas Est and Others v France*, Application 37971/97.

[17] Idem, paras 54, 71 and 76.

[18] Idem, para 46.

[19] See CS Kerse, *EC Antitrust Procedure,* 4th edn (Sweet & Maxwell, 1998) section 3.40.

[20] Pursuant to Article 20(4) of Regulation No 1/2003, this right to have the decision reviewed must be indicated in the decision.

[21] This power is new compared to Regulation No 17.

[22] Article 21(2) and (3) of Regulation No 1/2003. The addressees of the decision can also bring an application for judicial review before the Community Courts.

recognised by the Court of Justice, that the Commission cannot use its powers of investigation to take by force or to compel the production of lawyer-client communications, provided that such communications are made for the purpose and in the interests of the client's rights of defence and that they emanate from independent lawyers.[23] The limitations flowing from the privilege against self-incrimination are discussed separately in section 5.1.2 below.

498. Finally, refusal to cooperate with or attempts to obstruct the Commission in carrying out its investigations may constitute an aggravating circumstance leading to an increased fine for the antitrust violations found following the investigation.[24]

499. The powers of investigation of the competition authorities of the Member States are laid down in their respective national laws.[25] In several Member States these powers appear to be stronger than the Commission's powers.

500. In some Member States, these stronger investigative powers reflect stronger sanctions for violations of Articles 81 or 82 EC or related offences. Indeed, whereas Regulation No 1/2003 only allows the Commission to impose fines on undertakings and associations of undertakings for violations of Articles 81 or 82 EC, Article 5 of this regulation allows national authorities to impose 'any other penalty provided for in their national law', including in particular prison sanctions for directors or managers responsible for their companies' violation of Article 81 or 82 EC.[26] In those Member States where such criminal sanctions are provided for, or where criminal sanctions can be imposed not directly for violations of Articles 81 or 82 EC but for a related offence, it can be expected that correspondingly stronger criminal investigative powers are also provided for, including for instance powers to carry out directed surveillance and use covert human intelligence sources.[27]

501. Even in the absence of stronger sanctions for violations of Articles 81 and 82 EC or related offences, the national laws of several Member States give their national competition authorities stronger powers to investigate violations of Articles 81 and 82 EC than Regulation No 1/2003 gives to the Commission, for

[23] Judgment of the Court of Justice of 18 May 1982 in Case 155/79 *AM&S v Commission* [1982] ECR 1575; and Order of the Court of First Instance of 4 April 1990 in Case T–30/89 *Hilti v Commission* [1990] *ECR* II–163. See however also Order of the President of the Court of First Instance of 30 October 2003 in Joined Cases T–125/03 R and T–253/03 R *Akzo Nobel Chemicals v Commission*, not yet published in ECR, currently on appeal before the Court of Justice, Case C–7/04 P(R).

[24] See the Commission's Guidelines on the method of setting fines imposed pursuant to Article 15(2) of Regulation No 17 and Article 65(5) of the ECSC Treaty, [1998] OJ C9/3, point 2, second indent. Pursuant to Article 43(3) of Regulation No 1/2003, these guidelines continue to apply to fines imposed under Article 23(2) of Regulation No 1/2003.

[25] See n 6 above.

[26] On the need for prison sanctions to deter effectively the most serious violations of Article 81 EC, see my book *The Optimal Enforcement of EC Antitrust Law* (Kluwer, 2002) chs 8 and 9; and OECD, *Fighting Hard-Core Cartels: Harm, Effective Sanctions and Leniency Programs* (2002), accessible at http://www.oecd.org/pdf/M00036000/M00036562.pdf, pp 89–90.

[27] See for instance in the UK, the powers for investigating criminal cartels under the Enterprise Act 2002, described in OFT Guidance *Powers for Investigating Criminal Cartels* (January 2004), accessible at http://www.oft.gov.uk.

instance in that not only undertakings and associations of undertakings but also individual members of staff can be required to produce specified documents and information, and that failure to cooperate with investigations is a criminal offence, with directors, managers or other officers of companies or other bodies corporate being liable to punishment if they have consented to or connived at an offence or it is due to neglect on their part.[28]

502. On the other hand, in some Member States, the limitations on the use of mandatory powers of investigation flowing from legal professional privilege or the privilege against self-incrimination are stricter. In particular, in some Member States, including the UK and Belgium, legal professional privilege extends also to in-house legal counsel.[29]

503. Finally, Regulation No 1/2003 contains some provisions which allow the members of the European Competition Network to help each other with their investigations. Article 22(2) allows the Commission to request national competition authorities to undertake inspections on its behalf. The powers to be exercised are those provided for under national law. Article 22(1) provides for a possibility, not an obligation, for a national authority to carry out in its own territory 'any inspection or other fact-finding measure under its national law on behalf and for the account of the competition authority of another Member State'. Article 12(1) provides that '[f]or the purpose of applying Articles 81 and 82 of the Treaty the Commission and the competition authorities of the Member States shall have the power to provide one another with and use in evidence any matter of fact or of law, including confidential information.' However, Article 12(3) adds that the information exchanged on this basis,

> can only be used in evidence to impose sanctions on natural persons where: [first indent] the law of the transmitting authority foresees sanctions of a similar kind in relation to an infringement of Article 81 or Article 82 of the Treaty or, in the absence thereof, [second indent] the information has been collected in a way which respects the same level of protection of the rights of defence of natural persons as provided for under the national rules of the receiving authority. However, in this case, the information exchanged cannot be used by the receiving authority to impose custodial sanctions.[30]

5.1.2 The Privilege Against Self-Incrimination

504. The powers of investigation of the Commission and the competition authorities of the Member States are subject to certain limitations flowing from the privilege against self-incrimination. Roughly speaking, this privilege equals the

---

[28] See for instance in the UK, the powers of investigation of the Office of Fair Trading under the Competition Act 1998, described in OFT Guideline 404 *Powers of Investigation*, accessible at http://www.oft.gov.uk.

[29] As to the privilege against self-incrimination, see para 504 below.

[30] See sections 1.2.11 and 1.2.12 above.

right not to be obliged to produce evidence against oneself.[31] It encompasses the right to silence, ie the right not to answer questions.[32] The applicability of this privilege and the scope of the protection it grants have been clarified in a number of judgments of the Community Courts (the Court of Justice and the Court of First Instance) and the European Court of Human Rights.

505. With regard to the Commission's powers of investigation under Regulation No 17,[33] the Court of Justice addressed the question already in 1989 in *Orkem v Commission*.[34] On the basis of a study of the national laws of the then twelve Member States,[35] the Court of Justice found:

> In general, the laws of the Member States grant the right not to give evidence against oneself only to a natural person charged with an offence in criminal proceedings. A comparative analysis of national law does not therefore indicate the existence of such a principle, common to the laws of the Member States, which may be relied upon by legal persons in relation to infringements in the economic sphere, in particular infringements of competition law.[36]

506. The Court of Justice also found that, although Article 6 of the European Convention on Human Rights (hereafter: 'Article 6 ECHR') may be relied upon by an undertaking subject to an investigation relating to competition law, no judgment of the European Court of Human Rights existing at the time indicated that this provision upholds the right not to give evidence against oneself.[37]

507. Nevertheless, the Court of Justice held that the Commission 'may not, by means of a decision calling for information, undermine the rights of defence of the undertakings concerned', and therefore, 'may not compel an undertaking to provide it with answers which might involve an admission on its part of the existence of an infringement which it is incumbent upon the Commission to prove'.[38]

508. Applying this test, the Court of Justice thus held that the Commission was allowed to use its mandatory powers of investigation to secure factual information, such as the circumstances in which meetings of producers were held or the subject-matter of measures taken by the undertakings concerned, and that the Commission could also require the disclosure of documents in the undertaking's possession, but that the Commission could not require an undertaking to answer

---

[31] Dissenting Opinion of Judge Martens, *Saunders v United Kingdom*, judment of the European Court of Human Rights of 17 December 1996, *Reports* 1996–VI, p 2064, para 4.

[32] Idem.

[33] As explained above, the Commission's powers under Regulation No 1/2003 are wider in two respects, namely the wider power to ask questions on the spot during inspections (Article 20(2)(e) of Regulation No 1/2003. See n 12 above) and the new power to search private homes (Article 21 of Regulation No 1/2003. See n 21 above).

[34] Judgment of 18 October 1989 in Case 374/87 *Orkem v Commission* [1989] ECR 3343.

[35] See Opinion of Advocate General Darmon of 18 May 1989 in the same case [1989] ECR 3301, paras 98–117.

[36] *Orkem* judgment, n 34above, para29.

[37] Idem, para 30.

[38] Idem, paras 34 and 35.

questions relating to the purpose or the objectives of measures taken which would compel it to admit its participation in a violation of EC antitrust law.[39]

509. In a series of judgments posterior to the judgment of the Court of Justice in *Orkem v Commission*, the European Court of Human Rights has held that the privilege against self-incrimination forms part of the notion of a fair procedure under Article 6 ECHR.[40]

510. According to the European Court of Human Rights, the rationale of the privilege against self-incrimination 'lies, inter alia, in the protection of the accused against improper compulsion by the authorities thereby contributing to the avoidance of miscarriages of justice and to the fulfilment of the aims of Article 6 [ECHR]'.[41]

511. As to the scope of protection offered by the privilege against self-incrimination, the European Court of Human Rights has held that,

[t]he right not to incriminate oneself is primarily concerned [...] with respecting the will of the accused person to remain silent. As commonly understood in the legal systems of the Contracting Parties to the Convention and elsewhere, it does not extend to the use in criminal proceedings of material obtained from the accused through the use of compulsory powers but which has an existence independent of the will of the suspect such as, inter alia, documents acquired pursuant to a warrant, breath, blood and urine samples and bodily tissue for the purpose of DNA testing.[42]

512. The European Court of Human Rights has further held that,

the right not to incriminate oneself cannot reasonably be confined to statements of admission of wrongdoing or to remarks which are directly incriminating. Testimony obtained under compulsion which appears on its face to be of a non-incriminating nature—such as exculpatory remarks or mere information on questions of fact—may later be deployed in criminal proceedings in support of the prosecution case, for example to contradict or cast doubt upon other statements of the accused or evidence given by him during the trial or to otherwise undermine his credibility. Where the credibility of an accused must be assessed by a jury the use of such testimony may be especially harmful. It follows that what is of the essence in the context is the use to which evidence obtained under compulsion is put in the course of the criminal trial.[43]

---

[39] Idem, paras 37–40. See also judgment of the Court of First Instance of 8 March 1995 in Case T–34/93, *Société Générale v Commission* [1995] ECR II–547, paras 75–76.

[40] *Funke v France* (25 February 1993, A/256–A); *John Murray v United Kingdom* (8 February 1996, Reports 1996–I, p 49); *Saunders v United Kingdom* (17 December 1996, Reports 1996–VI, p 2064); *Servès v France* (20 October 1997, Reports 1997–VI, p 2173); *Condron v United Kingdom* (2 May 2000, Application 35718/97); *Averill v United Kingdom* (6 June 2000, Application 36408/97); *Coëme and Others v Belgium* (22 June 2000, Applications nos 32492/96, 32547/96, 32548/96, 33209/96 and 33210/96); *IJL and Others v United Kingdom* (19 September 2000, Application nos 29522/95, 30056/96 and 30574/96); *Heaney and McGuinness v Ireland* (21 December 2000, Application 34720/97); *Quinn v Ireland* (21 December 2000, Application 36887/97); *JB v Switzerland* (3 May 2001, Application 31827/96); *PG and JH v United Kingdom* (25 September 2001, Application 44787/98); *Beckles v United Kingdom* (8 October 2002, Application 44652/98); and *Allan v United Kingdom* (5 November 2002, Application 48539/99).

[41] *Saunders v United Kingdom*, n 40 above, para 68.

[42] Idem, para 69.

[43] Idem, para 71.

513. Finally, the European Court of Human Rights has held that,

the general requirements of fairness contained in Article 6 [ECHR], including the right not to incriminate oneself, apply to criminal proceedings in respect of all types of criminal offences without distinction from the most simple to the most complex. The public interest cannot be invoked to justify the use of answers compulsorily obtained in a non-judicial investigation to incriminate the accused during the trial proceedings.[44]

514. It has repeatedly been argued by lawyers defending undertakings investigated by the Commission under Regulation No 17 that the judgment of the Court of Justice in *Orkem v Commission* would no longer be good law in the light of the subsequent case law of the European Court of Human Rights. The argument is based on the fact that the Court of Justice in *Orkem v Commission* allowed the Commission not only to use coercive powers to obtain existing documents from the undertaking being investigated, but also to use its mandatory powers to ask questions of a factual nature which do not compel the undertaking to give directly incriminating answers, whereas the case law of the European Court of Human Rights equally allows the use of compulsion to obtain existing documents but excludes the use in evidence of any answers obtained from the accused through compulsory questioning during a non-judicial investigation, including answers to purely factual questions.

515. In *Mannesmannröhren-Werke v Commission*, the Court of First Instance basically ignored this argument, and merely repeated the judgment of the Court of Justice in *Orkem v Commission*.[45] Most recently, in the *PVC II* case, the Court of Justice itself appeared to recognize as a matter of principle that it would have to take into account in its case law the developments in the case law of the European Court of Human Rights, but, given that in the case at hand no use had been made of any answers obtained under compulsion, the Court of Justice did not find it necessary to decide in that case whether *Orkem v Commission* is still good law.[46]

---

[44] Idem, para 74. See also *Heaney and McGuinness v Ireland*, n 40 above, paras 57–58.

[45] Judgment of the Court of First Instance of 20 February 2001 in Case T–112/98 *Mannesmannröhren-Werke v Commission* [2001] ECR II–732. The *Orkem* rule has also been recalled by the Council in Recital 23 of Regulation No 1/2003, which reads as follows:

The Commission should be empowered throughout the Community to require such information to be supplied as is necessary to detect any agreement, decision or concerted practice prohibited by Article 81 of the Treaty or any abuse of a dominant position prohibited by Article 82 of the Treaty. When complying with a decision of the Commission, undertakings cannot be forced to admit that they have committed an infringement, but they are in any event obliged to answer factual questions and to provide documents, even if this information may be used to establish against them or against another undertaking the existence of an infringement.

[46] Judgment of the Court of Justice of 15 October 2002 in Joined Cases C–238/99 P, C–244/99 P, C–245/99 P, C–247/99 P, C–250/99 P to C–252/99 P and C–254/99 P, *Limburgse Vinyl Maatschappij (LVM) and Others v Commission* [2002] ECR I–8618, paras 274–92. The need to take into account the case law of the European Court of Human Rights has also been recognised by the Council in Recital 37 of Regulation No 1/2003, which reads as follows: 'This Regulation respects the fundamental rights and observes the principles recognised in particular by the Charter of Fundamental Rights of the European Union. Accordingly, this Regulation should be interpreted and applied with respect to those rights ans principles.' As the Charter ([2000] OJ C364/1), through its Article 52(3) and its preamble, refers to the European Convention on Human Rights and the case law of the European Court of Human Rights, the need to take into account the case law of the European Court of Human Rights is thus recognised. See further ch 2 above.

516. It does not appear obvious that the *Orkem* case law of the Court of Justice could not be maintained in the light of the subsequent case law of the European Court of Human Rights. It is clear that in its judgments the European Court of Human Rights has objected to the use in evidence of any answers obtained from the accused through compulsory questioning during a non-judicial investigation, including answers to purely factual questions. It is also apparent from these judgments that the complexity of antitrust investigations or the public interest in detecting and punishing antitrust violations would probably not constitute acceptable justifications.[47] It should however be noted that all the judgments of the European Court of Human Rights concerned questions put to natural persons in investigations potentially leading to those natural persons being convicted to imprisonment or other sanctions in criminal trials. It is not obvious that the European Court of Human Rights would grant the same scope of protection under the privilege against self-incrimination to legal persons in proceedings such as those under Regulation No 17 or Regulation No 1/2003, to the extent that these proceedings can only lead to the imposition of fines on legal persons.[48]

517. In those Member States whose national law allows the imposition of criminal sanctions on natural persons for violations of Articles 81 or 82 EC or for related offences, the stricter case law of the European Court of Human Rights is of course applicable to the corresponding investigations by national competition authorities.[49]

518. The Commission would probably also have to follow the stricter case law of the European Court of Human Rights if ever it were to investigate an infringement of Articles 81 or 82 EC committed by an undertaking consisting of an unincorporated business (a single trader, with or without employees, who has not incorporated his or her business, or a professional exercising his or her profession alone and unincorporated, or several natural persons operating a single business without any employment relationship between them and without any form of legal person).[50]

519. The fact that under Article 20(2)(e) of Regulation No 1/2003 the Commission can ask questions to staff members of the undertaking or association being investigated[51] does not appear relevant, given that Regulation No 1/2003 does not allow any penalty to be imposed on such staff members, and that the information thus obtained by the Commission could not under Article 12 of the

---

[47] See n 44 above.

[48] In the United States, corporations are not protected under the Fifth Amendment privilege against self-incrimination; *Braswell v United States* 487 US 99 (1988). See also n 35 and n 36 above as to the laws of the (12 oldest) Member States of the European Union, and para 548 below.

[49] See n 27 above for the case of the United Kingdom. Moreover, national law may grant a wider scope of protection against self-incrimination in investigations by national competition authorities than available under *Orkem v Commission* or than required under Article 6 ECHR. See *Mannesmannröhren-Werke v Commission*, n 45 above, paras 80–81, as to German law.

[50] This situation has however apparently never occurred. See *The Optimal Enforcement of EC Antitrust Law*, n 26 above, section 8.1.1.

[51] See n 12 above.

regulation be used in evidence by national authorities to impose on natural persons custodial sanctions or any other sanction of a nature which would make the stricter case law of the European Court of Human Rights applicable.

5.1.3 Leniency

520. Under the instrument of leniency, the competition authorities invite undertakings or members of their staff to come forward and voluntarily provide information in exchange for immunity from punishment or reduced punishment.

521. The Commission has set out its current leniency policy in a notice published on 19 February 2002 (hereafter: 'the Commission's leniency notice' or 'the notice').[52] The Commission's leniency notice only concerns certain types of violations of Article 81 EC, namely 'secret cartels between two or more competitors aimed at fixing prices, production or sales quotas, sharing markets including bid-rigging or restricting imports or exports'.[53]

522. According to points 8 to 11 of the notice, 'the Commission will grant an undertaking immunity from any fine which would otherwise have been imposed' in two cases:

(a) 'the undertaking is the first to submit evidence which in the Commission's view may enable it to adopt a decision to carry out an [inspection in the sense of Article 20(4) of Regulation No 1/2003]' and 'the Commission did not have, at the time of the submission, sufficient evidence to adopt [such] a decision […]', or

(b) 'the undertaking is the first to submit evidence which in the Commission's view may enable it to find an infringement of Article 81 EC', while 'the Commission did not have, at the time of the submission, sufficient evidence to find [such] an infringement […]' and 'no undertaking had been granted […] immunity' under (a).

523. In either case, three additional conditions must be fulfilled: (1) the undertaking cooperates fully, on a continuous basis and expeditiously throughout the Commission's administrative procedure and provides the Commission with all evidence that comes into its possession or is available to it relating to the suspected infringement. In particular, it remains at the Commission's disposal to answer swiftly any request that may contribute to the establishment of the facts concerned, (2) the undertaking ends its involvement in the suspected infringement no later than the time at which it submits evidence […], and (3) the undertaking did not take steps to coerce other undertakings to participate in the infringement.

---

[52] Commission notice on immunity from fines and reduction of fines in cartel cases, [2002] OJ C45/3. This notice has replaced the earlier Commission notice on the non-imposition of fines or reduction of fines in cartel cases, [1996] OJ C207/4.
[53] Idem, para 1.

524. According to points 20 to 23 of the notice,

undertakings that do not meet the conditions [for immunity from fines] may be eligible
to benefit from a reduction of any fine that would otherwise have been imposed. In order
to qualify, an undertaking must provide the Commission with evidence of the suspected
infringement which represents significant added value with respect to the evidence
already in the Commission's possession and must terminate its involvement in the suspected infringement no later than the time at which it submits the evidence.

The level of reduction of the fine will be determined essentially on the basis of
the timing of the submission of the evidence and the amount of added value which
the evidence represents to the Commission. The first undertaking will receive 'a
reduction of 30–50%', the second 'a reduction of 20–30%' and subsequent undertakings 'a reduction of up to 20%'.

In addition, if an undertaking provides evidence relating to facts previously
unknown to the Commission which have a direct bearing on the gravity or the
duration of the suspected cartel, the Commission will not take these elements into
account when setting any fine to be imposed on the undertaking which provided
this evidence.

525. According to point 29 of the notice: 'The Commission is aware that this
notice will create legitimate expectations on which undertakings may rely when
disclosing the existence of a cartel to the Commission.'

526. The Commission's use of the instrument of leniency has been approved by
the Court of Justice. Indeed, the Court of Justice has held that,

Article 15(2) of Regulation No 17 does not lay down an exhaustive list of the criteria
which the Commission must take into account when fixing the amount of the fine. [...]
The conduct of the undertaking during the administrative procedure may therefore be
one of the factors to be taken into account when fixing that fine [...]. Moreover, the
Commission cannot be criticised for having adopted guidelines to direct the exercise of
its discretion concerning the fixing of fines, and for thus better ensuring equal treatment
of the undertakings concerned.[54]

527. The Court of Justice has rejected the argument that the use of the instrument of leniency would be contrary to fundamental rights:

Nor [...] can the complaint of infringement of the rights of defence be upheld. An undertaking which, when challenging the Commission's stance, limits its cooperation to that
which is required under Regulation No 17 will not, on that ground, have an increased fine
imposed on it. If the Commission considers that it has proved the existence of an infringement and that the infringement can be imputed to the undertaking, the undertaking will
be fined in accordance with criteria which may lawfully be taken into account and which
are subject to review by the Court of First Instance or the Court of Justice.[55]

---

[54] Judgment of the Court of Justice of 16 November 2000 in Case C–298/98 P *Metsä-Serla
(Finnboard) v Commission* [2000] ECR I–10171, paras 56 and 57. The Court's reasoning remains
equally valid under Regulation No 1/2003, Article 23(2) of Regulation No 1/2003 being identical in this
respect to Article 15(2) of Regulation No 17.
[55] Idem, para 58.

528. The use of the instrument of leniency does not raise any objections either with regard to the privilege against self-incrimination as recognised in the case law of the European Court of Human Rights. Indeed: 'Persons are always free to incriminate themselves if in doing so they are exercising their own will'.[56] Nor does legal professional privilege stand in the way of lawyer-client communications being produced in the framework of leniency, since 'the principle of confidentiality does not prevent a lawyer's client from disclosing the written communications between them if it considers that it is in his interest to do so'.[57]

529. The Commission's leniency notice only concerns the Commission itself. Some national competition authorities have their own leniency policy, others have none.[58] In those Member States where national law provides for criminal sanctions for natural persons in relation to violations of Articles 81 or 82 EC, a leniency policy may also exist for natural persons who have committed such criminal offences.[59]

5.2   AN ECONOMIC ANALYSIS

530. In order to create deterrence, and thus to ensure that the antitrust prohibitions are not or less often violated, the competition authorities need to detect and punish violations.[60] The logic of deterrence is to create a credible threat of sanction in case of violation, so as to alter the potential antitrust violator's cost/benefit calculation, and thus make him or her refrain from committing antitrust violations. For deterrence to be effective, the expected sanction must exceed the expected benefit of the violation. The expected sanction depends on the probability that the violation will be detected and successfully prosecuted, as well as on the sanction which will then be imposed.[61] Hence the importance of detecting violations and collecting the necessary evidence to enable the imposition of sanctions.

531. Detecting antitrust violations and collecting the necessary evidence to have them punished is a costly activity. It consumes not only the resources of the competition authorities or other authorities which help in the investigation, but also imposes significant costs on the undertakings or persons subjected to the investigations. These costs should be weighed against the benefit in terms of

---

[56] Concurring Opinion of Judge Walsh in *Saunders v United Kingdom*, n 40 above. See also *The Optimal Enforcement of EC Antitrust Law*, n 26 above, section 3.5.2.

[57] *AM & S v Commission*, n 23 above, para 28.

[58] As argued in section 3.5.2 above, it would appear desirable for leniency policies to be harmonized, either spontaneously or by regulation, within the European Competition Network, and such harmonization is likely to happen under the pressure of the principle of *ne bis in idem*. See also section 1.2.14 above.

[59] See in the case of the United Kingdom: Enterprise Act Guidance, *The cartel offence: Guidance on the issue of no-action letters for individuals* (April 2003), accessible at http://www.oft.gov.uk.

[60] On the role of deterrence in relation to other objectives of antitrust enforcement, see section 4.2 above.

[61] See further *The Optimal Enforcement of EC Antitrust Law*, n 26 above, in particular section 2.1.3.

increased deterrence, so as to determine which investigatory measures are justified. In any event, whenever the same benefit in terms of increased deterrence can be achieved through different means, the least costly method should be preferred.

532. For certain types of antitrust violations, in particular exclusionary practices, but also non-covert exploitative practices, the competition authorities may be able to obtain at relatively low cost the necessary intelligence and evidence through interested third parties.[62] For other types of violations, however, in particular for secret price cartels, the undertakings that committed the violations and their staff may be the only ones holding the information which the competition authorities need to detect and punish these violations.

533. Competition authorities could use three possible methods to obtain the necessary intelligence and evidence from the undertakings that committed the antitrust violations or from their staff. First, they could use direct, physical force to obtain evidence in the hands of the undertakings or their staff. Secondly, they could use compulsion in the form of threatened sanctions for refusal to cooperate to make the undertakings and their staff provide the necessary information. Thirdly, instead of using the 'stick' of threatened sanctions for non-cooperation, they could also create incentives to cooperate by using the 'carrot' of a promise of immunity or reduced punishment in case of cooperation. The effectiveness and costs of these three methods are discussed in the following three sections.

5.2.1 Direct Force

534. The competition authorities can try to obtain information from the undertakings that committed the antitrust violations or from their staff by using direct, physical force, ie by forcibly entering the premises of the undertakings or the homes of their staff and taking the documents, computer files or other records they find there. As described above, the Commission has such powers under Articles 20 and 21 of Regulation No 1/2003, or at least can call upon the assistance of the Member States to use such powers.[63]

---

[62] These third parties have an incentive to help the competition authorities, so as to bring to an end violations from which they suffer. The possibility of obtaining damages following the establishment of the violation by the competition authorities may provide an additional incentive. The latter consideration could provide an argument in favour of encouraging private follow-on actions for damages, an argument not considered in ch 4 above. The strength of this argument depends however on the questions whether there is indeed a need for such an additional incentive on top of the existing incentive to avoid the continuation of the harm suffered from the violation (see KG Elzinga and W Breit, *The Antitrust Penalties: A Study in Law and Economics* (Yale Univertiy Press, 1976) 143–44; S Shavell, 'The Optimal Structure of Law Enforcement' (1993) 36 *Journal of Law and Economics* 255, 267–70) and whether or not the costs of such private damages actions outweigh the benefit resulting from the additional incentive to help the competition authorities, or are higher than the cost of the competition authorities' collecting the same information using their mandatory investigative powers.

[63] Paras 491–96 above.

535. This method has at least two drawbacks. Firstly, it can only be used to obtain existing documents or other existing physical or electronic evidence. Secondly, without help from the undertakings or staff concerned, and unless the competition authorities already have precise intelligence as to what documents or records they can find at what exact place, the method is a very expensive one, in that the authorities would have to go through many documents, files or records before finding relevant information.

536. More generally, even if the authorities have the necessary intelligence to make a more narrowly focused search, the method is generally a costly one, because of resources needed on the side of the competition authorities and the police or other authorities assisting them, and because of the substantial cost which it imposes on the undertakings and their staff subjected to the search, including both the economic cost flowing from the disruption of their business activities and the psychic cost resulting from the invasion of their privacy. As far as the cost to the competition authorities themselves is concerned, one can expect these authorities, whose resources are limited, fully to take this into account when deciding to use their search powers.[64] However, as they do not bear the costs imposed on the undertakings and staff subjected to the investigation, the authorities, if left to decide on their own, risk making excessive use of their search powers. Hence the need to have a control mechanism, such as a possibility for those subjected to the search to have the search decision judicially reviewed or the requirement for the authorities to obtain judicial authorisation before conducting a search, so as to ensure that the expected benefit from the search, in terms of gathered information and ultimately increased deterrence, exceeds its expected costs.[65] As described above, such control mechanisms are indeed provided for in Community law and under the European Convention on Human Rights.[66] These control mechanisms however add further cost to this method of collecting information.

5.2.2 Compulsion

537. In order to avoid the limitations and costs of the first method of obtaining information through the direct use of force, competition authorities could alternatively try to make the undertakings cooperate in handing over the information sought by using compulsion in the form of threatened sanctions for refusal to cooperate.

---

[64] One should however also consider the risk that the competition authorities would for whatever reason want to use their search powers for other purposes than the purpose of detecting and punishing antitrust violations. See n 65 below.

[65] Such control mechanism can at the same time address the risk of abuse of search powers for other purposes. See n 64 above.

[66] Paras 493 and 495 above. Proportionality is the main legal heading under which the expected benefit and costs are weighed.

538. The threatened sanctions for refusal to cooperate could be of two kinds. Refusal to cooperate with investigations could be punished as a separate offence, and such refusal could also be punished through an increase in the amount of punishment imposed for the antitrust violations established following the investigation.

539. To have the effect of inducing the undertakings or persons concerned to cooperate with the investigation, the expected penalties for refusal to cooperate must outweigh the expected costs of cooperation for the undertaking or person concerned. These costs essentially consist of the increased expected sanctions for the antitrust violation, as the cooperation will increase the probability of the violation being detected and punished.[67]

540. As described above, Articles 18 and 20 of Regulation No 1/2003 provide for obligations to cooperate with requests for information and inspections ordered by Commission decisions, under the threat of fines and periodic penalty payments for refusal to cooperate, or possibly increased fines for the antitrust violations established following the investigation.[68]

541. Compared with the first method of direct force, the second method of making the undertaking or its staff cooperate through the threat of punishment for non-cooperation has two advantages. Firstly, its use is not limited to obtaining information contained in already existing documents or records. Indeed, the undertaking or its staff can be induced not only to hand over such documents or records, but also to provide in response to questions information which is not contained in any existing physical records. Secondly, the method is less costly in that the undertaking and its staff will be able to locate or bring together more easily the required elements of information than the competition authorities' inspectors searching without help through a mass of business records with which they are unfamiliar.

542. The method of inducing cooperation through the threat of sanctions also has its problems, however. Firstly, as in the case of the first method of direct force, the competition authorities already need to have some level of intelligence concerning the antitrust violation. Indeed, if the authorities know very little about the violation, they would only be able to make wide, unfocussed requests for cooperation. The undertakings or their staff would understand from the vagueness of the request that the authorities know very little, and that they would thus have a good chance of getting away with only pretending to cooperate and giving misleading answers, as the authorities would not be able to establish a refusal to cooperate, and the threat of sanctions for non-cooperation would thus not be credible.

543. Secondly, even if this second method has the above mentioned advantage of lower search costs, in that the undertaking and its staff are more familiar with the business records than the competition authorities' inspectors, it still imposes a

[67] The expected sanctions include the sanctions which the investigation authority may impose or seek to have imposed, as well as possible follow-on private damages awards or sanctions imposed in other jurisdictions.
[68] Paras 490, 492 and 498 above.

significant cost on the undertakings and staff concerned, including the economic cost in terms of resources spent on complying with the requests for cooperation as well as the psychic cost where individuals are subjected to on the spot oral questions for explanations. As with the first method of direct force, the fact that significant costs are imposed on the undertakings and staff subjected to the investigation entails the risk that the competition authorities, if left to decide on their own, would make excessive use of their powers. Hence again the need for a control mechanism to ensure that the expected benefit of the use of compulsion, in terms of gathered information and ultimately increased deterrence, exceeds its expected costs.[69] As explained above, under Regulation No 1/2003 undertakings have the right to seek judicial review of decisions requesting information or ordering inspections.[70]

544. Because of the psychic cost imposed on individuals who are subjected to on the spot oral questions for explanations under compulsion, a cost which is likely to be especially high if the information obtained through this questioning could possibly be used as evidence to prosecute that same individual for a criminal offence, additional restrictions on the authorities' using such questioning may be needed. As explained above, the privilege against self-incrimination, as recognised by the European Court of Human Rights on the basis of Article 6 ECHR, prohibits the use in evidence against an individual in criminal proceedings of any answers obtained from the accused through compulsory questioning during a non-judicial investigation.[71] As explained above, whereas under Article 20(2)(e) of Regulation No 1/2003 the Commission can in the course of an inspection ask on the spot oral questions to staff members of the undertaking or association under investigation, the regulation does not allow any penalty to be imposed on such staff members, and the information thus obtained by the Commission could not under Article 12 of the regulation be used in evidence by national authorities to impose on natural persons custodial sanctions or any other sanction of a nature which would make the stricter case law of the European Court of Human Rights applicable.[72]

545. Thirdly, the problem of reliability constitutes a specific drawback of the second method of obtaining information under compulsion. Information obtained under compulsion may be unreliable for two sets of reasons. On the one hand, as already explained in the discussion of the first problem above, undertakings that have indeed committed antitrust violations or their staff may give misleading answers when questioned, in the hope of wrongfooting the investigating authorities and thus escaping detection and punishment. The threat of sanctions for untruthful answers may not be effective to the extent that the authorities are believed not to be able to obtain the necessary information to establish the

---

[69] Again such control mechanisms could at the same time address the risk of abuse of powers for other purposes than the purpose of detecting and punishing antitrust violations. See n 64 and n 65 above.

[70] Para 489 and n 22 above.

[71] Paras 509–13 above.

[72] Para 519 above. See also n 7 above with regard to the 'power to take statements' provided for in Article 19 of Regulation No 1/2003.

untruthfulness. On the other hand, where the undertakings or persons being investigated are in reality innocent, there is a risk that ingenious questioning will lead less sophisticated respondents to make seemingly inculpatory statements, or, in situations of on the spot oral questioning where psychological or physical pressure is created or felt, the individuals questioned may end up making untruthful inculpatory statements so as to escape from the pressure.

546. The risk of obtaining unreliable information depends essentially on two factors, namely the type of information sought and the context in which the compulsion takes place. As to the type of information sought, there is a relatively low risk of unreliability if existing documents or other physical evidence are asked for, as the content of such evidence is not affected by the nature of the questioning or the nature and the impact of the compulsion used to obtain it. Conversely, there is a higher risk of unreliability of answers to questions other than requests for existing documents or other physical evidence, in particular if the information sought is not of a purely factual nature but rather concerns more subjective notions such as intentions, objectives, motives or purposes. As to the context in which the compulsion takes place, there is obviously a much lower risk of unreliable answers if the questions are addressed in writing to a sophisticated company, which can take the time to prepare a written answer with the help of its lawyers, than where a common criminal is subjected to on the spot questioning in a police station.

547. The problem of the guilty providing misleadingly exculpatory information when questioned under compulsion does not seem to create a need for a specific legal rule, as the competition authorities spontaneously have an incentive to question the truthfulness of exculpatory statements.[73] On the other hand, the problem of the innocent making seemingly inculpatory statements needs to be addressed, as it risks leading to false convictions.[74]

548. The privilege against self-incrimination, as recognised in the case law of the Court of Justice and the European Court of Human Rights, indeed addresses this problem of unreliable inculpatory statements.[75] The low risk of unreliability with existing documents or other physical evidence explains why the case law of both courts allows the use of compulsion to obtain such evidence. Given the lower

---

[73] A justification for regulation may however exist if, because of a pooling effect, the fact that guilty suspects make false exculpatory statements would undermine the credibility of exculpatory statements by innocent suspects. See DJ Seidman and A Stein, 'The Right to Silence Helps the Innocent: A Game—Theoretic Analysis of the Fifth Amendment Privilege' (2000) 114 *Harvard Law Review* 430.

[74] False convictions are obviously undesirable, in that they entail costs (including the suffering of the wrongly convicted, the administrative costs of the proceedings, and the weakening of deterrence through reduction of the difference in expected punishment for illegal conduct as compared to legal conduct) without any benefit.

[75] It also simultaneously addresses the problem of unreliable exculpatory statements, to the extent that there is a need for this. See n 73 above. As explained above (para 544), the privilege against self-incrimination has not only the function of excluding the use of unreliable information but also the function of preventing the imposition of excessive psychic cost on individuals being questioned under compulsion. The view that these are the (only) two purposes of the privilege against self-incrimination has also been expressed i.a. by Judge Martens of the European Court of Human Rights in his Dissenting Opinion in *Saunders v United Kingdom*, n 31 above, para 8, and by AR Amar and RB Lettow, 'Fifth Amendment First Principles: The Self-Incrimination Clause' (1995) 93 *Michigan Law Review* 857.

risk of unreliability for answers to purely factual questions than for answers to questions relating to more subjective notions such as the purpose or objectives of conduct, and given that requests for information under Article 18 of Regulation No 1/2003 are addressed in writing to companies, which can take the time to prepare a written answer with the help of their lawyers, it also makes sense that the case law of the Court of Justice allows the Commission to use its mandatory powers to ask questions of a factual nature which do not compel the undertaking to give directly incriminating answers, whereas the case law of the European Court of Human Rights, which applies to individuals at risk of criminal convictions and to the use of compulsion in various contexts, for instance oral questioning in police custody, excludes the use in evidence of any answers obtained from the accused through compulsory questioning during a non-judicial investigation, including answers to purely factual questions.[76]

5.2.3 Leniency

549. Instead of using the threat of sanctions for refusal to cooperate so as to induce undertakings that have committed antitrust violations or their staff to hand over the necessary intelligence and evidence to establish the antitrust violations, competition authorities can try to create incentives for cooperation by offering in return immunity or reduced punishment for the antitrust violations.

550. Compared to the first and second method, direct force and compulsion, this third method has clear advantages. Indeed, contrary to the first method, it can be used to obtain all kinds of information, not just existing documents or other existing physical evidence. Like the second method, it saves on search costs in that the collecting of relevant information is done by the undertaking and its staff, who are most familiar with it. But contrary to the second method, it does not suffer from the same reliability problems, as there is no clear incentive for the cooperating undertakings or persons to provide unreliable information, given that they risk losing the benefit of immunity or reduced punishment if they provide misleading information and given that immunity from punishment is the highest benefit they can obtain.[77]

---

[76] Paras 514–16 above.

[77] See also Opinion of Advocate General Mischo of 18 May 2000 in Case C–298/98 P *Finnboard v Commission* [2000] ECR I–10159, paras 24–27. In his paper 'Optimal Leniency Programs' (13 May 2000, accessible at http://papers.ssrn.com/sol3/papers.cfm?abstract_id=235092), G Spagnolo has argued in favour of a system where self-reporting parties would be granted not just immunity but also a positive bounty, in particular the proceeds of the fines subsequently imposed on the other parties. The argument is based on a belief that such additional benefits are necessary to make leniency programs effective. I would disagree with both the perceived problem and the proposed solution. Practical experience with leniency policy, both in the United States and in the European Community, does not suggest that the offer of immunity is insufficient to induce self-reporting. See also OECD, n 26 above. As to the proposed grant of positive bounties, in particular the proceeds of the fines imposed on co-violators, it would create a serious risk of undertakings or persons providing unreliable information to the competition authorities in the hope of obtaining the bounty, with the resulting risk of false convictions. The proposal would thus remove one of the major benefits of leniency as a method to collect information, namely the absence of serious reliability problems.

551. However, for leniency to be effective in inducing undertakings or their staff to cooperate, they must expect to be better off when cooperating than when not cooperating. Whether or not this will be the case, will depend in the first place on the probability of the antitrust violation being detected and the undertaking or person being punished if they do not cooperate. This probability depends on the ability of the competition authorities to find the necessary intelligence and evidence themselves through the use of force or compulsion,[78] as well as on how the leniency policy is set up. In particular if the benefit of immunity is restricted to the single first cartel member to self-report, each cartel member may be made to fear that another cartel member will be the first to cooperate with the competition authorities. Whether an undertaking or person will be better off when cooperating than when not cooperating will further depend on the size of the sanctions which can be avoided by cooperating and on the size of the sanctions or other costs which the undertaking or person will have to bear as a consequence of its violation becoming established. For instance, the presence of prison sanctions in the United States and some EU Member States increases the incentive to cooperate in comparison with those parts of Europe where only fines are imposed for antitrust violations, whereas the relative absence of private damages suits in Europe increases the incentive to cooperate in European leniency programs.[79] The costs of cooperation also include possible sanctions in other jurisdictions, to the extent that the cooperation in one jurisdiction will have the result of alerting competition authorities in other jurisdictions and that leniency cannot be obtained simultaneously in those other jurisdictions,[80] as well as possible private actions in other jurisdictions,[81] loss of profits from the continuation of the cartel, and possible reprisals by other cartel members.

552. Whereas the leniency offered must be sufficient to make the cooperating undertaking or person expect to be better off when cooperating than when not cooperating, the use of the instrument of leniency only makes sense from the perspective of antitrust enforcement if its overall effect on deterrence is positive. This explains why the Commission's leniency notice only applies to cartels,[82] which involve always at least two parties, and why immunity is only available to the

---

[78] Leniency does thus not allow to dispense with the other two methods of obtaining information from antitrust violators.

[79] Unless the sanctions against which immunity can be obtained are correspondingly increased, in particular through the introduction of prison sanctions, the effectiveness of leniency in Europe would thus suffer from any attempts to stimulate private enforcement of the EC antitrust prohibitions. See further n 3 and n 26 above.

[80] See n 58 above.

[81] See pp 12–13 of the brief for the United States and the Federal Trade Commission as amici curiae in support of petition for rehearing en banc in the US Court of Appeals for the District of Columbia in *Empagran v Hoffmann-LaRoche* (23 March 2003), accessible at http://www.usdoj.gov/atr/cases/f200800/200866.pdf.

[82] The Commission's Guidelines on the method of setting fines, n 24 above, under para 3, sixth indent, however also provide for the possibility to take into account as an attenuating circumstance in the calculation of the fine 'effective cooperation by the undertaking concerned, outside the scope of [the leniency notice]'; for an example, see the Commission's Decision of 30 October 2002 in Case COMP/35.706 *Nintendo*, press release IP/02/1584.

single first party to self-report, thus ensuring that for every party granted immunity at least one other party will be punished. Even for cartels with only two participants, the overall effect on deterrence will still be positive, as the cartel participants, when deciding to enter into the cartel arrangement or to continue it, will face uncertainty as to which of the two will be the first to self-report.[83] Similarly, the fact that under the Commission's leniency notice fine reductions are only granted to the extent that the cooperation represents significant added value to the investigation serves to ensure that the overall effect on deterrence remains positive.[84]

553. Comparing finally the three methods to obtain intelligence and evidence from undertakings that committed antitrust violations and from their staff (direct force, compulsion and leniency), it appears that a combination of these instruments is required for effective and efficient antitrust enforcement. The effectiveness of both direct force and compulsion is limited by the need for initial intelligence. Leniency allows this limitation to be overcome. Moreover, leniency suffers neither from the limitation to existing physical or electronic evidence and the high search costs which characterize the use of direct force nor from the reliability problems which affect the use of compulsion. However, leniency will only work if cartel participants perceive a risk that the competition authorities will detect the antitrust violation without recourse to leniency, and granting immunity to a self-reporting antitrust violator only makes sense if this allows at least one other violator to be punished. The instrument of leniency therefore does not make it possible to dispense with the other two methods of obtaining information from antitrust violators.

---

[83] See also OECD, n 26 above; and *The Optimal Enforcement of EC Antitrust Law*, n 26 above, sections 3.3.4 and 3.4.

[84] See n 52 above. In this respect the Commission's current leniency notice clearly improves on its predecessor. See *The Optimal Enforcement of EC Antitrust Law*, n 26 above, section 3.4.3.

6

The Combination of the Investigative and Prosecutorial Function and the Adjudicative Function

6.1 INTRODUCTION

6.1.1 Overview

554. In the current system of EC antitrust enforcement, the European Commission combines the investigative and prosecutorial function with the adjudicative or decision-making function.[1] The purpose of this chapter is to analyse the advantages and disadvantages of this system, in comparison with a system in which the adjudicative function is separated from the investigative and prosecutorial function, such as the US system in which the Department of Justice or the Federal Trade Commission (under the pre-merger notification programme) investigates and prosecutes before a federal court.[2]

555. This introductory section 6.1 contains a description of the current EC system, a comparative description of the US system (or rather the US systems, as there are two), an overview of the legal debate on the compatibility of the current EC system with Article 6 of the European Convention on Human Rights (ECHR) and on the scope for change under the current EC Treaty, and an introduction to the wider policy debate, identifying the criteria for choosing the better system, namely accuracy and administrative cost.

---

[1] It could be argued that in the current EC system there is not really a prosecutorial function, only investigative and adjudicative functions. The prosecutorial function only emerges in a system in which the adjudicative function is separated from the investigative function. However, this does not alter the analysis in this chapter, as I do not distinguish between an investigative function and a prosecutorial function, but rather consider the investigative and prosecutorial function as a single function.

[2] Section 1.2.10 above deals with the question how Regulation No 1/2003 accomodates the differences which exist between the Commission and the competition authorities of the various Member States as to the combination or separation of the investigative, prosecutorial and adjudicative functions.

6.1.2 The Current EC System

556. Even if they are very similar, it may be useful to describe separately the existing rules as to the enforcement of Articles 81 and 82 EC, on the one hand, and
under the EC Merger Regulation, on the other hand.

6.1.2.1 Articles 81 and 82 EC

557. The basic rules concerning the enforcement of the prohibition on restrictive
agreements (Article 81 EC) and of the prohibition on abuse of a dominant position (Article 82 EC) are laid down in Regulation No 1/2003.[3] The European
Commission has considerable powers to detect and investigate possible violations
of Articles 81 or 82 EC. Where it considers that it has found evidence of such a violation, it addresses to the companies concerned a statement of objections, setting
out its preliminary findings. The companies have the opportunity to respond both
in writing and at an oral hearing to the allegations set out in the statement of objections. If the Commission considers that its preliminary findings can be maintained, it then adopts a decision finding an infringement of Articles 81 or 82 EC,
ordering its termination and/or imposing fines (up to 10% of annual turnover) on
the companies concerned.

558. The Commission's decision is binding upon the undertakings to whom it
is addressed. They can however bring an action for annulment of the decision
before the Court of First Instance of the European Communities. The application
for annulment can be based on both factual and legal grounds. A further appeal,
on legal grounds alone, lies before the Court of Justice of the European
Communities. Actions before the Community Courts have no suspensory effect,
but the companies can add to their application for annulment a request for suspension of the application of the Commission's decision or for other interim measures. Such a request will however only be granted by the Courts if it is established
that their adoption is *prima facie* justified in fact and in law, that their adoption is
necessary to avoid serious and irreparable damage, and that the balance of interests favours such an order. With regard to fines, the Commission has developed a
practice of allowing companies that have brought an action for annulment before
the Courts to avoid paying the fine immediately, on condition that they provide
an acceptable bank guarantee covering both the fine and subsequent interest.

559. As a matter of internal organisation within the Commission, the investi-
gation is conducted by officials of the Commission's Directorate-General for
Competition (hereafter: 'DG Competition'), working under the authority of the
Member of the Commission with special responsibility for competition matters

---

[3] Council Regulation (EC) No 1/2003 of 16 December 2002 on the implementation of the rules on
competition laid down in Articles 81 and 82 of the Treaty, [2003] OJ L1/1. Since 1 May 2004, this
Regulation has replaced Council Regulation No 17 of 6 February 1962, [1962] OJ 13/204 (Special
English Edition 1959–62, p 87).

(hereafter: 'the Competition Commissioner'). The sending of a statement of objections is normally decided by the Competition Commissioner, after consultation of the Commission's Legal Service, which operates under the authority of the President of the Commission, and, where appropriate, also after consultation of other Commission services. The oral hearing is presided by a Hearing Officer, an official who does not belong to DG Competition but who also reports to the Competition Commissioner. The hearing is not attended by any Member of the Commission, but rather by the officials from DG Competition dealing with the case, sometimes by officials from other Commission services, and by officials of the Member States. The Commission's final decision is drafted by officials from DG Competition, normally the same officials who conducted the investigation and drafted the statement of objections. It is adopted by majority vote by the Commission, on a proposal of the Competition Commissioner, and after consultation of the Legal Service and sometimes other Commission services, as well as of the Advisory Committee, composed of officials of the Member States.

560. The internal organisation of DG Competition has recently been strengthened in two respects.[4] First, a new position of Chief Competition Economist has been created. The Chief Competition Economist, who is assisted by a team of specialised economists, provides economic guidance in individual cases throughout the investigation process. He reports to the Director-General of DG Competition and presents his views to the Competition Commissioner. In agreement with the Director-General, he may also provide a written opinion to be submitted to the Commission together with the proposed final decision. Second, a system of peer review panels has been introduced. The peer review panel, composed of experienced officials, scrutinises the case team's conclusions with a 'fresh pair of eyes'. The panel reports to the Director-General of DG Competition and presents its views to the Competition Commissioner. As a rule, the peer review takes place before the sending of the statement of objections is decided, normally in all cases applying Article 82 EC and, where appropriate, also in cases applying Article 81 EC, but in principle not in cartel cases.

6.1.2.2 The EC Merger Regulation

561. The basic rules concerning merger control are laid down in the EC Merger Regulation.[5] Concentrations (mergers or acquisitions) with a Community dimension must be notified to the Commission. The concentration cannot be put into effect either before its notification or until it has been cleared by the Commission.

---

[4] See speech by Commissioner Monti, 'EU Competition Policy After May 1994', at the 30th Annual Fordham Conference on International Law and Policy (New York, 24 October 2003), available at http://www.europa.eu.int/comm/competition/speeches.

[5] Council Regulation (EC) No 139/2004 of 20 January 2004 on the control of concentrations between undertakings (the EC Merger Regulation), [2004] OJ L24/1. Since 1 May 2004, this Regulation has replaced Council Regulation (EEC) No 4064/89 of 21 December 1989 on the control of concentrations between undertakings, [1990] OJ L257/13, amended by Council Regulation (EC) No 1301/97 of 30 June 1997, [1997] OJ L180/1.

Within a first phase of 25 working days following the notification (a period which can be extended to 35 working days if the companies concerned propose modifications to their plans so as to remove competition concerns), the Commission must either take a clearance decision or, if it has serious doubts, an Article 6(1)(c) decision, opening a second phase investigation. If, in the course of the second phase investigation, the Commission comes to the preliminary view that the proposed concentration would significantly impede effective competition, it must address to the companies concerned a statement of objections, setting out its findings. The companies have the opportunity to respond both in writing and at an oral hearing. At the latest 90 working days after the opening of the second phase (a period which can be extended to 105 working days if the companies concerned propose modifications to their plans so as to remove competition concerns), the Commission must adopt a final decision, either authorising the concentration (possibly subject to divestments or other commitments proposed by the companies concerned) or prohibiting it.

562. As with decisions applying Articles 81 or 82 EC, the Commission's decision is binding upon the undertakings to whom it is addressed, but they can bring an action for annulment of the decision before the Court of First Instance, on both factual and legal grounds, with a possible further appeal before the Court of Justice only on legal grounds. There are no specific deadlines within which the Courts have to reach judgment, and the action for annulment has no suspensory effect, unless the Courts grant a request for suspension or other interim measures, which is only possible under strict conditions. If the Courts annul the Commission's decision in a merger case, the case is returned back to the Commission, which must reexamine the notification and take a new decision, under the same 25 working days and 90 working days deadlines for the first and second phases of the investigation. The concentration cannot be put into effect until it has been cleared by the Commission.

563. As to the Commission's internal organisation in merger cases, the situation is similar to that regarding cases under Articles 81 or 82 EC. A team of officials from DG Competition, working under the authority of the Competition Commissioner, conducts the investigation, drafts the Article 6(1)(c) decision and the statement of objections, attends the hearing (presided by a Hearing Officer and normally also attended by officials from other Commission services, as well as by officials of the Member States), conducts possible negotiations over commitments, and drafts the final decision. The Article 6(1)(c) decision is normally adopted by the Competition Commissioner, in agreement with the President of the Commission, and after consultation of the Legal Service and, where appropriate, also other Commission services. The statement of objections is normally adopted by the Competition Commissioner alone, after the same consultations. The final decision is adopted by majority vote by the Commission, on proposal by the Competition Commissioner, and after the same consultations, as well as consultation of the Advisory Committee.

564. The recent strengthening of the internal organisation of DG Competition through the creation of the position of Chief Competition Economist and the

introduction of a system of peer review panels affects merger cases in the same way as cases under Articles 81 and 82 EC.[6] As a rule, the peer review takes place before the sending of the statement of objections is decided.

6.1.3 The US System(s)

565. In discussions on the combination of the investigative and prosecutorial function and the adjudicative function in EC antitrust enforcement, a comparison is often drawn with the US system of federal antitrust enforcement. In fact, there are two US systems to be taken into account: on the one hand the system in which the Department of Justice or the Federal Trade Commission (FTC) (under the pre-merger notification programme) investigates and prosecutes before a federal court, and on the other hand the FTC's administrative procedure.

6.1.3.1 The Department of Justice and the FTC
(under the Pre-Merger Notification Programme)

566. In non-merger matters, the Department of Justice has extensive powers to investigate potential violations of Sections 1 and 2 of the Sherman Act (the US equivalent of Articles 81 and 82 EC). It does not however have any power to adopt decisions finding an infringement, ordering termination or imposing sanctions. Instead the Department of Justice has to bring in a federal district court either criminal or civil suits against the corporations and individuals which it accuses of violations of Sections 1 or 2 of the Sherman Act. In criminal cases, the district court can impose fines on corporate defendants, and fines and prison sentences on individual defendants. In civil cases, the district court can forbid continuation of illegal acts and may also force the defendant to dispose of the fruits of its wrong and restore competitive conditions. The decision of the federal district court can be appealed before the Court of Appeals for the corresponding circuit, on legal grounds alone. The Supreme Court can subsequently be petitioned to hear the case, but the Supreme Court only rarely agrees to hear such an appeal.

567. As to mergers, under the pre-merger notification programme established by the Hart-Scott-Rodino Act, certain proposed acquisitions of voting stock or of assets must be reported to the Department of Justice and the Federal Trade Commission prior to consummation. Following the assignment of the notified matter to one of these two agencies, the parties must then wait a specified period, usually 30 days. If the assigned agency determines during the waiting period that further inquiry is necessary, it can request additional information or documentary materials from the parties to the reported transaction (a 'second request'). A second request extends the waiting period until usually 30 days after all parties have complied with the request. If the reviewing agency then comes to the view

---

[6] See para 560 above.

that the proposed transaction would substantially lessen competition, it cannot itself halt the transaction beyond the waiting period. Instead it has to seek an injunction in a federal district court to prohibit consummation of the transaction. The district court's decision can be appealed on legal grounds before the Court of Appeals, and exceptionally further before the Supreme Court. If the case is brought by the FTC and the district court grants the injunction (and the reviewing Court of Appeals upholds the injunction), the FTC may then initiate an administrative proceeding that will decide on the legality of the transaction, if the parties do not abandon the transaction (as is frequently done at this stage). If it is a Department of Justice case, the legality of the transaction is litigated entirely in the federal court system.

6.1.3.2 The FTC's Administrative Procedure

568. Unlike the Department of Justice, which has only investigative and prosecutorial functions, the Federal Trade Commission also has adjudicative powers when cases proceed to the administrative stage. Under the Federal Trade Commission Act, it can issue civil injunctive orders (cease and desist orders) to halt unfair methods of competition, including the equivalent of violations of Sections 1 or 2 of the Sherman Act.

569. Investigations are opened by the FTC's Bureau of Competition under a general grant of authority delegated by the Commissioners. The investigating Bureau (in conjunction with the Bureau of Economics), upon completing its investigation, decides whether to close the investigation pursuant to authority delegated to it by the FTC, to recommend that the FTC accept a settlement with the parties under investigation, or to recommend that the FTC proceed with its complaint to litigation. The Commission decides by majority vote whether to accept the Bureau's recommendation. In administrative proceedings, if the Commission decides to issue a complaint, the complaint is referred to an Administrative Law Judge and the Commissioners are 'walled-off' from discussion of the matter with FTC staff while the matter is under adjudication. The Administrative Law Judge conducts a trial at which the FTC's Complaint Counsel and the respondent present their respective sides of the case. Upon conclusion of the trial, the Administrative Law Judge issues an initial decision which includes findings of fact and conclusions of law, determining whether to dismiss or affirm the complaint. The Administrative Law Judge's decision may be appealed by either side to the Commission, with the five Commissioners sitting as a kind of appeals court reviewing the Administrative Law Judge's initial decision on the facts and the law. The Commissioners may, by majority vote, affirm, modify or overturn the Administrative Law Judge's initial decision. If the Commission's decision is adverse to the respondent, the latter may appeal the Commission's decision to the federal Court of Appeals, only on legal grounds. Either side may seek Supreme Court review of the Court of Appeals decision, but the Supreme Court only rarely agrees to hear such cases.

570. The Federal Trade Commission thus combines prosecutorial and adjudicative functions in that it first decides to issue a complaint and may later hear the appeal against the Administrative Law Judge's initial decision. However, the situation differs from the European Commission's combination of investigative and prosecutorial with adjudicative functions in that a different system of internal checks and balances has been built into the FTC procedure. This system covers three aspects. First, the initial decision is taken by an independent Administrative Law Judge, following a full trial in which both sides of the case are presented. Second, the Commissioners are 'walled-off' from discussion of the matter with FTC staff while the matter is under adjudication. Third, when deciding on the appeal, the Commissioners sit as judges, with both sides of the case being directly presented to them. By contrast, in European Commission proceedings there is no independent initial adjudicator and no 'walling-off', and the Commissioners do not sit as judges hearing directly both sides of the case. Instead, apart from the opinion of the Advisory Committee, and possibly opinions of other Commission services,[7] the Commissioners receive only the proposal of the Competition Commissioner, who has not attended the hearing him-or-herself either, but has been briefed by the DG Competition officials dealing with the case, including the Chief Competition Economist and the peer review panel if they have been involved in the case, as well as by the Hearing Officer and possibly other Commission officials.

6.1.4 The Legal Debate: Compatibility with Article 6(1) ECHR and Scope for Change Under the Current EC Treaty

571. The combination of the investigative and prosecutorial function and the adjudicative function in EC antitrust enforcement raises two legal questions. The first is whether the current system is compatible with Article 6(1) of the European Convention on Human Rights. The second is whether the current EC Treaty would allow an alternative system under which the adjudicative function would be separated from the investigative and prosecutorial function and transferred to the Community Courts.

6.1.4.1 Compatibility With Article 6(1) ECHR

572. The combination of investigative and prosecutorial with adjudicative functions in EC antitrust enforcement has led to a legal debate relating to Article 6(1) of the European Convention of Human Rights. In scholarly articles as well as in (so far

---

[7] The Commissioners also receive a report from the Hearing Officer, but this report comments only on possible procedural incidents during the administrative procedure, not on the substance of the case. As indicated in para 560 above, the Commissioners may also receive a written opinion from the Chief Competition Economist, but only where the Director-General of DG Competition has agreed to such a written opinion being provided.

always unsuccessful) applications before the Community Courts,[8] it has been argued that the current system in which the Commission investigates and prosecutes as well as decides is incompatible with the requirements of Article 6(1) ECHR.

573. Article 6(1) ECHR reads as follows: 'In the determination of his civil rights and obligations or of any criminal charge against him, everyone is entitled to a fair and public hearing [...] by an independent and impartial tribunal [...].'

574. To determine whether EC antitrust procedures concern the 'determination of [...] civil rights and obligations or of [a] criminal charge', a distinction has to be made between, on the one hand, the procedures under Regulation No 1/2003 concerning violations of Articles 81 or 82 EC, and, on the other hand, procedures under the EC Merger Regulation.

575. In answering the question whether procedures under Regulation No 1/2003 which may lead to the imposition of fines relate to the 'determination of a criminal charge' within the meaning of Article 6(1) ECHR, the provision in Article 23(5) of Regulation No 1/2003, according to which decisions taken under those regulations 'shall not be of a criminal law nature', is not decisive. Indeed, according to the case law of the European Court of Human Rights, the indications furnished by domestic law as to the criminal nature of the offence 'have only a relative value', the notion of 'criminal' as conceived of under Article 6 ECHR being 'autonomous'.[9]

576. For Article 6 to apply by virtue of the words 'criminal charge', 'it suffices that the offence in question should by its nature be "criminal" from the point of view of the Convention', because it relates to 'a general rule, whose purpose is both deterrent and punitive', 'or should have made the person concerned liable to a sanction which, in its nature and degree of severity, belongs in general to the "criminal" sphere'.[10] As I have argued in detail elsewhere,[11] it appears difficult to deny that the application of the criteria set out in the case law of the European Court of Human Rights leads to the conclusion that proceedings based on Regulation No 1/2003, leading to decisions in which the Commission finds violations of Articles 81 or 82 EC, orders their termination and imposes fines relate to 'the determination of a criminal charge' within the meaning of Article 6 ECHR.[12]

---

[8] See ie D Waelbroeck and D Fosselard, 'Should the Decision-Making Power in EC Antitrust Procedures be Left to an Independent Judge?—The Impact of the European Convention on Human Rights on EC Antitrust Procedures' (1994) 14 *Yearbook of European Law* 111–42; and Judgment of the Court of First Instance of 15 March 2000 in Joined Cases T–25/95 ao *Cimenteries CBR ao* [2000] ECR II–700, paras 712–24.

[9] Judgment of 21 February 1984, *Öztürk v Germany*, A/73 paras 52 and 50.

[10] Judgments of 25 August 1987, *Lutz v Germany*, A/123 para 55, and of 24 February 1994, *Bendenoun v France*, A/284 para 47.

[11] See WPJ Wils 'La Compatibilité des Procédures Communautaires en Matière de Concurrence Avec la Convention Européenne des Droits de l'Homme' (1996) 32 *Cahiers de Droit Européen* 329.

[12] See also Opinion of Judge Vesterdorf acting as Advocate General in Case T–1/89 *Rhône- Poulenc v Commission* [1991] ECR II–867, 885; Opinion of Advocate General Léger in Case C–185/95 P *Baustahlgewebe v Commission* [1998] ECR I–8422 para 31; and Judgment of the Court of Justice of 8 July 1999 in Case C–199/92 P *Hüls v Commission* [1999] ECR I–4383 paras 149–50; as well as K Lenaerts and J Vanhamme, 'Procedural Rights of Private Parties in the Community Administrative Process' (1997) 34 *Common Market Law Review* 531, 557.

577. As to proceedings under the EC Merger Regulation, they are in all likelihood to be regarded as relating to the determination of civil rights or obligations within the meaning of Article 6(1) ECHR, in that the result of these proceedings is decisive for the parties' right to merge or make an acquisition.[13]

578. Although the Commission combines the investigative and prosecutorial with adjudicative functions, and thus cannot be qualified as an independent and impartial tribunal, this does not as such make the current system incompatible with Article 6(1) ECHR. Indeed, the European Court of Human Rights has ruled that, for reasons of efficiency, the determination of civil rights and obligations or the prosecution and punishment of offences which are 'criminal' within the wider meaning of Article 6 ECHR can be entrusted to administrative authorities, provided that the persons concerned are able to challenge any decision thus made before a judicial body that has full jurisdiction and that provides the full guarantees of Article 6(1) ECHR.[14] The latter condition is currently satisfied because the addressees of Commission decisions imposing fines can bring an action for annulment before the Court of First Instance, which manifestly provides the full guarantees of Article 6(1) ECHR and which undertakes a comprehensive review of the Commission's decisions.[15] The Court of First Instance's judgments in cases such as *Airtours* clearly show that, not only in cases under Articles 81 or 82 EC but also in merger cases, the Court undertakes an exhaustive review of both the Commission's substantive findings of fact and its legal appraisal of those facts.[16]

579. In the US, the argument that the mere combination of prosecutorial and adjudicative functions by the FTC violates due process has also been made, but never accepted by the courts absent a strong factual showing of actual bias.[17]

---

[13] See WPJ Wils referred to in n 11 above, p 335–37; D Waelbroeck and D Fosselard, n 8 above, p 124–25.

[14] Judgments of of 23 June 1981, *Le Compte, Van Leuven and De Meyere v Belgium*, A/43 para 51; and of 1 February 1983, *Albert and Le Compte v Belgium*, A/58 para 29; as well as *Öztürk* and *Bendenoun* judgments, n 9 and n 10 above, at para 56 and para 46 respectively. This alternative means of satisfying the requirements of Article 6(1) ECHR does not appear to be available in more traditional areas of criminal law or in areas considered criminal under domestic law. See judgments of 26 October 1984 in *De Cubber v Belgium*, A/86 paras 31–32; and of 25 February 1997 in *Findlay v United Kingdom*, Reports 1997–I para 79.

[15] See WPJ Wils referred to in n 11 above, p 337–38; K Lenaerts and J Vanhamme, n 12 above, p 559–62.

[16] See Judgment of 15 March 2000 in Joined Cases T–25/95 *Cimenteries CBR ao* [2000] ECR II–701, para 719 ('When the Court of First Instance reviews the legality of a decision finding an infringement of [Article 81(1) and/or Article 82 EC], the applicants may call upon it to undertake an exhaustive review of both the Commission's substantive findings of fact and its legal appraisal of those facts.'); and Judgment of 6 June 2002 in Case T–342/99 *Airtours* [2002] ECR II–2592.

[17] See *FTC v Cement Institute*, 333 US 683 (1948); and the lower court judgments cited in ABA Antitrust Section, Monograph No 5, *The FTC as an Antitrust Enforcement Agency* (1981) Vol II, 69, n 259 and n 260.

6.1.4.2 Scope for Change Under the Current EC Treaty

580. It has been argued that the transfer of the decision-making power in antitrust cases from the European Commission to the Community Courts would require a modification of the EC Treaty, because it would require the enlargement of the existing catalogue of tasks of the Courts as established in the Section of the EC Treaty specifically concerning the Courts (Articles 220 to 245 EC).[18]

581. I doubt whether this argument is decisive. With regard to Articles 81 and 82 EC, Article 83(1) EC gives a wide mandate to the Council, acting by a qualified majority on a proposal from the Commission and after consulting the European Parliament, to lay down 'the appropriate regulations or directives to give effect to the principles set out in Articles 81 and 82'. Article 83(2) specifically adds that the Council's regulations and directives 'shall be designed in particular: (d) to define the respective functions of the Commission and of the Court of Justice in applying the provisions laid down [under Article 83(1)]'. This provision would appear precisely to allow the Council to transfer the decisional power with regard to Articles 81 and 82 EC from the Commission to the Courts. Indeed, that the Commission would prosecute before the Court appears also to have been the understanding of the Spaak Report preceding the adoption of the EC Treaty.[19]

582. Moreover, Article 229 EC provides that regulations adopted by the Council may give the Community Courts 'unlimited jurisdiction with regard to the penalties provided for in such regulations'. That such 'unlimited jurisdiction' can take the form not only of an unlimited review of a Commission decision, but also of imposition of penalties directly by the Community Courts, is apparent from the German language version of Article 229 EC which refers to giving the Court a competence 'which includes the power of unlimited control of judgment and the power to modify or impose such penalties'.[20]

583. With regard to merger control, the situation is however different, because the main legal basis of the EC Merger Regulation is not Article 83 EC but Article

---

[18] See ie F Montag, 'The Case for a Radical Reform of the Infringement Procedure under Regulation 17' (1996) 8 *European Competition Law Review* 428, 436; CD Ehlermann, 'Decision Making at the Centre' in CD Ehlermann and LL Laudati (eds), *Robert Schuman Centre Annual on European Competition Law 1996* (Kluwer, 1997) 36.

[19] Comité intergouvernemental créé par la Conférence de Messine, Rapport des Chefs de Délégation aux Ministres des Affaires Etrangères, Mae 120f/56 corrigé (Bruxelles, 21 avril 1956) p 56:

Pour l'application concrète, il conviendra d'établir une procédure qui évite autant que possible une multiplication de procès devant la Cour. A cette fin, la Commission européenne constituerait un comité consultatif des ententes et discriminations qui l'aiderait dans une tâche de conciliation et d'arbitrage. A défaut d'une solution acceptée par les parties à l'expiration d'un délai qui pourrait être de deux mois, les Etats ou la Commission européenne elle-même pourraient introduire une plainte devant la Cour. Dans tous les cas, l'affaire sera instruite par la Commission européenne.

[20] Emphasis added; my translation from 'eine Zuständigkeit [...] welcher die Befugnis zu unbeschränkter Ermessensnachprüfung und zur Änderung oder Verhängung solcher Maßnahmen umfaßt.

308 EC, and because merger control, at least in the way it is currently structured, is not based on the imposition of 'penalties' within the meaning of Article 229 EC.

6.1.5 The Wider Policy Debate: Criteria for Choosing the Better System

584. The wider policy debate concerns the relative merits of the current system of EC antitrust enforcement and an alternative system, inspired by the American example, under which the investigative and prosecutorial function and the adjudicative function would be separated. This raises the preliminary question regarding the criteria by which antitrust enforcement systems are to be judged.

585. With regard to mergers where, as a result of pre-merger notification obligations, the number of cases to be decided is not determined by the Commission,[21] the two main criteria appear to be accuracy and administrative cost. Accuracy refers to the extent to which a procedural system leads to correct decisions, in that those concentrations which, according to the material standard of legality, should be prohibited are indeed blocked, and those which should not be prohibited are indeed allowed to proceed. By administrative cost I mean the entire societal cost of the merger control procedures, which includes not only the resources used by the enforcement authority and the courts but also the costs borne by all the private parties involved, including complainants. The optimal enforcement system is the one which achieves maximal accuracy at minimal administrative cost.

586. With regard to violations of Articles 81 and 82 EC, the equation is somewhat more complicated, since the number of cases is dependent on action by the Commission. Indeed, the concern here is not only that those cases which are pursued are accurately decided, but also that deterrence is served through the detection and successful prosecution of a sufficient number of antitrust violations, with priority being given to the most harmful.[22]

6.2 ACCURACY: THE RISK OF PROSECUTORIAL BIAS

6.2.1 Introduction

587. A large number of factors may have an impact on the capacity of an enforcement system to lead to correct decisions, such as the level of expertise of the persons involved and the availability of sufficient resources.[23] For the purposes of this chapter, which is limited to a comparison between the current system of EC antitrust enforcement, in which the European Commission combines the investigative and

---

[21] I omit here the additional task of detecting possible violations of the pre-merger notification obligation.

[22] See n 27 below.

[23] On the need for sufficient resources, see J Kay, 'The Missing Element', *Financial Times*, 18 June 2002, p 10.

prosecutorial function with the adjudicative function, and an alternative system in which these functions would be separated and the decision-making power transferred to the Community Courts, most of these factors do not need to be discussed, as there is no reason to assume that these factors would tend to favour the one system over the other.[24]

588. The one issue which needs to be discussed is whether there is a risk of prosecutorial bias in a system in which the investigative and prosecutorial function is combined with the adjudicative function. Indeed, a repeatedly voiced criticism of the existing combination of functions in EC antitrust enforcement relates to alleged prosecutorial bias. 'The frequent opinion of industry is that a view, once entrenched in the Commission's thinking, cannot be dislodged: "I have made up my mind. Do not try to confuse me with the facts".'[25] This is explained by the observation that a case handler 'naturally tends to have a bias in favour of finding a violation once proceedings have been commenced'.[26] Such alleged prosecutorial bias would lead to erroneous prohibition decisions or to companies being led to offer unjustified commitments to avoid such decisions being adopted.[27]

589. How can we judge whether such risk of prosecutorial bias really exists? Two types of approach are possible: either we try to find empirical evidence of an abnormal incidence of erroneous prohibition decisions (not explained by other causes), or we try, through theoretical reasoning informed by insights from economics and psychology, better to understand the possible sources of prosecutorial bias.

---

[24] The question whether a system in which the Commission would prosecute before the Community Courts would be inherently more costly than the current system is discussed in section 6.3 below. As to the possible problem of expertise of the judiciary in some developing and transition countries, see *Capacity building and technical assistance: Building credible competition authorities in developing and transition economies*, report prepared by the ICN Working Group on Capacity Building and Competition Policy Implementation, June 2003, available at http://www.internationalcompeti tionnetwork.org.

[25] AJ Burnside, 'Comment: Merger Control Green Paper: SLC' in *Competition*, (December 2001), http://www.linklaters.com/in_competition/200112.htm. This opinion was indeed expressed (in different words) in many of the submissions on the Commission's 2001 Green Paper on the Reform of the Merger Regulation, see http://europa.eu.int/comm/competition/mergers/review. See also A Burnside, 'Mario Monti Should Not Be Judge and Jury', *Financial Times*, 21 October 2002, p 17; and A Winckler, 'Some Comments on Procedure and Remedies under EC Merger Control Rules: Something Rotten in the Kingdom of the EC Merger Control?' (2003) 26 *World Competition* 219, 231–32.

[26] E Fox, in CD Ehlermann and LL Laudati (eds), *Robert Schuman Centre Annual on European Competition Law 1996* (Kluwer, 1997) 76.

[27] As indicated in para 586 above, with regard to violations of Articles 81 and 82 EC, the concern is not only that those cases which are pursued are accurately decided, but also that deterrence is served through the detection and successful prosecution of a sufficient number of antitrust violations, with priority being given to the most harmful. The risk of prosecutorial bias in a system in which the investigative and prosecutorial function is combined with the adjudicative function is also relevant in this respect. Indeed, whenever, as a result of prosecutorial bias, unsound prohibition proceedings would be pursued, or would be pursued beyond the point at which they should have been abandoned, scarce enforcement resources which would otherwise be spent on pursuing other cases would be wasted.

6.2.2 Empirical Evidence

590. Claims by companies which have been addressees of prohibition decisions or by their lawyers or economic advisors that the prohibition decision concerning them is erroneous can obviously not be taken at face value. Indeed, one would expect them to make such claims, whether these claims are founded are not, just as one would expect the Commission to claim for each of its decisions that it is correct, whether or not that is true.

591. One possible approach is to consider how the Commission's prohibition decisions fare when subjected to review by the Community Courts.[28] For instance, the annulment of the Commission's *Airtours* merger decision by the Court of First Instance[29] has been interpreted as 'rais[ing] further doubts about the Commission's combined role as prosecutor, judge and jury'.[30] The difficulty with this approach is that a single erroneous decision does not necessarily constitute evidence of a systemic problem of prosecutorial bias. Indeed, errors are likely to occur from time to time in any antitrust enforcement system.[31] The question is whether there is an abnormal incidence of erroneous prohibition decisions.

592. To my knowledge, the only attempt at showing statistically the existence of prosecutorial bias in EC antitrust enforcement was made by Frank Montag.[32] Focusing on Commission decisions imposing fines for violation of Articles 81 or 82 EC, Dr Montag found that, out of the 29 decisions imposing fines of 3 million ECU or more adopted since the entry into force of Regulation No 17 until 1996, the date of his writing, 24 decisions were challenged before the Community Courts. Of the 18 of these 24 decisions which had been decided at the date of his writing, only 4 had been confirmed by the Courts, whereas 12 were annulled in their entirety, or fines were quashed with regard to some companies and reduced with regard to all other companies fined, and in the 2 remaining cases fines were upheld with regard to some companies and cancelled or reduced with regard to others. Dr Montag concluded: 'Even if these results should not be generalised owing to the limited sample of decisions, they nevertheless provide remarkable evidence of the Commission's poor record in reaching decisions imposing fines which come under scrutiny in Community Courts'.[33]

593. The very high percentage of annulments which Dr Montag found may in fact only be representative of a relatively limited time period. On the one hand, as

[28] For such an approach to be useful, one must of course assume that the Community Courts make objectively correct judgments.

[29] See n 16 above.

[30] C Ahlborn, 'Comment: Airtours/First Choice: CFI Clips MTF's Wings' in *Competition*, (June 2002), http://www.linklaters.com/incompetition/200206.htm.

[31] See also President Vesterdorf of the Court of First Instance, questioned by the Financial Times (19 December 2003; full transcript at http://www.ft.com) on the annulments in the Airtours case and two other merger cases: 'I'm personally very impressed by the work that these guys do. They do a very good job. But you win some and you lose some.'

[32] F Montag, n 18 above, p 430–33.

[33] Idem, at 432.

his sample only included decisions with fines of at least 3 million ECU in nominal terms, it included only 7 decisions preceding 1986.[34] On the other hand, at the time of his writing, appeals against decisions dating from after 1992 were still pending before the Court of First Instance. The sample thus essentially concerned decisions adopted by the Commission in the 1986–92 time period. These cases happened to be the first wave of cases decided in the first half of the 1990s by the newly created Court of First Instance. The very high percentage of annulments in that period may be explained by the fact that the Court of First Instance in its judgments in this period substantially raised the procedural requirements which the Commission has to respect in its administrative proceedings, for instance with respect to access to the file.[35] After these judgments, the Commission adjusted its practice to the new, higher standard, and far fewer decisions have been annulled on procedural grounds in later years. Indeed, some of the decisions which were annulled in the first half of the 1990s on procedural grounds were even readopted by the Commission and have since been confirmed by the Community Courts.[36]

6.2.3   Three Possible Sources of Prosecutorial Bias

594. One could identify three possible sources of prosecutorial bias in a system such as the current EC system, in which the investigative and prosecutorial function is combined with the adjudicative function: (1) confirmation bias, (2) hindsight bias and the desire to justify past efforts, and (3) the desire to show a high level of enforcement activity.[37]

6.2.3.1   Confirmation Bias

595. Many psychologists have proposed that human reasoning is subject to confirmation bias, ie a tendency to search for evidence which confirms rather than challenges one's beliefs, and to accept more readily the conclusion to a syllogism if

---

[34] In real terms many more fines of the same magnitude were imposed before 1986, but the nominal figures are much smaller because of the high inflation during the 1970s and 1980s. For statistics on fines in real terms (ie corrected for inflation), see my book *The Optimal Enforcement of EC Antitrust Law* (Kluwer, 2002) 10–12.

[35] See the 'Soda Ash' judgments of 29 June 1995 in Cases T–30/91 *Solvay v Commission* [1995] ECR II–1775; T–36/91 *ICI v Commission* [1995] ECR II–1847; and T–37/91 *ICI v Commission* [1995] ECR II–1901.

[36] See the 'PVC II' judgment of the Court of Justice of 15 October 2002 in Joined Cases C–238/99 P, C–244/99 P, C–245/99 P, C–247/99 P, C–250/99 P to C–252/99 P and C–254/99 P, *Limburgse Vinyl Maatschappij (LVM) ao v Commission* [2002] ECR I–8618. The whole process of adoption, annulment and readoption of decisions is however administratively costly and thus also problematic. See para 619 below.

[37] Other possible sources of prosecutorial bias, such as the desire to attract attention by pursuing cases which innovate by stretching the law, or the temptation to intervene in the market beyond what is strictly necessary to resolve the antitrust issues, are not dealt with here, as I am not sure that there is less risk of such bias in a system in which courts decide.

it corresponds to one's beliefs than if it does not, irrespective of its actual logical validity.[38]

596. If such confirmation bias is indeed a general tendency of human reasoning, there is no obvious reason why the persons within the European Commission dealing with an antitrust case would be immune from it. The question is however why they would start from an initial belief that there is an antitrust violation. In merger cases, there is no obvious reason why they would do so. As all mergers and acquisitions with a Community dimension are notified to the Commission and investigated by DG Competition, and most of them are found to be unproblematic, the officials handling a new merger case may start from an initial belief that the merger will be yet another unproblematic one rather than one of the more rare problematic ones. The situation may be different with regard to Articles 81 and 82 EC where, certainly after the abolition of the notification system by Regulation No 1/2003, an investigation will normally be started only if the officials from DG Competition hold the initial belief that an antitrust violation is likely to be found.[39]

6.2.3.2 Hindsight Bias and the Desire to Justify Past Efforts

597. It is a fact of life that resources are limited, and this is certainly true in antitrust enforcement. The European Commission and its DG Competition have only limited resources to devote to antitrust enforcement, and their officials have themselves only a limited amount of time and energy to devote to their multiple tasks. At all levels there is thus a constant need to allocate these resources efficiently. Both to the outside world, inside the institution, and to themselves, the persons involved will want to justify that they do not waste their scarce resources, time or energy.

598. Given the complexity of antitrust investigations, it is inevitable that from time to time, in a second phase investigation or after the sending of a statement of objections, it will become apparent, once all newly uncovered elements are taken into account, that there is not really an antitrust problem or violation to be found, or at least a lesser one than initially thought. Logically, this does not necessarily mean that the opening of the second phase investigation or the sending of the

---

[38] See i.a. J Klayman, 'Varieties of Confirmation Bias' in J Busemeyer, R Hastie and DL Medin (eds), *Decision Making from a Cognitive Perspective* (1995) 32 *Psychology of Learning and Motivation* 365–418; KC Klauwer, J Musch and B Naumer, 'On Belief Bias in Syllogistic Reasoning' (2000) 107 *Psychological Review* 852–84; CG Lord, L Ross and MR Lepper, 'Biased Assimilation and Attitude Polarization: The Effects of Prior Theories on Subsequently Considered Evidence' (1979) 37 *Journal of Personality and Social Psychology* 2098; and M Rabin, 'Psychology and Economics' (1998) 36 *Journal of Economic Literature* 11, 26–29.

[39] In merger cases a problem of confirmation bias might however arise at a later stage in the handling of the case. Indeed, if a second phase investigation has been opened, or a statement of objections has been issued, this has necessarily been done on the basis of a belief that there is (likely to be) an antitrust problem or violation. During the subsequent part of the administrative proceedings, this belief might lead to confirmation bias.

statement of objections was not fully justified as a matter of efficient allocation of scarce enforcement resources. Indeed, on the basis of the information available at the time, the opening of the second phase or the sending of the statement of objections may very well have been entirely justified, even if afterwards, with the benefit of subsequently uncovered information, there does not appear to be a real antitrust problem or violation.

599. However, both the officials who are handling the cases, their hierarchical superiors and outside observers judging the Commission or DG Competition's resource allocation decisions may falsely deduce from the fact that it becomes apparent in the second phase of the investigation or after the sending of the statement of objections that there is no basis for a prohibition decision that the initial decision to open a second phase investigation or to send a statement of objections was unjustified.

600. Such false beliefs would follow from the well-documented psychological phenomenon of hindsight bias. This is the tendency for people with the benefit of hindsight, to falsely believe that they could have predicted the outcome of an event. Once outcomes are observed, there is a tendency to assume that they are the only outcomes that could have occurred and to underestimate the uncertainty in outcomes that could have happened.[40]

601. At the level of each individual dealing with the case inside DG Competition or the European Commission (from the case handler up to the Competition Commissioner) the result of such hindsight bias would be a situation of cognitive dissonance,[41] in that the (false) belief that the opening of a second phase investigation or the issuing of a statement of objections was unjustified would conflict with their (psychologically entirely normal) general confidence in their own judgment. Cognitive dissonance being psychologically uncomfortable, people are generally motivated to avoid it by avoiding information likely to create such dissonance. All the individuals within DG Competition or the European Commission who participated in the decision to open a second phase investigation or to issue a statement of objections may thus psychologically be motivated to avoid discovering subsequently that there is no case for a prohibition decision, or only a much more limited one.

602. Pressure to avoid discovering in a second phase investigation or after the sending of a statement of objections that there is no case for a prohibition decision, or only a case for a much more limited one, could not only result from this

[40] See ie SA Hawkins and R Hastie, 'Hindsight: Biased Judgment of Past Events after the Outcomes Are Known' (1990) 107 *Psychological Bulletin* 311–27, JJJ Christensen-Szalanski and CF Willham, 'The Hindsight Bias: A Meta-analysis' (1991) 48 *Organizational Behavior and Human Decision Processes* 147–68; NJ Roese and JM Olson, 'Counterfactuals, Causal Attributions, and the Hindsight Bias: A Conceptual Integration' (1996) 32 *Journal of Experimental Social Psychology* 197–227; and M Rabin, n 38 above, p 29–30.

[41] See L Festinger, *A Theory of Cognitive Dissonance* (Row Peterson, 1957); E Harmon-Jones and J Mills (eds), *Cognitive Dissonance: Progress on a Pivotal Theory in Social Psychology* (American Psychological Association, 1999); GA Akerlof and WT Dickens, 'The Economic Consequences of Cognitive Dissonance' (1982) 72 *American Economic Review* 307–19.

internal psychological tendency to avoid cognitive dissonance. It could also result from the need externally to justify the past decision to open a second phase investigation or to issue a statement of objections to hierarchical superiors or outside observers suffering from hindsight bias.

6.2.3.3 The Desire to Show a High Level of Enforcement Activity

603. Assuming that the European Commission's task with regard to the enforcement of Articles 81 and 82 EC is to create deterrence by detecting and adequately punishing a sufficient number of violations, with priority being given to the most harmful, one should expect the Commission, the Competition Commissioner and DG Competition to want to show to the outside world that they are fulfilling this task well. One should thus not be surprised to observe that statistics of the number of decisions imposing fines and the amounts of these fines are being published.[42] Similarly, to further their career and to earn the respect of their colleagues and friends, officials within DG Competition will want to show the contribution that they or their organisational division is making to fulfilling this task.

604. The problem is however that the observers for whom these statistics are destined are most often unable to judge themselves whether the prohibition decisions and the amounts of the fines imposed are indeed justified by the detection of real antitrust violations sufficiently serious to justify the amounts of the fines. To the outside observer, statistics of numbers of decisions and amounts of fines are equally impressive, irrespective of whether or not these decisions are correct. The result is a potential risk of abuse, in that dubious cases might be pursued or fines might be inflated in order to keep up the statistics.

605. This risk arguably does not exist, or at least not to the same extent, with regard to mergers, since the number of merger notifications is given, the European Commission has to adopt decisions on all of them, and outside observers do not know either what percentage of mergers being prohibited would be optimal.

6.2.4 Professional Ethics and Credibility of the Enforcement System

606. When reading the above explanations of the three possible sources of prosecutorial bias, one may wonder whether it is not all just a matter of professional ethics. Certainly with regard to the third possible source of prosecutorial bias, the desire to show a high level of enforcement activity, it would seem that there is no problem as long as the officials of DG Competition and the Competition

---

[42] See for instance Commission press release IP/01/1892 of 20 December 2001, containing such statistics for the year 2001, speech 02/384 by Commissioner Monti before the Economic and Monetary Affairs Committee of the European Parliament on 11 September 2002 (available at http://www.europa.eu.int/comm/competition/speeches), citing the same statistics and adding: 'The Commission will seek to maintain the level of activity in future.'; and the foreword by Commissioner Monti to the Commission's XXXIst Report on Competition Policy 2001, SEC (2002) 462 final, p 3.

Commissioner respect the standards of professional ethics as one would normally expect. Unfortunately, the problem might arguably be more complex with regard to the first possible source of prosecutorial bias, confirmation bias, as well as with regard to the second source, at least to the extent that the Commission officials and the Competition Commissioner are themselves subject to hindsight bias and do not merely react to outside observers suffering from hindsight bias. As confirmation bias, hindsight bias and the avoidance of cognitive dissonance would appear to be general psychological tendencies, it cannot be excluded that even the most ethical professionals might not be entirely immune from them.[43]

607. In any event, even assuming that prosecutorial bias never really materialises, a problem may remain in that, because of the theoretical risk of prosecutorial bias, the addressees of prohibition decisions and their advisors might always be able (either in good faith, suffering themselves also from confirmation bias, or in bad faith) to claim with some credibility that the decisions concerning them are erroneous.[44]

6.2.5 Separation of the Adjudicative Function from the Investigative and Prosecutorial Function

608. The problem of prosecutorial bias does not arise in a system in which the antitrust enforcement authority prosecutes before an independent court, as is the case in the US with the Department of Justice, as well as the FTC under the pre-merger notification programme. Indeed, however much the officials of the Department of Justice may be subject to confirmation bias, hindsight bias and the desire to justify their past efforts, the final decision to find an antitrust infringement and to impose any sanction or remedy remains unaffected, as it is taken by an independent court. As to the desire to show a high level of enforcement activity, there is no risk of abuse either, as the Department of Justice will have to show statistics of fines and prison terms imposed by the courts.

609. One may object that in the US a significant number of cases are closed through a negotiated settlement, under which the defendant agrees to cease or refrain from certain activities, or accepts certain penalties, in exchange for a promise by the Department of Justice to forego litigation. Such a settlement must

---

[43] With regard to hindsight bias, see JJ Rachlinski, 'A Positive Psychological Theory of Judging in Hindsight' (1998) 65 *University of Chicago Law Review* 571, 603; RB Korobkin and TS Ulen, 'Law and Behavioural Science: Removing the Rationality Assumption from Law and Economics' (2000) 88 *California Law Review* 1051, 1097 ('Unfortunately, psychologists have yet to find a method of eliminating the hindsight bias, and even reducing its effects has proven quite difficult.'). See also M Rabin, n 38 above, p 31–32.

[44] To the extent that this would lead to a loss of credibility of the antitrust enforcement system as a whole, it might have a negative effect on the overall level of observance of antitrust law. See generally TR Tyler, *Why People Obey the Law* (Yale University Press, 1990). A lack of credibility of the system may also lead to an increase in the number of appeals against Commission decisions, and thus to increased administrative costs. See F Montag, n 18 above, and para 619 below.

however be approved by a court through a consent decree. There is no such intervention by a court if, in the area of merger control, the companies concerned decide to drop their merger plans faced with the Department of Justice's or the FTC's decision to file suit.[45] However, the fact that, if the parties do not abandon their transaction, the Department of Justice or the FTC will have to convince an independent judge of their case, will still affect both their decision to file suit and the parties' decision whether or not to abandon their transaction.[46]

6.2.6 Internal Checks and Balances

610. If it is clear that any (real or perceived) risk of prosecutorial bias in EC antitrust enforcement could be removed by separating the investigative and prosecutorial function from the adjudicative function, and transferring the latter to the Community Courts, one may wonder whether an equivalent solution could not be reached through internal checks and balances inside the European Commission's administrative proceedings, or indeed has not already been achieved in the current system.

611. Without doubt, internal checks and balances can significantly reduce the risk of prosecutorial bias. If, for instance, inside DG Competition a second team of officials reviews the work of a first team of case handlers, as now occurs under the recently introduced peer review panel system,[47] this removes the risks of confirmation bias and hindsight bias at the level of the first team of case handlers. It does however not remove the risks flowing from hindsight bias or from the desire to show a high level of enforcement activity at the level of DG Competition as a whole, of the Competition Commissioner and of the Commission itself. The only way to remove those risks would be to provide for some person or body with sufficient time and resources to check the entire investigation and with a real power to veto the final decision. But this would in reality come down to separating the investigative and prosecutorial function from the adjudicative function, and transferring the latter power to this person or body.

612. The difficulty of fully eliminating prosecutorial bias through internal checks and balances would appear to be illustrated by the FTC's administrative procedure. This procedure provides for far-reaching internal checks and balances

---

[45] See para 252 of the European Commission's Green Paper on Review of the Merger Regulation, COM (2001) 745/6 final of 11.12.2001, available at http://europa.eu.int/comm/competition/mergers/review.

[46] See various submissions on the European Commission's 2001 Green Paper on Review of the Merger Regulation, all available at http://europa.eu.int/comm/competition/mergers/review, in particular p 26 of the submission of the American Bar Association and p 26 of the submission of Cleary Gottlieb Steen & Hamilton; as well as AJ Burnside, 'Comment: Judges and Merger Control: A Brewing Controversy' in *Competition*, (March 2001), http://www.linklaters.com/incompetition/200103.htm, quoting Joel Klein, former Assistant-Attorney General for Antitrust at the US Department of Justice, as saying that, if there had not been the very real inhibition of having to stand before a judge within a few weeks, and argue the case on its full merits, he would have blocked many more deals.

[47] See paras 560 and 564 above.

in that the initial decision is taken by an independent Administrative Law Judge, following a full trial in which both sides of the case are presented, in that the Commissioners are 'walled-off' from discussion of the matter with FTC staff while the case is under adjudication, and in that, when deciding on appeal, the Commissioners sit as judges, both sides of the case being directly presented to them. Notwithstanding these strong guarantees, an econometric study by Malcolm Coate and Andrew Kleit suggests that there might remain a problem of prosecutorial bias.[48] For a sample of 70 mergers challenged by the FTC from 1950 to 1988 and decided under its administrative procedure between 1956 and 1992,[49] they looked at how many of the five Commissioners deciding each case on appeal had also taken part in the initial decision to file the complaint. Through a regression analysis they found a statistically significant impact of the number of Commissioners taking part in both decisions on the final outcome of the case, in that the number of same Commissioners significantly increases the likelihood of the merger being ultimately prohibited.

6.2.7 Subsequent Judicial Review

613. Finally, one may wonder whether any (real or perceived) problem of prosecutorial bias is not solved through judicial review, such as that exercised by the Court of First Instance over the European Commission's decisions. It is undeniable that the possibility of judicial review significantly reduces any risk of prosecutorial bias. Indeed, the risk of prosecutorial bias would even be entirely eliminated if there existed a possibility of judicial review which was not only complete, in that the Court would be able to make its own full assessment of all the factual and legal aspects of the case, but also fast, in that there would be no important time lag between the administrative decision and the judgment upon review. In practice it is however difficult for both conditions to be fulfilled simultaneously: a complete review is unlikely to be fast, and a fast review is unlikely to be complete.

614. To the extent that the judicial review is not complete, in that certain relevant assessments in the administrative decision are not reassessed, the risks of prosecutorial bias remain unaltered with respect to those assessments. To the extent that there is an important time lag between the administrative decision and the judgment upon review, the beneficial effect of the judicial review in neutralising the risks of prosecutorial bias is weakened. A judgment annulling an administrative decision several years later may fail to neutralise the risks of prosecutorial bias. This is especially true if one considers the risk of prosecutorial bias flowing

---

[48] MB Coate and AN Kleit, 'Does it Matter that the Prosecutor is Also the Judge? The Administrative Complaint Process at the Federal Trade Commission' (1998) 19 *Managerial and Decision Economics* 1–11.

[49] These procedures either predate the entry into force of the 1976 Hart-Scott-Rodino Act or relate to the administrative proceedings following the grant of a court injunction suspending the consummation of the merger.

from the desire to show a high level of enforcement activity. With respect to decisions imposing fines for violations of Articles 81 or 82 EC, it may easily take 5 years before it is known through the process of judicial review whether the European Commission's decision was correct or not. By that time, the officials having taken credit for the fining decision may for instance have been granted a promotion on the basis of their record in enforcement activities, and the judgment is unlikely to reverse such effects.

6.3 ADMINISTRATIVE COST

615. The main argument in favour of the current EC system of antitrust enforcement, in which the European Commission combines the investigative and prosecutorial function with the adjudicative function, is that this system is administratively less costly than a system based on prosecution before the Community Courts. In one of the submissions on the Commission's 2001 Green Paper on Review of the Merger Regulation, Professor Barry Hawk, James Venit and Henry Huser pleaded for this reason for a strengthening of internal checks and balances in the Commission's administrative proceedings in merger cases, as they 'believe[d] these intermediate steps would help "level the playing field" by addressing the strongest due process and legitimacy concerns identified by most observers, without incurring the substantial costs of a pure US-style system'.[50]

616. Indeed, the high cost of litigation in the US is a well-known problem, not only in the area of antitrust but more generally in all areas of litigation. It could however be argued that this problem is related to certain characteristics of American procedural law and practice which are not found in Continental Europe, and which should thus also be avoidable at the Community Courts. The essence of this difference between the American and the Continental litigation traditions is that in the Continental tradition the bench takes a much more active role in managing the case, in particular by directing to a much greater extent the selection and presentation of evidence, so as to limit the litigants' (or their lawyers' and experts') tendency wastefully to produce distorted or superfluous and mutually cancelling evidence.[51]

---

[50] Para 4.3 of the submission by Skadden Arps, available at http://europa.eu.int/comm/competition/mergers/review. Internal checks and balances have indeed been strengthened since. See paras 560 and 564 above.

[51] See JH Langbein, 'The German Advantage in Civil Procedure' (1985) 52 *University of Chicago Law Review* 823–66; G Tullock, *Trials on Trial* (Columbia University Press, 1980); F Parisi, 'Rent-Seeking through Litigation: Adversarial and Inquisitorial Systems Compared' (2002) 22 *International Review of Law and Economics* 193; Mr Justice Lightman, 'The Civil Justice System and Legal Profession—The Challenges Ahead', 6th Edward Bramley Memorial Lecture, University of Sheffield, 4 April 2003, available at http://www.lcd.gov.uk/judicial/speeches/jl040403.htm. See also RA Kagan, 'Should Europe Worry About Adversarial Legalism?' (1997) 17 *Oxford Journal of Legal Studies* 165; RA Kagan, *Adversarial Legalism: The American Way of Law* (Harvard University Press, 2001); RA Posner, 'An Economic Approach to the Law of Evidence' (1999) 51 *Stanford Law Review* 1477.

617. Even if the excesses of US-style litigation could be avoided if the decision-making power in EC antitrust enforcement were to be transferred to the Community Courts, the question would remain whether a system in which the European Commission prosecuted before the Community Courts would not be administratively more expensive than the current system in which the Commission can itself decide.

618. It is certainly true that a pure system in which one person or one group of persons both investigate and decide is administratively cheaper than a system in which one person or group of persons investigates and a second person or group of persons decides, because in the latter system there will inevitably be some duplication in that the second person or group of persons has to acquire at least part of the knowledge of the case which the first person or group of persons will already have.

619. The cost advantage is less obvious however when, as is the case in the current system of EC antitrust enforcement, there are, on the one hand, internal checks and balances in the administrative proceedings, which imply that other persons or groups of persons than the first investigator or group of investigators have to acquire knowledge of the case, and, on the other hand, frequent subsequent applications for judicial review, which again require other persons, notably the judges and their clerks, to acquire the necessary knowledge of the case. Not only does the cost advantage of the system of combined investigation and decision-making then tend to disappear, but it might even be inverted into a cost disadvantage. Indeed, the decision-taking phase of the administrative proceeding risks becoming a superfluous anticipation of the work which will anyway be done by the reviewing court. Moreover, when the reviewing court annuls the administrative decision, the administrative procedure may have to be taken up a second time, as the Courts cannot substitute their decision for that of the Commission, save as regards the amount of fines. The recently concluded saga of the PVC cartel, where the initial Commission decision was first declared non-existent by the Court of First Instance, then upon appeal annulled by the Court of Justice, on strictly formal grounds, to be subsequently readopted by the Commission and confirmed by the Community Courts, clearly illustrates the resulting waste of resources.[52]

620. A similar reasoning could be applied to the question whether a system in which the Commission prosecutes before the Community Courts would necessarily be slower than the current system. It is certainly true that a pure system in which one person or one group of persons investigates and decides is faster than a system in which this first person or group, after having investigated the case, subsequently has to prosecute before a second person or group of persons which will then adjudicate. However, this speed advantage becomes less obvious when internal checks and balances are introduced or when there is a subsequent judicial review. With regard to mergers, internal checks and balances cannot lead to delays, because of the fixed deadlines applying to the whole of the administrative procedure under the EC Merger Regulation, but in cases under Articles 81 and 82 EC,

---

[52] See n 36 above.

internal checks and balances are likely to slow down the process. The speed advantage may even be inverted to the extent that the decision-making phase of the administrative procedure becomes a superfluous anticipation of the subsequent court proceedings, and to the extent that, following annulment of the administrative decision upon judicial review, the case is returned to the administrative authority for a new decision.[53] This reversal of the speed advantage is more likely to happen with regard to Articles 81 and 82 EC than with regard to mergers, as the addressees of negative Commission decisions appear to have more frequently recourse to judicial review in the former cases than in the latter.

6.4 SUMMARY AND CONCLUSION

621. This chapter has analysed, from a legal and economic perspective, the current system of EC antitrust enforcement, in which the European Commission combines the investigative and prosecutorial function with the adjudicative function, in comparison with the alternative system in which the adjudicative function would be separated from the investigative and prosecutorial function and transferred to the Community Courts. The current scheme does not pose any legal problems, as it appears fully compatible with Article 6 ECHR, as interpreted by the European Court of Human Rights. The policy question whether the current system is the better system is more difficult to answer.

622. As far as accuracy is concerned, ie whether the current system leads to correct decisions, there does not appear to be a simple answer to the question whether the current system suffers from a problem of prosecutorial bias or risk of prosecutorial bias, as compared to a system in which the Commission would prosecute before the Community Courts. Even if the allegation of bias is often voiced, there does not appear to exist convincing empirical evidence confirming such allegations. Through theoretical reasoning informed by insights from economics and psychology, one can identify, at least with regard to Articles 81 and 82 EC, three possible sources of prosecutorial bias: (1) confirmation bias, (2) hindsight bias and the desire to justify past efforts, and (3) the desire to show a high level of enforcement activity. With regard to mergers, only the second of these three sources appears equally relevant. One can also see that the risk of prosecutorial bias is significantly reduced, but not entirely eliminated, by the possibility of judicial review as well as by internal checks and balances, such as the recently introduced peer review panel system, which normally applies in all cases under Article 82 EC and in all merger cases, but not in cartel cases. Finally, it is possible that the professional ethics of the officials of DG Competition and the Competition Commissioner could ensure that prosecutorial bias never really materialises, but it cannot be excluded that even the most ethical professionals might not be immune from the first and second of the three possible sources of bias. In any

---

[53] See again the PVC example, n 36 and para 619 above.

event, even assuming that prosecutorial bias never really materialises, a problem may remain in that, because of the theoretical risk of prosecutorial bias, the addressees of prohibition decisions and their advisors might always be able (either in good faith, suffering themselves also from confirmation bias, or in bad faith) to claim with some credibility that the decisions concerning them are erroneous.

622. As far as administrative cost is concerned, it is not easy to draw simple conclusions either. In principle a system in which the investigative and prosecutorial function is combined with the adjudicative function is administratively cheaper, but this cost advantage risks being reduced, and might even be inverted, as a result of internal checks and balances and frequent judicial review.

623. On balance, the arguments in favour of the alternative system in which the European Commission would prosecute before the Community Courts would appear to be stronger with regard to Articles 81 and 82 EC than with regard to mergers. Indeed, confirmation bias and the desire to show a high level of enforcement activity are more likely to lead to prosecutorial bias in cases under Articles 81 and 82 EC than in merger cases.[54] Moreover, the recently introduced peer review panel system, which significantly reduces the risks of confirmation bias and hindsight bias at the level of the case team, normally applies in all merger cases (as well as all Article 82 cases), but in principle not in cartel cases.[55] Judicial review, which undermines the cost advantage of the current enforcement system, also appears to be more frequent in cases under Articles 81 and 82 EC than in merger cases.

624. Finally, with regard to Article 81 EC, the transfer of the adjudicative function from the European Commission to the Community Courts would have the advantage of making possible the introduction of individual penalties, and in particular the introduction of prison sanctions for those individuals responsible for horizontal, naked price fixing and market allocation schemes.[56]

---

[54] See sections 6.2.3.1 and 6.2.3.3 above.

[55] See paras 560 and 564 above.

[56] As I have argued in detail elsewhere (see my book The Optimal Enforcement of EC Antitrust Enforcement (Kluwer, 2002) chs 8 and 9, and CD Ehlermann and I Atanasiu (eds), European Competition Law Annual 2001: Effective Private Enforcement of EC Antitrust Law (Hart Publishing, 2003) panel four), the introduction of prison sanctions appears to be the only way generally to achieve effective deterrence of price cartels and other antitrust violations of comparable profitability and ease of concealment. Indeed, the current exclusive reliance on corporate sanctions is ineffective because the fines which would generally be required to deter effectively such violations, which appear to be at least in the order of 150% of the annual turnover in the products concerned by the violation, are impossibly or unacceptably high, in particular because they would often exceed the companies' ability to pay and would be likely to raise fundamental objections of proportional justice. Moreover, in a number of circumstances firms may not, in reality, be capable of adequately controlling the behaviour of their agents, with the result that exclusive reliance on corporate sanctions will not lead to effective deterrence. Individual fines or other lesser sanctions than imprisonment are also unlikely to be sufficient, in particular because of the problem of indemnification. The introduction of prison sanctions would require the transfer of the decisional power from the European Commission to the Community Courts. The need for a judicial decision follows in particular from Article 5(1) ECHR, which provides that no one shall be deprived of his or her liberty save in the cases listed in Article 5(1)(a) to (f). Of these six cases, the only one which could cover the imprisonment of antitrust offenders would be the one in Article 5(1)(a), being 'the lawful detention of a person after conviction by a competent court'. The need for a judicial decision also follows from Article 6 ECHR. See De Cubber and Findlay judgments, n 14 above.

Table of Legislation

Table of Cases

Opinions

COURT OF FIRST INSTANCE

Judgments

Opinions

EUROPEAN COURT OF HUMAN RIGHTS

Subject Index